DEMOCRACY
IN JONESVILLE

RESEARCHES IN THE SOCIAL, CULTURAL AND BEHAVIORAL SCIENCES

EDITED BY
BENJAMIN NELSON

In Preparation

DEMOCRACY IN JONESVILLE

A Study in Quality and Inequality

By W. LLOYD WARNER

With the collaboration of

WILFRID C. BAILEY
ARCH COOPER
WALTER EATON
A. B. HOLLINGSHEAD
CARSON McGUIRE
MARCHIA MEEKER
BERNICE NEUGARTEN
JOSEPH ROSENSTEIN
EVON Z. VOGT, JR.
DONALD WRAY

HARPER TORCHBOOKS
The Academy Library
HARPER & ROW, PUBLISHERS
NEW YORK

TO THE MEMORY OF

Émile Durkheim

Contents

List of Tables

List of Charts

Foreword To The Torchbook Edition

WHAT THIS BOOK IS ABOUT

QUALITY AND INEQUALITY

Jonesville, 1963, and Jonesville, 1949, (when the first edition of this book was published) are very much the same. It has grown a little and spread its dwelling areas a little, but outwardly it looks very much today as it did when we completed our research.

Throughout the years we have maintained close contact with this city. Most of us have visited it many times, some of its citizens have visited us, and a few of us have also reexamined parts of it for new research purposes. But we have not restudied the total community; with very few changes, this Torchbook is the same as the first edition. We know that since we studied Jonesville, this community and the other small cities of this country, the agricultural counties, and the great metropolitan areas have continued changing their relations to each other and to the expanding national society. Later in this foreword some of the changes in Jonesville will be briefly discussed.

The American social system, which organizes and controls the lives of all of us, is permeated with two conflicting social principles: The first says that all men are equal before God and man and emphasizes the spirit of the great ritual documents of our nation, such as the Declaration of Independence, the Gettysburg Address, and the Bill of Rights. It expresses the religious and political ideals of America, explicitly stated in the official beliefs of our countrymen and in their basic codes of conduct. The second, contradictory to the first, more often found in act than in words, in oblique reference than direct statement, declares that men are of unequal worth, that a few are superior to the many, that a large residue of lowly ones are inferior to all others.

In a social system where such reckonings are made, it is not necessary for research to reveal that there are men who are above, below, and at the Common Man Level in all American communities. But science does tell us much and can answer vital questions which common sense cannot about social class and equality in the lives of our people. Because all levels of men and their families are identifiable, their ways of life can be studied, and the reasons for some of the conduct in their social classes can be scientifically understood. The more precise language of social science tells us that above the Common Man Level, in the towns and cities of America, is a dominant upper class with varying claims to aristocracy; below it, a stratum of substantial upper-middle class people; at the Common Man Level are the little people of the lower-middle and upper-lower classes; and beneath them, the ne'er-do-wells and unfortunates of the lower-lower level, sometimes referred to in this volume as the Level Below the Common Man.

As we have said earlier, these social levels are not categories invented by social scientists to help explain what they have to say; they are groups recognized by the people of the community as being higher or lower in the life of the city. The social scientist, when he hears that certain groups are superior or inferior, records what he hears and observes and tries to understand what it means. The designations of social levels are distinctions made by the people themselves in referring to each other.

Some families stay at one level for generations, and within the same period others rise to the top and stay or sink to the bottom and remain there. Why do these things happen to people? What are the secrets which have made some men victims of downward mobility and carried others to the high places of power and prestige? In finding the answers to these questions we must learn how the seemingly unreconcilable principles of equality and aristocracy are reconciled in American thought and action. This book seeks to present some of the answers to these basic problems.

With this and other purposes in mind, our search through the pages which follow will first take us into the structure of the laboratory where we sought the answers—the social system of the city of Jonesville, U. S. A.

By forsaking the extremes of studying the whole of America and, in the blur of the forest, seeing none of the trees, or of devoting ourselves to the intensive study of a few individuals and seeing none of the social forest of which they are important parts, we were able to turn for our answers to the study of Americans living in a representative community in the United States. By such a study, we could see and understand the larger design of American life.

The city we call Jonesville was chosen because it satisfied the exacting requirements we had established. Jonesville, the City of the Common Man, is an actual place which we have come to know well because we studied it for several years. Although we chose it above all other places for its particular qualifications for our study, we know that most other places, for purposes of evidence, might have done equally well. The Jonesvilles, Smithtowns, Greenfields, and all the other -villes, -towns, and -fields of America are essentially alike. Sometimes the road signs at their entrances say Dallas, Seattle, or maybe Indianapolis or Buffalo, or they might spell out Atlanta, Springfield, or Walla Walla, but no matter what the signs say or how the alphabetical letters are arranged they still spell Jonesville. No two American habitations are identical, but all of them, big or little, bear the strong family resemblance of the same parentage.

Jonesville has been our laboratory for studying Americans. The social structure governing American capitalism lies within the actions of its people, for the lives of the ten thousand citizens of Jonesville express the basic values of 180,000,000 Americans. The life of the community reflects and symbolizes the significant principles on which the American social system rests. Borrowing from the Gospel of John, we can say that Jonesville is in all Americans and all Americans are in Jonesville, for he that dwelleth in America dwelleth in Jonesville, and Jonesville in him. This is true for the urbanite office dweller, living his life in a Broadway canyon, for the devout acolyte buried in a priestly cell of a monastery, and for the six generations of Jonesville who were born on the banks of The River and lie buried where they lived their lives.

To study Jonesville is to study America; it is a laboratory, a clinic, a field study for finding out what we are as a people and for learning why we think and feel and do the things we do.

Near the time the field study of Jonesville began (1940), over 6,000 people lived inside its corporate limits and a few more than 18,000 were in Abraham County. Jonesville is its county seat. At that time, some fifty-odd miles away, 4,600,000 individuals lived in metropolitan Chicago and 132,000,000 made up the total population of the United States. In 1950, a year after the first edition of Jonesville was published, there were just under 7,000 people and a little over

19,000 in Abraham County. Meanwhile, metropolitan Chicago had grown to over 5,000,000 and the population of America had increased to 152,000,000. At the last census (1960), there were 180,000,000 in the United States, over 6,000,000 in metropolitan Chicago. Jonesville had increased to 7,600 and Abraham County to just over 22,000.

From 1950 to 1960 the American population had increased by 18.5 per cent, Chicago's by 20 per cent, and Abraham County's by 16 per cent. Jonesville lagged a little behind with only 9 per cent. However, this increase compares favorably with the increases of many other small cities and towns in America.

The growth of great cities since well back in the last century has been a notable and significant process in the development of our American society.

Twenty-four metropolises, those with over 1,000,000 population, with other big ones, all well spread throughout the country, have grown enormously. All the great metropolitan areas in the United States, as everyone knows, have increased much more than the country itself. The so-called Standard Metropolitan Statistical Areas (212 of them) in their totality have increased by 26 per cent during the last decade. Much of our national growth for several decades has been in the great cities. The rural areas and small towns have lost, made minor gains or have barely held their own. These great cities are now centers of dominance and integral and highly important parts of the American society. They are closely related economically and socially to each other and to the smaller communities which increasingly and sometimes unknowingly are becoming in effect satellites of the near and distant great cities. In this intricate web of relations, Jonesville in 1950 and 1960 plays its part. Some small cities had been swallowed and absorbed by the great cities nearby. Jonesville is still very much itself, an independent city. Yet, all American communities now, big and little, are increasingly interdependent and less autonomous—more and more interconnected parts of the one great primary society which is the American national community. Despite its separateness, despite its continuing autonomy, Jonesville is a necessary part of this enormous process. The great primary national society that is coming into being has taken over many of the old functions of the local communities and, for the common good or not, is now demanding new tasks be performed by them. In the tightening "social space" and the quickening "social time" Jonesville is now more closely related to Chicago, to

Los Angeles, to New York and to the national society than it ever was before. But although Jonesville has changed, Jonesville is still very much Jonesville.

A few small factories have moved into the community and a few more, following the modern trend, have located in what was once entirely rural Abraham County. The most important industry in Jonesville, what we call "The Mill," has been purchased by a very large corporation and its headquarters moved from nearby Chicago to a distant metropolis in one of the middle Atlantic states. The industry previously was big for Jonesville but small for America. The new corporation is now among *Fortune* magazine's top 500, with plants scattered from Illinois through Ohio to the Atlantic coast states. It has over 6,000 employees and has slightly less than $100,000,000 in annual sales. It is big business and Jonesville's plant now is only one part of an elaborate, complex large-scale organization that is one of the characteristic "organs" of the growing and developing America that has now emerged.

The City of the Common Man still lies serene and lovely on the banks of The River and across The Canal. Jonesville—center of Abraham County, State of North Prairie, United States of America. Down the river are Athens, Rome, and Alexandria. Up the river are La Belle France, Carthage, and Pekin. The men of the prairie borrowed these august symbols of ancient cultures to cover the nakedness of their villages and to announce to everyone that they meant to get their share of the bigger and better world of tomorrow. The proud founders of Jonesville, embarrassed by a common name too casually acquired, sought a higher-sounding word to christen their new-born city that would agreeably express its true significance and fit their town for future greatness.

Those who deliberated unanimously chose Xenia. But, unfortunately for the classical tradition in American place names, a violent dispute arose, for there were those among them who said Xenia must always be spelled with an X, and others equally positive who knew it could only be started with a Z. Meanwhile, for the common man who settled there, Jonesville—not hard to remember and easy to spell—went on being Jonesville. And today, over a hundred years after its founding, the City of the Common Man is still Jonesville, U. S. A.

This book is devoted to the story of what has been learned from several years' research in the Jonesville clinic about Americans. In the expressive language of our people, those who collaborated on this book wanted to find out what makes Americans tick. In the language of the social scientist, we were interested in the question: How do the dominant factors of democracy and social class and other factors such as social change control individual and group behavior in the communities where Americans live?

We tried to find out how wealth, education, beauty, sex, marriage, and many other social characteristics contribute to the rise of an individual or family. We thought it important to ask and find out what the instigations are which urge some people to climb, whatever be the prize, and yet seem to have no force in the lives of others? That whole mysterious area of American behavior, hidden shamefully as though it were a social disease by those who experience it—downward mobility—is examined. When they lose their wealth, why do some families drop rapidly into oblivion? And why do others refuse to surrender, fight desperate rearguard actions, and re-establish themselves in the security of their original positions? During the course of the pages to follow we will report on social mobility as a natural phenomenon of American life.

A dominant theme in the life of all American communities is social change. For most people cultural change is without form. Events to them have no more form than their serial order. For them the live, cultural realities of yesterday become the dead myths of today and, tomorrow, disappear into a dull record of a dead past not worth carrying in their memories. But for the observant, cultural change is not chaotic but ordered, and conforms to the basic principles which make up the social structure of any culture. To these people, history is never dead; the past is alive in the present. We shall see how the conflicting principles of social class and equality and other factors dominate the changes which compose the town's social history, for we shall see that the past still lives in the present lives of the people of America's Jonesvilles.

Jonesville's living comes largely from the immense cornfields which surround it, where the farmers and their families earn the money to buy the goods and services of the businessmen of the town. A large factory and several small ones provide a substantial part of the town's income. The changes taking place in the rural life of Abraham County and in the urban existences of managers and workers of Jonesville are typical of much that is happening for good or evil in the lives of millions of Americans. We tell the story of the farmers and the urban workers in several chapters.

Not all social endeavor in Jonesville is social climbing. Many men are not mobile in fact or fancy. Some institutions, deeply conscious of the spirit of equality and fraternity, teach and practice the beliefs and values of Christian brotherhood. It is no happenstance that the equalitarian values of democracy were born in a Christian society. Although the churches are never free from the values of social class, many of them come nearer to practicing as well as preaching democracy, equality, and the brotherhood of man than does any other American institution. We will see how the church functions in Jonesville. We will analyze the lives of the ministers and their congregations and study the sermons of the preachers to ascertain their deeper meanings in the life of the community.

Lodges, secret societies, Rotary clubs, women's organizations and associations—diverse in form, often contradictory in function—make up one of the more significant and powerful groups of American life. It is necessary to study their place in our social order and to understand their functions to know what their beliefs and practices mean to the two sexes, the old and the young, and the several social classes, and to see how potent they are in American culture. For this purpose, two chapters will be devoted to the associations of Jonesville as typical examples of such groupings in the larger life of America.

The school, instrument of democracy for giving American youth an equal chance but above all promoter and advocate of upward mobility, will be studied as a system of control for the maintenance of the *status quo* and as a vehicle used on one of the main routes of the upward mobile.

The factory, by its very nature a rigid social hierarchy, where men work to live but strive to advance themselves, will be examined to learn what it does to Jonesville and what Jonesville does to it, that we may find out how it aids and hinders managers and workers when they try to climb the social ladder and how the industrial structure orders, and is ordered by, the American social system.

Jonesville, like most American communities, could not exist without the support of its rural background. A full understanding of Jonesville, and of similar cities, can only be reached through seeing it as a part of the larger mesh of the region of which it is a part. A chapter will be devoted to the agricultural life of Abraham County, which uses Jonesville as its economic and social center.

The political organization of Jonesville fits the rest of the social structure, conforming to democracy here or, there, curving or bulging with the class outlines of the body politic.

Deeply and securely knitted into the cultural web of Jonesville are several ethnic groups—European peoples who carry variant cultures, yet preponderantly conform to most of the mores of the common life. A full knowledge of their adjustments is necessary to gain insight into how people become Americans, one of the basic themes of the social life of the United States.

During our study World War II began. The departure, absence, and return of the young men profoundly affected the people of the town, and the war deeply influenced its social life. A full and detailed study was made of what happened to these young men and to the town that sent them to fight.

Finally, in the last chapter we shall re-examine the ideology of status in Jonesville and other communities of the United States and attempt to state a set of principles which operate in our social order. Again, we shall face the problems of how the antagonistic principles of equality and aristocracy are reconciled and how well these principles serve the social system of the United States. We shall give careful attention to the beliefs and values of Americans, to the forms and functions of these values and beliefs, and tell what we think the several ideologies commonly carried by Americans mean to them. We will learn about these matters of such great importance to all Americans in Jonesville, U. S. A., the City of the Common Man.

W. LLOYD WARNER

University of Chicago, 1949
Michigan State University, 1963

Chapter 1

THE COURSE OF HUMAN EVENTS

THE PAST OF THE PRESENT

When Will Taylor unhitched his team from the prairie schooner to end the journey that had brought him from the green hills of New England to settle on the prairie he became a reckoning point for those who came after him in the history of Jonesville. Since he was there to stay, Jonesville began with him. Before his arrival there had been only Indians and occasional Frenchmen on the prairie. After him came more settlers, some from New England, others from the South. A village grew into a town, and then into the city of Jonesville. Will Taylor came in 1834.[*]

The prairie in which Jonesville is located and through which The River flows is rich and capable of supporting a multitude of people. Father Marquette, with Louis Jolliet the first Europeans to sail the waters, reported to his Jesuit superiors, "We have seen nothing like this river for the fertility of the land, its prairies, woods, wild cattle, stag, deer, ducks, parrots, and even beaver." Jolliet concurred in this and called the area "the most beautiful and most suitable for settlement." When Jonesville was born, William Cullen Bryant was visiting a pioneer family down The River. Feeling his "heart swell" with the prairie's grandeur, he wrote:

> These are the gardens of the desert, these
> The unshorn fields, boundless and beautiful,
> For which the speech of England has no name—
> The Prairies. I behold them for the first,

[*] By W. Lloyd Warner. See List of Authors.

And my heart swells, while the dilated sight
Takes in the encircling vastness . . .

Will Taylor and the English-speaking people who settled along the banks of The River were armed invaders. They were part of the Caucasoid race's attacking army of migratory people which, for three centuries, had been engaged in deadly combat with the Mongoloid people for the living space on the two American continents. Ten millennia had passed since the forefathers of the Indians had left their Asiatic kinsmen, passed over Bering Straits, and migrated southward until finally they had established themselves over all the living space of the two American continents. Their people had grown and multiplied. They had developed hundreds of separate nations and, in Mexico and Peru, produced cultures of grandeur that rivaled classical antiquity. Some of the Indian cultures were at least the equal of the white invaders' in all aspects but one: their weapons and the technical equipment for producing them were inferior. This technical failure dominated in their destruction.

It sounds melodramatic to say that the conflict between the invading whites and the defending yellow people was "a struggle to the death"; but even this is an understatement. The whites wanted the land and substance which maintained the Indians as a biological group and nourished their arts and industries. The guns of the whites got them what they wanted. In less than four centuries they destroyed the cultures of the Indians, obliterated most of them as biological groups, and reduced a surviving few to receiving the bounty of the white man and his degrading pity.

Before the white man came, the Indians living in the valley of The River had fought among themselves. When La Salle was there, warriors from the great military nation, the Iroquois, had come down the Great Lakes and had driven the local tribes down The River to the Mississippi. La Salle aided the indigenous people in their war against the invaders. The struggle among the Indian nations was followed by the conflict between the Indians and whites and between the French and the English for control of the country. All this culminated in the Treaty of Paris in 1763 which gave the future state of North Prairie to the English. The hierarchical structures of the French, with king and cardinal at each apex, were succeeded by a culture which emphasized local control, in which each community was largely autonomous. The organized chain of French forts reaching from Mobile to Montreal gave way to English improvisation which often approached chaos. The civil war between the English of Europe and those of North America in 1783 gave the land where Jonesville was to be located to the United States; and shortly before 1820 North Prairie was admitted as one of the states of the Union.

When Will Taylor arrived there the battle with the Indians for The River and for the state of North Prairie had been won. Daniel Boone and the hunters and woodsmen from the South had crossed the mountains and infiltrated the valleys of the streams of the Ohio as far as the Mississippi. In the southern part of the state, villages and towns were everywhere. The year before Taylor's arrival, the Indians in his region had been banished across the western banks of the Mississippi River. Black Hawk and his tribesmen, returning hungrily to the cornfields of their ancestors from which they had been driven by the whites, were met at the Battle of Bad Axe and there, after the slaughter and scalping of Indian men, women, and children by the military of the prairie states, they and all their tribes once and for all gave up the land of their ancestors to the white conquerors and fled to oblivion.

Edgar Lee Masters, in his fine poem, "Black Hawk,"[1] has written an epitaph to the Indian period which closed when Jonesville, U. S. A., was founded.

> He had returned from Iowa, thereby
> Breaking his word not ever to return,
> But forced by hunger and the need of corn
> To seek his land and village . . .
> From which he had been driven . . .
>
> .   .   .   .
>
> So Black Hawk made a prisoner
> Was taken in chains on a triumphal tour
> Over America, to show him the mighty stir
> Of the White man in the cities,
> To show him the cities magnificent, secure,
> Springing like blossoms from the Indian land;
> To show him the unconquerable American cities,
> Where neither justice was, nor pities,
> To show him how the Indians could not stand
> Against the White man—it could be no more.

[1] Edgar Lee Masters, "Black Hawk," in *More People* (New York: D. Appleton-Century Co., 1939).

Our Fathers Brought Forth . . .

The County of Abraham, in which Jonesville is located and the land to which Will Taylor came after Black Hawk's departure, was quickly settled by people largely from New England, New York, Ohio—in general, people of the North. However, from the beginning a strong minority of Southerners from Virginia, Kentucky, and Tennessee located there. The basic beliefs and sentiments which brought the people of the North and South into conflict elsewhere sometimes caused bitterness in the relations of the two migrant groups.

When the Erie Canal opened in 1825, followed a little later by steam navigation on the lake, thousands of people from the Atlantic states and Ohio moved westward and filled the northern parts of Indiana, Illinois, and the states of Wisconsin and Michigan. Not content, and ever restless, many of them were soon on their way to California and Oregon and the other states west of the Mississippi. Will Taylor's son, born the year after the family arrived, had not reached voting age before Jonesville was no longer on or near the frontier but part of a settled, well-ordered, populous region. When the child was born, St. Louis and New Orleans were the principal trading centers for the whole of North Prairie and for the few people who had come that far north to locate on the river banks. St. Louis was the principal distribution point for the Mississippi Valley. The Germans and the Irish were already filling its streets and competing with the men of Kentucky for dominance. New Orleans was a city of 40,000 souls. Its shipping receipts from the interior alone were over $45,000,000. A sizable percentage of this vast wealth came from the men of The River.

When Jonesville was settled, Chicago was rapidly gaining population and preparing for dominance. Until the opening of The Canal which connected The River with Lake Michigan, all water traffic on The River had been southward. Steam boats had not reached Jonesville, but by 1837 they were coming up from St. Louis to towns only a short distance down The River. At the beginning of 1832 Chicago had a population of 1,850; at the end of that year 2,000 people were located there. In 1837, with a population of 8,000, the town was incorporated. Chicago soon became a center to which the northern communities sent their goods. Lines of wagons thirty and forty strong, loaded with wheat, took the produce of the region to this new metropolis to fill the holds of the ships which carried their cargoes eastward to New York.

The several townships of the County of Abraham, during this period, were soon filled with farmers. The early settlers took their land by pre-emption and shortly after this were permitted to buy it at $1.25 an acre at public auction. In a few years, almost half of the land of the county was under cultivation. Once the prairie was broken, the settling of Jonesville by substantial farmers was rapid and involved few changes in the kind of inhabitant who settled there. There was not an earlier period of woodsmen and hunters as there had been in the southern part of the state. The original settlers were all farmers. Their first homes were log cabins, and the land cultivated by each farmer was not extensive. But soon modern houses were built, farms enclosed, and the rude cooking and eating utensils were supplanted by importations from the East.

Will Taylor had built the first log cabin on the site of Jonesville in 1834. In 1841, Jonesville consisted of two or three log buildings, a frame store, a small public house, and a few laborers' cabins along the banks of The Canal. When the town was selected as a county seat, a number of other people moved in and various business enterprises were started. In 1843, the first school was opened and a post office was established. Two Protestant church groups were formed early: the Methodist in 1842 and the Congregationalist in 1848. Up The River a Catholic church had been built in 1842 to provide a place of worship for the Irish workers who were digging The Canal. However, until The Canal was completed in 1848, the growth of Jonesville was slower than that of communities in other counties. But after that the city boomed. Several warehouses were built along its banks and barges could transport goods to and from Jonesville. In 1848 the population was 150. In 1850, it had increased to 627 and that year the town was incorporated and village trustees were elected. By this time Jonesville had established dominance over the surrounding towns and villages and had become the most important community in the county.

In 1850 the county was still almost entirely agricultural. The population represented all nationalities; but even at this early date the Norwegians were present in large numbers. They had come there in 1847-48 and had settled in two of the townships where their descendants live today.

With the completion of The Canal the farmers for the first time had a means of shipping their produce to market. The Canal ushered in a new era for the town. Shipping yards were established along its banks and the introduction of adequate transportation facilities brought an opportunity to establish manufacturing industries. In the next decade several industries located there.

THE CANAL—LAST PRODUCT OF THE OLD CULTURE

The portage was a low, marshy land which soon led Father Marquette into a river that carried him to the foot of Lake Michigan. The priest, a devout man, and his companion, Louis Jolliet, explorer and man of the world, had voyaged up the Mississippi into The River and, with the help of the Indians living nearby in the future County of Abraham, had journeyed to the portage which separated the transportation system of the Mississippi River Valley from Lake Michigan and the transportation system of the Great Lakes and St. Lawrence River.

"The place at which we entered the lake," Marquette wrote in 1673, "is a harbor very convenient for receiving vessels and sheltering them from the wind." In the state of North Prairie, all the children of the grade schools know that "the place" was Chicago. They also know that Marquette was wise enough to realize the full significance of his experience for he continued writing, "a very great and important advantage" lay in the low limestone ridge over which he had carried his boat and equipment. "It would only be necessary to make a canal by cutting through half a league of prairie to pass from the foot of the lake of the Illinois to the River St. Louis which falls into the Mississippi. The bark when there would easily sail to the Gulf of Mexico."

It is possible that the Indians who brought Marquette to the portage had long been aware of the value of such a water connection between the two drainage systems. It is certain that all men who came after him—French, British, and American—recognized the truth and importance of his observations. Most of them reiterated what Marquette had said. Their words had no result until 1808 when agitation was begun in Congress to construct The Canal.

An Indian treaty was drawn up with this project in mind, extinguishing all titles to the land along the proposed route. In 1822-27 Congress authorized The Canal, granting the right of way across public lands, giving the route and ninety feet of way on each side. After various vicissitudes, digging commenced on July 4, 1836.

Difficulties continued because labor was scarce and it was soon realized that the total cost was going to be much more than had been expected. Meanwhile, the country went through a national panic. In 1842 the state of North Prairie was no longer solvent. The following year work was stopped before The Canal was completed. Finally, The Canal Commission managed to negotiate an additional loan of one million dollars, and work was resumed in 1845. In April 1848 The Canal was completed, at a total cost of more than six million dollars. By means of tolls, leased water power, and the lease and sale of land along the banks, the total debt was paid off in 1871.

The years immediately following its opening were the busiest and most productive for The Canal. The first boat, carrying sugar, sailed from New Orleans to Chicago and Buffalo. For the first time, Chicago's exports were greater than her imports. The farmers now had an easy and efficient means of shipping their produce to market. The Canal, open 230 to 250 days a year, carried corn, lumber, wheat, sugar, flour, beef, and beeswax. During the early fifties, it moved two-thirds of over three million bushels of corn that came into Chicago and, in turn, carried quantities of lumber into the interior.

Jonesville soon became a distributing and transportation center for the surrounding country and for Abraham County. The steamers and towboats docked at its wharves bringing goods from Chicago and the outside world and taking the corn, oats, and other products of the country to the world market. Jonesville corn and livestock were becoming increasingly dependent on the larger world for a profitable market. The year before the completion of The Canal, Chicago's exports were slightly over $2,500,000; the year The Canal opened they rose to almost $11,000,000. In a very few years, meat from cattle fattened in the fields along The River and processed in Chicago was being sold in the butcher shops of London. The people of the prairie and the urban men of New York and London, through the mediation of Chicago and The Canal, were becoming interdependent and necessary to each other.

During the period of The Canal's greatness, packets such as *The Avalanche, Queen of the Prairie,* and *Bird of the Prairie,* loaded with passengers coming north from New Orleans and St. Louis and going south with travelers from New York and Philadelphia and other eastern cities, brought the people of Jonesville into constant and direct relation with the affairs of the outside world. Some of these "palaces" boasted in their advertisements "of the well known urbanity and unwearied attentions" of their officers for the comfort of their passengers and of cabins that were fifty feet long, nine feet wide, and seven feet high. They were pulled by steamboat or by horses on the towpath at the rate of six miles per hour. They stopped frequently for freight and passengers. Many of the European immigrants who arrived on them, particularly Germans, Irish, and Scandinavians, settled permanently along The Canal and The River.

In 1854 the railroad opened through the region and within six months practically all passenger traffic had gone to it, though the contest for freight between the railroad and The Canal was a long and spirited one. High-class freight went to the railroad, but lumber, grain, coal, and stone continued to be transported on The Canal in large quantities. Because the railroad could reach all parts of the country and was constantly adding innovations, The Canal fought a losing battle during the latter half of the century. The railroad soon robbed The Canal of its significance and importance to the people of Jonesville. The old canal, with its towpaths and winding channels, is gone. Jonesville is now land-minded. It moves by automobile and train. Yet The River has again become an important artery of transportation. The deep waterway, built in 1933 by the machinery of mass technology and of the new culture, with modern boats, locks and dams, and connecting Chicago with The River above Jonesville by a new canal, has succeeded the old canal. Great barges once again move up and down The River, some of them stopping at Jonesville for grain and other produce. The towpaths are no longer used.

A mile or so outside Jonesville, not far from the old towpaths, stands a large boulder. It marks the grave where Shabonee, great chief of the Pottawatomie, was buried by white men. Shabonee, friend of the white man, was given a small farm by the "grateful white people" for saving their lives and their lands—a farm now barren and worthless, given him to replace the prairie empire taken from him and his people by the white invaders.

The towpath and The Canal, grown over with grass and underbrush, decaying symbols of the power of an older culture, are now public parks dedicated to a dead past. In the tourist guides, a few paragraphs below the description of Shabonee's boulder, they are briefly listed as public monuments, "full of history"—a history in which the myths of the present effectively destroy the realities of the past.

THE RAILWAY AND THE NEW TECHNOLOGY

The grandiose dreams which became the commercial realities of the canals connecting lake and river for Jonesville and North Prairie State were the same dreams and same realities of the people of New York, of Ohio, Indiana, Illinois, and the other states and towns of the great Northwest. The history of Jonesville's canal, its rise to power and its early defeat by the railway, is a classic example of similar histories of those years throughout the regions inhabited by white Americans.

Whereas The Canal was an invention known to the men of the Nile and Euphrates, the steam railroad was something new under the sun. It had within itself the potential power of revolutionizing the civilizations of the world. Within less than three generations, with the aid of similar inventions, a new civilization was produced.

When the railway came to Jonesville in 1854, Will Taylor was forty-five and his son, John, only nineteen. The road was one of the many that were spreading out from Chicago. A railway center in spite of itself, Chicago had envisaged itself as a great inland port and had neglected the railway, while its merchants campaigned in and out of Congress for The Canal. The main line of the Illinois Central was first constructed from Cairo to La Salle. Afterwards, and as an afterthought, a "branch" line was extended to Chicago. Eastern capitalists, granted 2,500,000 acres of land by Congress, had built the railway. In this ten-year period, dozens of railways—among them the one that went through Jonesville—were completed in North Prairie State. In a short period of only twenty-five years, which included ten years following the Civil War, the major era of railroad building in North Prairie was over.

The amount and kind of social interaction, as well as economic interchange, among the people of North Prairie and with the people of the world were enormously increased and accelerated. Jonesville, feeling the new rhythm and responding to it, literally turned its back on The Canal and The River and, facing the railway, became a modern city. The rhythm of the railway and of the way of life brought with it was the rhythm of the Machine Age, born in the industrial revolution and matured in the world wars of the twentieth century. Machine invention piled upon machine invention while masses of men congregated in great cities to run the factories and spread their products to the farms and small towns.

The year before the first boat steamed past Jonesville on its way to Chicago, a Virginian by the name of Cyrus Hall McCormick landed in Chicago. He built his factories along the Chicago River, and the year The Canal opened he built seven hundred reapers. By the time several of the great railways were running, his factories were building fifteen mechanical reapers a day, and the farms of North Prairie and Abraham County were reacting to, and being changed by, the machine.

Soon after Will Taylor arrived in Jonesville, he and the other settlers were using the new steel plow. The breaking and settling of the prairie had to wait for this new invention. At about the time of Taylor's arrival, John Deere started building steel plows for public sale. In time the plowed fields of Abraham County were fenced with barbed wire invented within the state and adapted to the needs of the prairie farmers.

In 1865, the legislators of North Prairie incorporated the Union Stockyards, and 345 acres of swamp land south of Chicago were enclosed to become a huge corral and a gigantic pigsty for the cattle and hogs of the farmers of all the prairie states. Nelson Morris came from Germany, Armour and his brothers from Milwaukee, and Gustavus Swift from Massachusetts to butcher the hogs and cattle of the prairie farmers for the world meat markets. They made great fortunes, and their descendants became Carl Sandburg's "hog butchers of the world."

Meanwhile, factories, commensurate with its size, came to Jonesville. They were small and seemingly insignificant in their beginnings, but in time of the greatest importance to the economy of the town. A plow manufactory was opened, a grist mill was built, and a pottery plant started. The factory and the industrial age, with the problems of managers and workers, had made their appearance in Jonesville.

Throughout the state, and in Jonesville as well as Chicago, the "tycoons," emerging from the common men of the prairie, rose to prestige and power and created a new way of life at a social status "above the Common Man Level." Men like David Davis, Jesse Fells, and W. D. Green, who were important and powerful instruments in Lincoln's nomination of 1860, incorporated railways, developed corporations, or, in times of panic and depression, bought the farms of the destitute and thereby amassed fortunes. They built their mansions in the restricted areas of the growing towns and cities; and their wives and daughters, importing the social institutions of Eastern and European culture to form a social system, distinguished themselves in fact and symbol from the common run of people. Before Jonesville turned to the railway the city had developed its own level above the Common Man. In the neighborhood of the towpath and the district across The Canal on which the city had turned its back, there developed a people also set off from the Common Man—a lower class, a Tobacco Road. James Gray, who knows The River well, writes:[2]

Sinclair Lewis has said that Main Street is a highway that stretches through every state of the Union. It might be said that Tobacco Road is another such national highway.

Looking for the site of Father Marquette's mission to the Indians, for the actual land where he baptized them under the Virgin's banners, one comes upon the Illinois section of Tobacco Road. . . .

One passes the dismal huts of squatters. Heaps of garbage decay in the sun. A rusty bedspring completes a bit of sagging fence.

An all but unintelligible inhabitant of Tobacco Road points out across the fields and tells you in broken English, "All over! Much Indians! Much fighting!"

The railway and the new technology helped destroy more than The Canal when they came to Jonesville. But it would be too much to say that this industrial revolution destroyed an existing society in which all men were equal and introduced social and economic classes to the city. It merely accelerated a process and accentuated what was already present, perhaps in nascent form, within the social order of the towns of The River.

LAND FOR THE FAMILY AND FOR A PROFIT

The early settlers who came with Will Taylor to Jonesville, in the state of North Prairie, carried with them and planted the seeds out of which grew a new agricultural empire; within themselves they carried social sentiments from which the contemporary social system of Jonesville came into being. Those historians who depict them as men in pursuit of life, liberty, and happiness, seeking land

2 James Gray, *The Illinois* (New York: Farrar and Rinehart, Inc., 1940).

with the sole intent of settling in a secure place to rear their families, draw a true picture; but they leave out important dimensions whose exclusion distorts reality and makes their representations more often symbolic than real. No doubt each man who came to these happy surroundings wanted to find a fair land where he could raise bountiful crops, build great houses and barns, and rear a fine family. No doubt in such men the sentiments of democracy and equality were deeply placed. Each knew he was as good as anybody else and was prepared to prove his point by word, deed, and, when necessary, by force. Each believed in plain living and was opposed to him who thought himself better than anyone else. Yet, despite all this, all of them were intent on getting ahead and bettering themselves. When these aspirations are examined in the actions and lives of such men, we learn that they meant much more than sharing the good things of life with other common men. Each was striving to achieve a higher level and to get to a better position than that occupied by his fellows.

The land for these people was more than a place to establish a family and become the head of many generations of kindred who would count themselves from this beginning. Land was for the family, but it was also capital which could be exploited for a profit.

All these men were incipient or true capitalists. They tilled their land and sold their produce and made a profit. The simple economic process might not make them capitalists. But all of them wanted more land than they could till because possessing it increased their prestige and selling it for more than it cost increased their capital. Their farms were often viewed much as a modern shareholder evaluates his stock in a business enterprise. It was hoped that by getting in early, by more people coming into the area, and by local and national improvements, the dollar value of the land would greatly increase, and the owner would become rich or be well on his way to wealth.

During the whole period of Jonesville's settlement, the entire country was involved in speculation in western lands. Great corporations were formed in the East to buy up the new lands, settle them, and reap the profit from the sale of the property. Local men bought land and sold it for purposes of profit only. Whole communities mortgaged their farms and bought railway stock. Panic after panic resulting in part from over-speculation reduced many men to penury and lifted others to wealth and power. Down The

River at Pekin, after a panic, David Davis, shrewd lawyer, bought 14,000 acres of land from the farmers and made himself a man of wealth and power. His activities as a friend of Lincoln's and an early leader in the Republican Party were rewarded when Lincoln made him an associate justice of the Supreme Court of the United States in 1862.

The first farms of Jonesville, U. S. A., were acquired by pre-emption and then bought at public auction for $1.25 an acre by those who had settled there. Speculators, many no doubt the same men who settled the farms, inflated values to many times their actual worth. When the land was put up for sale at the first public auction in Chicago, hordes of people came there to realize quick profits by speculation. So many attended the auction that the building broke down and the sale had to be moved to another part of town. The speculators expected to bid on the pre-empted land and hold it for higher prices. Overnight they bought up all of the timber land in the northeast part of Illinois. Before The Canal was actually constructed, earlier histories of Abraham County tell us, "The land and town lot fever broke out in the state in 1834-35. It took a malignant type in Chicago—the disease spread over the entire state and adjoining states. It was epidemic. It cut up men's farms without regard to locality, and cut up the purses of the purchasers without regard to consequences. . . ."

Another early account which concerns the development of Abraham County reports: "Every ship that left her port [Chicago] carried with it maps of splendidly situated towns and additions, and each vessel that returned was laden with immigrants. It was said at the time that the staple articles of Illinois were town plots and that there was danger of crowding the state with towns to the exclusion of land for agriculture."

Meanwhile, bonds of the states were sold all over the eastern part of the United States and in Europe. The legislatures of the several prairie states greatly contributed to the speculative fever and to the several inflations that ended in panics. The legislature of the state of North Prairie, in 1836-37, voted the laying of 1,300 miles of railroad. These tracks were to cross the state in every direction. Hundreds of miles of canal improvements were contemplated in this legislation, and any county that did not have a canal or railway going through it was compensated by a free grant of funds to be used as it saw fit. The speculators from the various parts of the several counties were so fearful of not getting their share that the legislature ordered the work on the railroads and canals to be started at each end and go to the center and improvements on the rivers to begin at every crossing. Ultimately, the inflated values of land and real property ended in panic, and another crop of speculators bought up the farms of the destitute, and many of them became very wealthy men.

From the beginning, in the minds of the men of Jonesville, U. S. A., the beliefs about being just as good as your neighbor, owning a little land to raise a family, and the concept that all men are equal have been joined in conflict with those about getting ahead, making a profit out of the land, and climbing up to the level above the common level of men. All that they did and everything they believed in embodied and expressed these antithetical ideals. It was in this environment that Abraham Lincoln grew to maturity. The culture of The River made Lincoln, the man. His country claimed him, transformed his image into its own likeness, and used it as a symbol of the perfect American.

Will Taylor and his son voted for Lincoln in 1860. They had heard him debate Douglas. These men with a New England heritage knew that the words of a man from Kentucky evoked within them the warm feelings that made them know he was the right man to represent them and to lead his country.

LINCOLN—A COLLECTIVE REPRESENTATION MADE BY AND FOR JONESVILLE AND THE U. S. A.

Lincoln, product of North Prairie's Jonesvilles, sacred symbol of American idealism, myth more real than the man himself, symbol and fact, was formed in the flow of events which composed the changing cultures of Jonesville and the towns of The River. He is the symbolic culmination of America. To understand him is to know what America means.

When the City of the Common Man began, Abraham Lincoln was twenty-five years old. When the future president was elected to Congress, Jonesville had become a town and the legal seat of Abraham County. By the time Abraham Lincoln contested with Stephen Douglas for the senatorship in the series of debates which brought the attention of the whole county, Jonesville had grown into a sizable community. Lincoln's first debate with Douglas was sufficiently near Jonesville to permit him to stay all night there before the day of the debate.

The country in which Abraham Lincoln grew up was down at the other end of The River from Jonesville. The culture of The River and of North Prairie formed his personality and fashioned him into Lincoln, the man. What he later became as myth and collective representation for Americans was first begun on The River by the peoples of Jonesville and the other towns in the state of North Prairie. The Lincoln image was completed by the people of the entire nation who found in the man Lincoln the necessary materials for a symbol of national unity and for the basic ideals sacred to most Americans.

In 1858 when Lincoln ran against Stephen Douglas for the United States Senate, he was Abraham Lincoln, the successful lawyer, the railroad attorney, who was noted throughout the state as a man above common ability and of more than common importance. He was an ex-congressman. He was earning a substantial income. He had married a daughter of the superior classes from Kentucky. His friends were W. D. Green, the president of a railway, a man of wealth; David Davis, a representative of wealthy eastern investors in western property, who was on his way to becoming a millionaire; Jesse Fell, railway promoter; and other men of prominence and prestige in the state. Lincoln dressed like them; he had unlearned many of the habits acquired in childhood from his lowly-placed parents and learned most of the ways of those highly-placed men who were now his friends. After the Lincoln-Douglas debates his place as a man of prestige and power was as high as anyone's in the whole state.

Yet in 1860 when he was nominated on the Republican ticket for the presidency of the United States, he suddenly became "Abe Lincoln, the rail splitter," "the rude man from the prairie and the river bottoms." To this was soon added "Honest Abe," and finally in death "the martyred leader" who gave his life that "a nation dedicated to the proposition that all men are created equal" might long endure.

What can be the meaning of this strange transformation?

When Richard Oglesby arrived in the Republican convention in 1860 he cast about for a slogan that would bring his friend, Lincoln, favorable recognition from the shrewd politicians of New York, Pennsylvania, and Ohio. He heard from Jim Hanks, who knew

Lincoln as a boy, that Lincoln had once split fence rails. Dick Oglesby, wise in the ways of politicians because he knew they would know what appeals are most potent in bringing out a favorable vote, dubbed Lincoln "the rail splitter." Fence rails were prominently displayed at the convention to symbolize Lincoln's lowly beginnings. Politicians, remembering the enormous popular appeal of "Tippecanoe and Tyler too," "Old Hickory," and "The Log Cabin and Cider Jug" of former elections, realized this slogan would be enormously effective in a national election. Lincoln, the rail splitter, was re-born in Chicago in 1860; and the Lincoln who had become the successful lawyer, intimate of wealthy men, husband of a well-born wife, and man of status was conveniently forgotten.

Three dominant symbolic themes compose the Lincoln image. The first, the theme of the common man, was fashioned in a form pre-established by the equalitarian ideals of a new democracy; to common men there could be no argument about what kind of a man a rail splitter is.

"From log cabin to the White House" succinctly symbolizes the second theme of the trilogy which composes Lincoln, the most powerful of American collective representations. This phrase epitomizes the American success story, the rags-to-riches motif, and the ideals of the ambitious. As the equal of all men, Lincoln was the representative of the Common Man, both as their spokesman and their kind; and, as the man who had gone "from the log cabin to the White House," he became the superior man, the one who had not inherited but earned that superior status and thereby proved to everyone that all men could do as he had. Lincoln thereby symbolized the two great collective but antithetical ideals of American democracy.

When Lincoln was assassinated a third powerful theme of our Christian society was added to the symbol being created by Americans to strengthen and adorn the keystone of their national symbol structure. Lincoln's life lay sacrificed on the altar of unity, climaxing a deadly war which proved by its successful termination that the country was one and that all men are created equal. From the day of his death thousands of sermons and speeches have demonstrated that Lincoln, like Christ, died that all men might live and be as one in the sight of God and man. Christ died that this might be true forever beyond the earth; Lincoln sacrificed his life that this might be true forever on this earth.

When Lincoln died the imaginations of the people of the eastern seaboard cherished him as the man of the new West and translated him into their hopes for tomorrow, for to them the West was tomorrow. The defeated people of the South, during and after the reconstruction period, fitted him into their dark reveries of what might have been, had this man lived, who loved all men. In their bright fantasies, the people of the West and Jonesville, young and believing only in the tomorrow they meant to create, knew Lincoln for what they wanted themselves to be. Lincoln, symbol of equalitarianism, of the social striving of men who live in a social hierarchy, the human leader sacrificed for all men, expresses all the basic values and beliefs of Jonesville, of North Prairie State, and of the United States of America.

Lincoln, the superior man, above all men, yet equal to each, is a mystery beyond the logic of individual calculators. He belongs to the culture and to the social logics of the people for whom contradiction is unimportant and for whom the ultimate tests of truth are in the social structure in which, and for which, they live. Through the passing generations of our Christian culture the Man of the Prairies, formed in the mold of the God-man of Galilee and apotheosized into the man-god of the American people, each year less profane and more sacred, moves securely toward identification with deity and ultimate god-head. In him Americans realize themselves.

THE PRESENT

The cheap and fertile agricultural lands of North Prairie continued to attract settlers from the eastern and southern parts of the country and immigrants from Europe. In the decade from 1850 the population of the state doubled. But as the frontier moved westward to the Pacific, and as transportation and machinery were developed and improved, making a living in North Prairie became more complex and varied. Experience with the soil taught the farmers that corn gave the best yield. In the northern part of the state the corn was shipped to the Chicago market but in other sections it was used to fatten hogs. Oats, also raised in large quantities, and wheat were the other important crops. Dairy farming never became important; cash grain crops yielded the agricultural income. The period of sustenance farming was over.

In this same period, the population of Abraham County tripled, and the number of foreign born increased in even higher proportions. Many of these were Norwegians; almost all settled on the land. Land under cultivation in North Prairie increased from 50,000 acres to 150,000. By 1860 the cash value of farmland in the state was the fourth largest in the country and the number of acres under cultivation ranked second.

Meanwhile, of course, national developments were having their effect on Jonesville and Abraham County. Granger Laws were passed in North Prairie in 1870—part of a national movement of farmers to organize their strength to fight for their interests, and especially aimed at the railroads, upon whom the farmers had become so dependent. National wealth was mounting rapidly in the years following the Civil War, in spite of the condition of the southern states. The purchase of Alaska in 1867, the transatlantic cable finally completed in 1866 by Cyrus Field, and the growing traffic of the western railroads were part of the national expansion. The development of the agricultural and mineral resources of the Mississippi Valley helped to lay the foundation of national wealth.

This decade saw the growing power of the independent farmer. The agricultural population reached its peak in the area surrounding Jonesville in 1870, more land was being utilized, and the number of farms in Abraham County increased from 1,307 to 1,781. Improved knowledge of the soil and the new techniques of farming, combined with the factor of greater land use, pushed the grain crop yield from 590 thousand' bushels to over four million.

The concentration of crop, the new type of machine farming, and the increased availability of markets through railways and waterways combined to attract the interest of large landholders. With 1880 the number of independent farmers began to decrease; size of farm and tenancy increased. Small farms were being consolidated into large holdings.

As the farm population of the county began to decline, more and more people came to live in Jonesville. The Canal had passed its period of importance except for the transportation of heavy freight; but several railroads now ran through the county, the most important passing through Jonesville. The location of the town on a transportation system, its proximity to Chicago, and the availability of labor, freed from the farms by new machinery, attracted new industries. A pottery company started about 1850, and a plow manufactory a few years later, but both failed The first bank was organized in 1853; it also failed. Then, a grain company opened, a cutlery company, and a grist mill. And in the next few years those industries came which developed into the chief economic interests of Jonesville during the next fifty or sixty years.

The mining of bituminous coal had become a dominant industry in the southern part of North Prairie in these years. Coal mining began in Abraham County in 1862 and by 1880 began to assume dominance over agriculture. The population of the mining towns of the county doubled in the coming decade, with a great increase in the number of foreign born immigrants—English, Scotch, and Italian. Most of the coal was loaded on railroad cars and shipped out of the area. Townships were re-formed to provide representative government to the farmers who were overwhelmed by the mining interests of the old townships. But mining reached its peak in Abraham County about 1900. The peak of population was reached at the same time, remained stable for about a decade, and then began to decline with the decline of the mining population.

The economic resources of the county were once more defined in terms of the wealth of the farmers, for whom Jonesville was the commercial center, and of the industries which had become permanently established in the sixties and seventies. One of these was a tannery which grew steadily until it was large enough to be incorporated in 1895. The original building burned, was rebuilt and enlarged, and an additional building was constructed about ten years later. When the founder died, his sons continued the operation of the company but had to close its doors in 1933. Whether failure was due to the incompetence of the sons, or whether heavy speculation in hides late in the First World War put a financial strain on the company from which it could not recover, no one knows.

A brewery started in 1866 and operated with some success until prohibition. A furniture company was established about the same time and was taken over and enlarged a few years later by new owners. The new enterprises and the increased activity of the community called for a bank, and the Abraham County National Bank was founded in 1864 and still operates today. A city hall was built four years later. In 1870 a bank from a nearby town was moved to Jonesville to become the First National Bank of Jonesville.

Then more industries came in: the Square Deal Grain Company, a lumber yard, the Jonesville Grain Company, and numerous smaller concerns. By 1900 Jonesville boasted of 103 manufacturing concerns. An idea of their size and activity is given in the figures which show a combined capital of $848,765, total products of $1,273,095, wages and salaries of $212,841.

The country had successfully weathered the panic of 1893 and entered a period of rising economy stimulated by the discovery of gold in the Yukon, several years of good crops, and the production demands of the Spanish-American War, which put the United States for the first time in the position of a first-class power. It was a period of rising industrialism.

In Jonesville, an industrial association was formed to attract and assist new industries. The association constructed a building on the edge of town to rent to newcomers as an aid in getting them started in Jonesville. Poles, who would work for lower wages, were brought in to help break a strike in the tannery. They settled in a separate section of town and are only now being partially assimilated.

An oatmeal company was started, a mail order clothing manufactory was opened in a nearby town, and another bank was founded. Then, in 1910, the industry which dominates the town today, The Mill, opened its doors.

Throughout the country there was an unprecedented growth of urban population at the expense of the rural areas, and Abraham County reflected this trend. Manufactured goods made up an increasingly large part of our exports. The outbreak of the World War in 1914 caused a high demand for American goods, and our exports increased to supply these new markets. Prices were inflated and reached a peak in the summer of 1920.

Farm prices, which had been rising steadily since the turn of the century, were greatly affected by the war. The demand for wheat and cattle started a speculation in land that sent the price in Abraham County to $235 an acre in 1920 for land that had sold for $56 in 1900. The crop was shifted from corn and oats to wheat. The trend to larger holdings and higher tenancy continued.

Since the great depression of the 1930's Abraham County has continued the population trend that it showed in the twenties: Jonesville has grown at the expense of the rural areas. Farm methods have been radically changed by the tractor; the value of farm machinery has risen while other farm values have continued to fall. Of course the number of hands needed in the fields dropped with the use of machinery.

New machinery has brought back successful mining in the county. A mine has begun to operate near Jonesville where giant electric power shovels scoop out the coal lying twenty to sixty feet under shale and sandstone. The capacity is sufficient to load sixty or seventy 50-ton railway cars a day. When one strip mine is exhausted another is opened up.

And another machine—the automobile—has also had its effect on the town, for the increase in commercial enterprises and the number of people they employ shows that Jonesville has become the center for an ever larger part of the surrounding country.

All of these influences have contributed their share to what Jonesville, as physical plant and community of men, is today. Indeed, to anyone with a sharp eye, an inspection of the physical arrangement of the city's business and dwelling areas will reveal many of the secrets of Jonesville's past and tell him much of its unspoken present. Better yet, anyone who understands the immaterial values of the social-class system of the city can predict how the material facts of the city's physical plant will be arranged. With these thoughts in mind, we will first acquaint ourselves with the social classes of Jonesville and then examine the city as a physical object which reflects these values.

Chapter 2

STATUS IN THE DEMOCRACY
OF JONESVILLE

LIVING ABOVE, BELOW, AND AT THE COMMON MAN LEVEL

Each family's private world and the life of each person are small facets which fit into the larger status mosaic of the city. Jonesville lets no one escape its all-pervasive rating system, for every man rates his fellows and is rated by them. All men and all women are thereby assigned their places in the status structure of the community. A comment of Mr. Walter Thomas, respected Jonesville citizen, is, in varying degrees, in the feelings and thoughts of everyone: "Almost everyone in this town is rated in some way; people can rate you in just a few minutes by talking to you. It's remarkable how you can size people up in a hurry—suppose I use a rating scale of zero to 100 and rate people on it. You can be sure this is not a hypothetical thing either. Not to the people of Jonesville. People like the Caldwells and Volmers [the Lowells and Cabots of Jonesville] rate 100. The Shaws would be up there, too. People like me, oh, a 70 maybe, and people like John [a janitor] about a 40, no better than that. Remember, this is the social rating. If we rated them financially, some of them would rank differently."*

Although each man gets individual recognition from those around him and has his own unique position, he and his family are classified into larger, more commonly recognized categories of status that ordinarily place everyone in the community. These larger categories of status are necessary because it is impossible for those

* By W. Lloyd Warner and Arch Cooper. See List of Authors.

who live in Jonesville to have a ready supply of several thousand separate status categories for each of the several thousand individuals who are members of the community. A few basic categories of status are necessary, among other reasons, to permit people who talk about status easily to recognize what each is talking about. No society has ever succeeded in socially recognizing thousands of separate statuses, and no humans are capable of carrying that much knowledge. In the society of Jonesville, categories which group all people into a few levels are used. These larger classes, being few in number, permit those who use them to rank large numbers of people and to designate the class of the family by simple and easily understood methods. Furthermore, since social differences along status lines are present, the terms used for the social classes adequately identify and designate the several layers of people who compose the Jonesville status system.

The most important and populous class in the status hierarchy of Jonesville is the Level of the Common Man. The layer above, divided into two parts and crowned by an elite, and the one below, filled with a mixed old American and ethnic proletariat, are recognized by everyone in Jonesville. The highest crust is rewarded with deference; the lowest, often with ridicule, pity, or scorn. Knowing and recognizing their superiors and inferiors, the common men of Jonesville learn how to act properly with them. Everyone in Jonesville knows that inferiors must come last in line when the prizes are being distributed and go first when there are heavy loads to carry and unpleasant tasks to perform. The etiquette of deference in the democracy of Jonesville between inferiors and their superiors more often demands inflections of speech than outspoken admittance of superiority or inferiority, lest the speaker convict himself of being a boot-licker by his superiors or a snob and undemocratic by his inferiors. These morals of democracy, designed specifically to protect the small man's self respect while they maintain the big man's prestige, usually protect inferiors from too frank and embarrassingly explicit appraisal of their humble position. Social superiors and inferiors must be subtly recognized lest these American dogmas of equality be flouted, but this same code does not protect the lowly from covert attack and exploitation by their superiors. It is well for such people to know their place and to know how to act in it.

In its lower reaches, the Jonesville upper class shades off and blends into the upper-middle class, the two comprising the Level Above the Common Man. The common men and those below them sometimes lump these two together into one stratum. The people of the upper-middle class, all of them class-conscious, desperately try to separate themselves from the lower groups and incorporate themselves with the elite. The elite, sometimes associating with the upper-middle class but always aware of their own superiority, recognize the more inclusive status which separates upper- and upper-middle-class people from everyone else, but they and the members of the class below them are well aware of the status differences between them. The upper class holds about three percent of the people of Jonesville.

Beneath these two classes are the lower-middle and upper-lower classes, who compose the common run of Americans and the great bulk of the population of Jonesville and other American communities. These are the two strata we have called the Common Man Level. Under certain conditions the members of the lower stratum of this level are thought by the people of Jonesville to be at the bottom of the social heap and are classed with the lowest level in the society. At times the lower-middle-class people are grouped with the upper-middle class. This classification occurs when people think only of the two extremes of society and the middle. We have retained and interrelated the two ways of classifying, and referring to, the social strata of Jonesville.

About three percent (2.67) of the people of Jonesville are upper-class and a little less than 11 percent are upper-middle. Since these percentages include only those who live in the town itself (for 6,108 individuals) and not the rural areas, it is possible to compare the composition of the classes of urban Yankee City with those of Jonesville. The percentages for the two top levels are similar, the upper class of Yankee City having exactly three percent of the population, while the upper-middle includes slightly over 10 percent of its citizens. (See "Yankee City Series" by Warner and associates, Yale University Press.)

The proportion of people in Jonesville's lower-lower class (14 percent) is smaller than for the New England community (25 percent). This means, of course, that the Common Man Level is much larger in Jonesville, 31 percent being in the lower-middle class and 41 percent in the upper-lower class, whereas 28 percent of the population of Yankee City is lower-middle and 33 percent belongs to the upper-lower class.

It is clear that the lowest class in Jonesville is not the largest but ranks third, the upper-lower being first, the lower-middle second, and the two higher levels ranking fourth and fifth. The size of the classes of Yankee City follows this same order. This probably means that basically similar forces are operating to produce these same results.

However, the discrepancies between the two sets of figures need further analysis. The figures for the lower-lower classes show the greatest differences. The principal reasons for them are not difficult to find. Yankee City is an industrial town. Jonesville, while depending on industry, is also an important market center. Market towns are more likely to have people who belong to the Common Man Level and less likely to produce a proletariat. In other words, the population of a market town resembles the people in its agricultural background where status differentiation is less advanced than in urban areas.

Another important reason for this difference is that there are fewer members of ethnic groups in Jonesville who have recently arrived in America than there are in Yankee City. Such people tend to swell the lower levels, for when they come into the community they start at the bottom. The chapter on the Norwegians, who are by far the largest ethnic group in Jonesville, shows that when they first came into the town the proportion of their people who were lower-class was much larger than it is now. The Norse as a group have put pressure on their members to force most of them into behavior that keeps them above the lower-lower class.

Finally, and perhaps most importantly, Yankee City is much older than Jonesville. The classes in an older community have had longer to become organized and recognized. It will be remembered that in the older regions, particularly those where social change has been slow, class differences are more pronounced. In Jonesville and similar cities most people of lower status continue to struggle for higher position, for their faith in social mobility for everyone is stronger than these same people have in Yankee City. Fewer people in Jonesville have given up.

The people of the upper class are divided into "old families" and "the new people." Usually the first term implies people who have had wealth and family position for several generations or who have managed to retain their social position despite loss of much of their wealth; the second refers to those who have recently climbed into this top position and succeeded in being accepted by the people who occupy it. In New England, the Deep South, and the older regions of the United States, the "old families" are securely placed above those in the "new family" group. But in Jonesville this is not true. The "new families," once accepted, in less than a lifetime can secure equality with the others at this top level. It must be remembered that only a few are accepted and that not every wealthy family which tries to reach the top succeeds.

The comparative recency of Middle Western settlement partly accounts for the difference in the class structure of the several regions. The great grandchildren of the original settlers are still alive in the Middle West. Jonesville has not had time to slough off awkward memories about the early immigrants and admit the claims of the "old families" as the social arbiters of who shall enter the realm of aristocracy. The power of the blood of the elite can only be infused into it by many generations of deference-giving from one community; yet large towns elsewhere in the Middle West have produced an "old family stratum," though admittedly weak and insecure. Their large populations make it possible for their older families to hold themselves aloof from the newly wealthy, and to insist upon recognition of their prestige by the deference of climbers. But in Jonesville the "old families" are not numerous enough to organize such a group. Their high status is more secure and more widely recognized when they join hands in friendship and marriage with the "new people," but not with all of them. Only some of the recently wealthy, only a few of the men who recently acquired professional prestige, and a few of those who have come to Jonesville from elsewhere are anointed with the manna of those who stand at the top of the social stairs.

The "old families" of Jonesville, North Prairie State, and of the Middle West generally are cursed with another social plague which constantly threatens the security of their status. The people who settled the Middle West were migrants from the East. Jonesville and the Middle West, for many of them, were midpoints on their westward journey. If one generation did not move on to the Far West, the next often did. Today the wealthy families, too frequently for the security of the upper class, sell their farms and move to California or Florida.

Worse still, the daughters and sisters of wealthy Chicago burghers, upper-class members of a city which should supply the keystone to the Middle Western class-arch, desert their home city and go East to Boston and New York (and sometimes London) to marry into the higher status of the East. The mere recognition by upper-class Middle Westerners of the superiority of the "old family" status in the older regions of the United States weakens their own class security and decreases the social height of the upper-class level of the Middle West. Despite the weaknesses of the "old family" position, the present necessity of accepting some of the newly arrived as equals may cease, for there are indications that a few generations will mature the society of Jonesville and North Prairie State sufficiently to put a strong "old family" crust over it. Even now, the fact that, to be accepted, all new families have "to work at it" and not all of them "make it" indicates that the "old families" are not without power in dealing with the "new money" and "new prestige" of the recently arrived.

The upper-middle class, active in all community activities, is composed of the people who are less wealthy than those at the top. They are the prominent, substantial people to whom common men very often pay deference. But they are anxious people, for in their eagerness to associate with those who are their social betters they are very fearful of doing something wrong and ruining their chances for advancement. They worry for fear they will overlook some opportunity for bettering their station in life. They are constantly on the alert to enter into worthy civic enterprises, particularly those in which men and women from the elite are active sponsors. They accept the necessity of offering deference to their betters sometimes with good grace, sometimes with concealed hostility and bitterness, but they accept it. In fact, some of them learn to like their deference roles so much that they seemingly lose their desire to climb to the position of the elect.

The small shopkeepers, the skilled workers, the clerks and others like them are, occupationally, characteristic of the top of the Common Man Level. They are the people who "belong to nice families but are nobody socially." More of them tend to be religious and more of them tend to provide themselves with the sentiments which are thought to be the backbone of the moral life of America. Below them are the little people, the poor but honest workers who fill the small houses that press against each other in the new developments and in the areas around The Mill and in the less well kept parts of town. These common men are worlds apart from the elite and from the upper-middle class.

The Level Below the Common Man, the lower-lower class, live in little houses which are sometimes tarpaper shacks, sometimes small bungalows that huddle together across The Canal and on the towpath down The River or on the other side of the railway tracks in "Polack Town" and "Ixnay." To many of the men of Jonesville they are the "god-damned Polacks" and "those dirty, poor whites," "the hill-billies," and "the poor and unfortunate."

The five classes blend into each other. The young people of each class tend to marry at their own level. Their children acquire the status of the parents, learn their way of life, and thus help maintain their part of the class system and insure its permanence. The people of each class more often than not form friendships at their own or adjacent levels. Some of them move to higher levels and some sink to lower ones. Some climb to higher levels by getting better jobs and more money; others do it by education; many women and a few men, by marriage; and still others, by being very successful in gaining recognition for a talent prized by the community. All of them must obtain the social acceptance of groups of people at higher levels if they are to consolidate their social mobility and securely acquire status for themselves and for their children. To do this, they need, and must have, the values and behavior of those who are their new associates or they will not gain approval and acceptance. From the point of view of social class, the people of Jonesville are ranked at inferior and superior levels where the prizes of life are unequally distributed, but with mobility possible either for ascent or descent. Such are the simple outlines of the class order.

Before presenting a detailed description of the social-class system of Jonesville, we will let a few well-informed people tell us what they think it is. Our interviews with these people are too full for complete presentation. Although we will hear from them in their own words, it will be necessary to cut their statements to a minimum. We will first learn how Lawyer Donnelley was rated by the people of Jonesville and what he and his wife think about the rating. And we shall also learn how, despite their feeling of superiority to the system that rated them, he and his wife have accepted the inferior rank assigned them by the upper crust.

He Was Trying to Place Me

Mr. and Mrs. Frank Donnelley are comparative newcomers to Jonesville. Mr. Donnelley, now prominent among the lawyers of the town, has been in Jonesville only twenty years. He has a good income, and his competitors and the people of the town consider him a successful man. Mr. Donnelley came there from a large city. "It seems to me," he said, "there's quite a lot of difference in the type of relation you have in a big town and a small town. In large cities people aren't so closely connected with one another. In small towns the people know all about their neighbors. They're much more closely connected. It's like a network; it's very closely intertwined. They even know when you bought your last pound of butter. They can see everything you do. And they follow all your goings and comings. People are held more tightly together."

Mrs. Donnelley, who belongs to the Woman's Club and other civic organizations, knows her position and is frank about it. "The first two or three years we were here we were more or less out of things. We were strangers, and it was a little hard to get acquainted."

Mrs. Donnelley's understanding of the closely-knit character of the social life of Jonesville is explicitly realized by her.

"We have become a part of a definite group here in town. Our group is not upper-class. I'm quite sure that all the people in our group are upper-middle-class. We eat around at one another's houses, play bridge, and have nice dinners. All the women pride themselves on being good cooks. We just drink, play bridge, talk business, and have a good time." Mrs. Donnelley then listed a number of people who belong to her level and said, "There's an older, upper-class group here in town. It's sometimes referred to as the older 'Federated' group. I hear them spoken of that way because they all more or less belong to the Federated Church, but I don't think they go very regularly. Mrs. Stanley Radcliffe is one of those. She is a snob, just plain snob. She holds herself aloof from practically everyone in town."

After listing a number of people who belong to that level she said, "There's also a younger, upper-class group here in town. They're sometimes spoken of as 'social register.' The Carl Stocktons, who live right over back of us, are in that group. Mrs. Stockton, I think, is exclusive. I just don't say she is a snob, but she certainly hasn't been at all friendly or neighborly. Here we have been neighbors for seven years, but she has never asked me in to one of her parties, and she has them all the time."

Mrs. Donnelley's list of names of those who belong to the upper and upper-middle classes corresponds almost name by name with those mentioned for these two classes by several other men and women in Jonesville.

Mr. Donnelley has a story about his place in the community. He preferred to tell it as one of his first experiences after settling in Jonesville.

"When I came here, twenty years ago," he said, "it didn't take me over two months to discover that this town is class-conscious. There's that 400 group at the top, and they look down on people like me. Now, you're new here and strange, and you might think I'm just complaining. But I'm willing to give you a concrete illustration of what I mean. When I first came here I went around to a few affairs and met some of the people. I don't remember where I was, but I met Clay Coolidge. One evening I was walking down the street and I saw Clay coming the other way and we met. He held out his hand and said, 'Good evening, Mr. Donnelley.' I held out my hand and we shook hands. I saw that he was kindly disposed. He began to ask me questions. Something like this:

" 'Mr. Donnelley, I understand that you are a new lawyer here in town.' I said, yes, I hoped to practice my profession here. He said, 'Well, my family has been around here for a long time.' As we strolled along the street he said, 'Mr. Donnelley, did you learn your law in a law office?' I said, no, I didn't. He said, 'Well, did you go to a law school?' I said, yes, I did. 'Well, Mr. Donnelley, what law school did you attend?' I said, oh, I went up to the University of Michigan and finished there. He went on, 'Oh, you did. Well, that's a very good school.' He was fumbling around for another question, but I just let him fumble.

"Then he said, 'Mr. Donnelley, did you belong to a fraternity?' And I said, yes, I belonged to a fraternity. 'Well, Mr. Donnelley, what fraternity did you join?' I said, Alpha Alpha Alpha. 'Oh, Mr. Donnelley, that's a very fine fraternity. All of the best people at the University I went to joined that fraternity.'

"Then he went on like this for a little bit, and then he said, 'Did you do your undergraduate work at Michigan?' I said to him, 'Mr. Coolidge, I have a kind and indulgent father. He had made a little money, so he wanted me to have an education, so he sent me away to college.' Then Clay went on, 'Ah, Mr. Donnelley, I see. Very good. And where did you attend college?' " Mr. Donnelley told him. "Then he asked, 'Did you belong to a fraternity when you were an undergraduate?' " According to Mr. Donnelley, Mr. Coolidge continued asking questions about his background. Mr. Donnelley said that at about the same time he asked about the fraternity, "I saw what he was up to. He was trying to place me socially."

Mr. Coolidge, by use of his little interrogatory, gathered much of the necessary evidence to give Mr. Donnelley and his family their original placement in Jonesville. Mr. Coolidge learned that Mr. Donnelley had "a higher education," that his father had sufficient wealth and interest to send Donnelley to college (at least Mr. Donnelley said that he had), that Donnelley belonged to "a good fraternity," filled with the sons of "the better people," and that he had gone to "a good college." He also learned that Mr. Donnelley had a superior occupation and that probably his principal income was from "fees," a highly respected source of income. It is possible that Mr. Coolidge had learned by then in what neighborhood Lawyer Donnelley lived and what kind of a house he had acquired to launch his fortunes in Jonesville. The lawyer's superior manners helped confirm what he had told Mr. Coolidge. Mr. Donnelley's original score on Mr. Coolidge's and other social arbiters' interrogatories, combined with his and his family's subsequent behavior, gave him an upper-middle-class position.

To make sure that we know what our informants are talking about, and to increase the representativeness of those who speak about status in Jonesville, let us call another expert witness, a substantial citizen who knows Jonesville well.

"I think generally you can put the people of this town into four groups and rank them socially so those in Group One are highest and those in Group Four are the lowest. In the first group, I would put such people as Mrs. Henry Coolidge, and I would put Mrs. Joseph Coolidge in there, too." He then named a number of families who belong to this level. "They are in the top brackets or the upper class. They are so high up they're just social history around here now, and it doesn't matter what they do. They can do anything they want and don't have to worry about what people are going to think of them. They bought up the county early and own most of it. They have been here so long that it really doesn't matter what they do. And they don't care what people think of them because they know their position is all right anyway.

"Of course, I think that that whole group is pretty secure. They don't have to worry much about what other people think of them. But that isn't true of all of them.

"Then, in the second group I would put such people as Mrs. Mary McKelvey and Mrs. Marjorie Kingman. I would say that the first group is more certain of itself than the second group. That second group hasn't gotten so far financially and they still worry about themselves and what people think of them. They're working to get some place, and they have to be more careful of what they do and what people think of them.

"The third group I would consider as more religious than intelligent, if you know what I mean. They have a lot of principles such as loving each other as Christians even though there's a war on. But they are not very logical about their ideas. They don't think through anything very well. They're just religious.

"Then, the fourth class, well, they're all composed of poorer people. I think the husbands of most of them are laborers or perhaps they have small office jobs.

"Really, you can say that the first group and the fourth group are alike in a lot of respects. They're both absolutely secure in their positions. That fourth group is sort of at the bottom of the pile, to be crude about it, and they're perfectly secure and perfectly settled in their position. They've resigned themselves to it and they know they won't get any place. It's only those people that are worrying about getting some place that think about other people's opinion."

Mr. George Brown, a long-time resident of the town who has kindred in what is called "the fancy crowd," divides the town into "social strata." These strata are "the top one," composed of old, wealthy families or "new people" who have a lot of money, the "upper-middle class," "a lower but middle stratum," and the "ordinary workmen, mostly ranked as lower class around here" who are not as low as "the canal renters and the older Poles" who are at the "bottom of the social structure." His rating, with few differences, corresponds closely with the preceding interview.

Our estimates of Jonesville status alignments so far come from adults. Americans generally believe that young people are more democratic; that they are not aware of, and care nothing about, class distinctions. Our own research indicates that this is not true, or at least is not true categorically. The daughter of a prominent merchant, of the upper-middle class of Jonesville, made the following comments:

"There's not supposed to be classes in this town, but actually there are. There's a higher class, and then there's a middle class, and then there's a lower class. Then, there are those in between. Well, families like us are in between the higher class and the middle class. We're not exactly middle-class, and we're not higher-class.

"Income, I guess, is the main thing in class, but—well, it's more than that, too. Part of it is the way you use your money, and the way that you act, and what you do in town. The things that you are in and stuff like that."

Mr. Ranney, a minor city official, was sitting in his office when he was interviewed. He was giving his attention to people of the Level Below the Common Man. His feelings about them are mixed. He said, "The class of people who come in here [lower-lower] aren't worth much. Most of them have been on relief the last ten years. Right now there's a lot of work, and a man can get ninety cents an hour for common labor over at the munitions plant. But ten years from now I bet those people will be right back in here.

"Every once in a while you will find someone who tries to make good. But if a family has a relief reputation it's pretty hard in a town like this to get any place. I always tell these young people to get out of town—go somewhere else where their family is not known and they will have a chance. They don't have any here. You take the Kula family. It's a mess. Those women don't live right. That woman isn't raising those girls right. They never go inside of a church or anything. They're one of the really immoral families we have in this community. Now, this is a family that's got three or four grown girls. The father was in trouble several times around here and he deserted them a number of years ago. The girls are trying to make an effort to get a job. I have tried to get them jobs. Now, the fellow down at the ABC Restaurant needed two girls recently, and I went over and talked to him about putting the Kula girls on, and he wouldn't do it. 'No, I can't have those girls in here,' he said, 'with the reputation their family has. Those girls just better leave town. They can do the work all right, but I just can't have them in my place.'

"I know that those girls are good, steady, honest workers, but they can't get work in this town.

"Now, some of the people aren't worth anything. Others try to help themselves, and they just can't because they have a bad reputation."

Mr. Ranney, a respectable member of the lower-middle class, distinguishes between the poor but honest worker who is trying to get off relief and the chronic reliefers. He listed a large number of families "who are no good." All of them belong to what another informant called "the lulu level." Our own research concluded they belong to what we call, less expressively, the lower-lower class.

Throughout the statements of all informants there is the constant theme of social inequality and class difference. All of them recognize several classes. The status levels outlined by them are in general agreement. Perhaps the most critical and decisive proof of the general recognition of class in Jonesville is the degree of conformance in placement among all of those who mention names.

The chances are few that this agreement among them is individualistic and not a well-recognized social phenomenon. It seems highly probable that the citizens of Jonesville know and think about class behavior and that this knowledge is one of the basic guides to proper and adaptive behavior for all of them.

Chapter 3

THE FACTS OF LIFE

LIVING SPACE

Even the casual observer of the present city of Jonesville notices that the town's living space is sliced into three large layers. In the north, the railway cuts through, dividing the top and the middle, and in the south the waters of The Canal separate the thick middle from the thin, lower layer. (See map, p. 37.) In Jonesville, everyone knows that if you live north of the tracks or south of The Canal, you are on the wrong side of town. The social reputation of these areas, in the minds of the people of the town, is sufficiently low to rank at the bottom of the social heap those who live there. "North of the tracks" and "across The Canal" are symbolic terms, emblematic of low status.*

"The poorest area in town," we were often told, "is south of The Canal and behind the old tannery [Towpath]. That's the original town. Most of the upper-class people here will not admit that this section exists, especially the women." Often a family known to be at the bottom of the social heap but living north of The Canal in one of the better regions is said to be "some of those people who live across The Canal." This kind of regional term in the democracy of Jonesville and the United States is an indirect and acceptable way of saying a family is of inferior status.

A glance at the map of Jonesville reveals that we were able to distinguish seventeen major and minor dwelling areas. Each was given an appropriate name and ranked according to its social reputation among the inhabitants of the town. The two major

* By W. Lloyd Warner. See List of Authors.

areas north of the tracks, Northwestern and Polish Town, are sometimes called Ixnay and Frogtown and a number of other derogatory terms equally unflattering. These terms, used with obvious intent to degrade, are applied to the areas and their people more often than not by those who live in the middle layer of Jonesville.

"This town is divided into sections," a man from this middle region said. "Across the tracks is Ixnay; the northeast part of that section is called Frogtown. It's full of Polacks. The whole west side (south of the tracks), barring The Canal, is all right. But the outskirts on the far west side are kind of bad."

Frogtown (Polish Town) is a region where one must drive carefully for the streets are like alleys bordered by broken fences that lean over into them. Sometimes it is almost impossible to drive through. Old women sit out in the yards in broken-down chairs watching the chickens running over the alleys and destroying the yards. Mr. Thomas, an upper-middle-class professional man who knew his Jonesville, said, "You'll talk to a lot of people here in town and they'll tell you we don't have any real poor section, but we do. Frogtown is one of our poorest sections. Then there's that part down by The Mill, East Canal. The worst section we have, though, is south of The Canal [Towpath]. You talk to Jonesville people here, and they just ignore those sections."

Oldtown and Towpath are the two oldest parts of town. The remains of the older industries are still there. The people in these areas live in abandoned stores, small industrial plants, or "squat" in rudely constructed shacks and small, insubstantial houses. Towpath is disordered and lacks any planned arrangement of houses.

To rank the town's evaluations of these several dwelling areas, we used a seven-point scale, ranging from very good to very poor. Towpath ranked 7. It is lower than Oldtown (ranked 6) or East Canal (6) which are on the right side of The Canal and do not so easily distinguish their residents from the rest of the town in the thinking of Jonesville's people. Frogtown, doubly stigmatized by being "infested with Polacks" and being on the wrong side of the tracks, but still with claims to respectability, was given a 6.

Residence and social status in Jonesville are so arranged that Top Circle (rated a 1), near the center of the city and identified as being superior to the Common Man Level, blends into middle-class West Side (2) and into upper-lower-class districts. In the

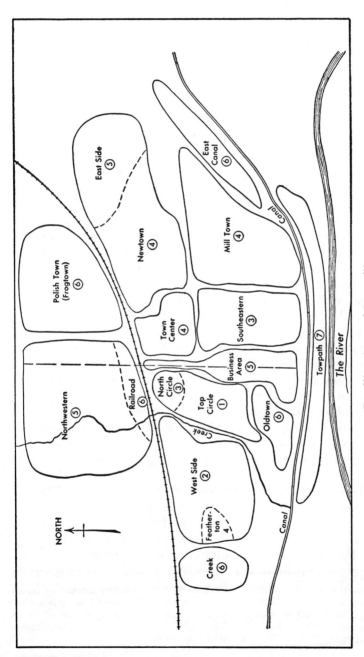

Dwelling Areas of Jonesville

east it shifts from Top Circle into the middle-class Southeastern (3) and drops into lower-class districts such as East Side (5) and East Canal (6). A diagram, arranged in concentric circles, simplifying the whole arrangement of status in dwelling areas, would show a progressive dropping off from Top Circle's social heights through the lower-ranking zones to the periphery of the town and the bottom social levels.

In their comments on their experiences in moving into Jonesville and attempting to find a proper place to live, a middle-class family's evaluation of the several areas is clearly given. Mr. Brown is talking: "When we first came here the layout of the town wasn't very clear to us. But we were told when we started to look for a house not to rent a house north of the railway tracks and to try to get something west of the center of town. If we couldn't find anything there we should get in close to it on the east side, say a block or two away. We were told that if we got over on the east side, down close to The Canal, we would be talked about and looked down upon."

From such statements and many similar ones it becomes obvious that each man in Jonesville carries a working map of the city in his head. He knows where things are and how to get to them. But the map that is carried by him and those like him in other American communities is not merely one that could be constructed by compass and surveyor's instruments, since most of the people of Jonesville and America know that railways, canals, and interstate highways which form the broad division of the major regions of the town are also the boundaries which often separate common men from their social superiors and inferiors. Where a man lives in America's Jonesvilles helps label and grade him.

HOUSES, INCOME, AND OCCUPATION; MARKS OF DISTINCTION

Dwelling area was but one of four social characteristics that we used to rate the families of Jonesville. The other three, also ranged on a seven-point scale running from very high (1) to very low (7), were house type, occupation, and source of income.[1] They, too, were excellent indicators of the social level of a family in Jonesville.

[1] Several other characteristics were used at first, including amount of income and education; many others could have been used. For the whole story on why these characteristics were chosen, see *Social Class in America: A Manual for the Measurement of Social Status*, by W. Lloyd Warner, Marchia Meeker, and Kenneth Eells (Chicago: Science Research Associates, 1949).

The houses of Americans are valued by them not only as utilities but because they are outward symbols of the social status of those who occupy them. The houses of Jonesville were ranked according to their size and condition of repair. As could be expected, there is a close relationship between the rank of the house and the class of the person who lives in it, the higher classes occupying the fine houses, and the lowest, the poorest ones.

I	71	Top Circle (82%) North Circle (60%)
II	41	West Side (41%) Southeastern (41%)
III	25	Mill Town (28%) Featherton (24%) Town Center (23%)
IV	14	Newtown (12%) Northwestern (14%) Creek (16%)
V	3	East Side (4%) Polish Town (5%) Business (3%) East Canal (5%) Oldtown (4%) Railroad (5%) Towpath (0%)

CHART I.   Where the Mansions and Fine Houses Are Located
(These houses are ranks 1 and 2)

The fine houses and the shanties are distributed throughout the dwelling areas of Jonesville, not by chance but in accordance with the dictates of social class. Chart I tells this story. It divides the areas into five ranks, showing the distribution of the better houses (a combination of the two highest ranks) in the several dwelling areas. (Table 1 gives the number and percentage of the seven ranks of houses in the several regions. The category "unknown" includes cases where evidence was not sufficient for class typing.) It will be noticed that 82 percent of the houses in Top Circle belong to the two highest ranks, and 82 percent of the families in Towpath live in houses ranked as sixth and seventh.

The people of Jonesville, and Americans generally, rank inher-

Area	1	2	3	4	5	6	7	Unknown	Total
Top Circle	23.13 / 31	58.96 / 79	2.24 / 3	8.21 / 11	0.75 / 1	2.99 / 4	- / -	3.73 / 5	6.40 / 134
West Side	10.53 / 14	30.08 / 40	31.58 / 42	10.53 / 14	3.01 / 4	14.29 / 19	- / -	- / -	6.35 / 133
Southeastern	3.54 / 9	37.80 / 96	24.41 / 62	16.54 / 42	6.69 / 17	8.66 / 22	- / -	2.36 / 6	12.12 / 254
North Circle	18.60 / 8	41.86 / 18	18.60 / 8	9.30 / 4	4.65 / 2	4.65 / 2	- / -	2.33 / 1	2.05 / 43
Mill Town	2.19 / 10	25.88 / 118	30.04 / 137	14.04 / 64	5.26 / 24	21.27 / 97	1.10 / 5	0.22 / 1	21.77 / 456
Featherton	5.88 / 1	17.65 / 3	35.29 / 6	- / -	5.88 / 1	35.29 / 6	- / -	- / -	0.81 / 17
Newtown	2.88 / 6	9.13 / 19	26.44 / 55	4.81 / 10	17.79 / 37	36.54 / 76	0.96 / 2	1.44 / 3	9.93 / 208
East Side	- / -	3.92 / 2	1.96 / 1	- / -	41.18 / 21	41.18 / 21	7.84 / 4	3.92 / 2	2.43 / 51
Town Center	- / -	22.50 / 27	47.50 / 57	15.00 / 18	1.67 / 2	11.67 / 14	0.83 / 1	0.83 / 1	5.73 / 120

Business Area	—	3.05 / 4	17.56 / 23	8.40 / 11	65.65 / 86	1.53 / 2	1.53 / 2	2.29 / 3	6.25 / 131
Northwestern	2.46 / 6	11.48 / 28	25.41 / 62	11.48 / 28	5.74 / 14	32.79 / 80	5.33 / 13	5.33 / 13	11.65 / 244
Oldtown	—	4.49 / 4	13.48 / 12	16.85 / 15	39.33 / 35	14.61 / 13	1.12 / 1	10.11 / 9	4.25 / 89
Creek	—	16.13 / 5	19.35 / 6	29.03 / 9	—	29.03 / 9	6.45 / 2	—	1.48 / 31
Polish Town	—	5.22 / 6	15.65 / 18	6.09 / 7	9.57 / 11	50.43 / 58	11.30 / 13	1.74 / 2	5.49 / 115
East Canal	—	5.41 / 2	—	8.11 / 3	5.41 / 2	54.05 / 20	24.32 / 9	2.70 / 1	1.77 / 37
Railroad	—	4.76 / 1	4.76 / 1	19.05 / 4	4.76 / 1	38.10 / 8	28.57 / 6	—	1.00 / 21
Towpath	—	—	9.09 / 1	—	—	9.09 / 1	72.73 / 8	9.09 / 1	0.53 / 11
Total	4.06 / 85	21.58 / 452	23.58 / 494	11.46 / 240	12.32 / 258	21.58 / 452	3.15 / 66	2.29 / 48	2,095

TABLE 1. House Type

ited wealth above all other sources, even above its nearest competitor, earned wealth, despite the feeling that a man who earns his own way has great virtue and is someone to admire. Just below these two top ranks are profits and fees; salary outranks wages; and wages are considered better than living on private philanthropy. Public aid is considered so low that it ranks seventh and last with

I	(18)	**Top Circle (19%)** **North Circle (16%)**	
II	(5)	**West Side (7%)** **Southeastern (5%)** **Creek (3%)**	
III	(2)	**Mill Town (2%)** **Town Center (2%)** **Business Area (2%)**	
IV	(1)	**Newtown (1%)** **Northwestern (1%)**	
V	(0)	**Featherton (0)** **East Side (0)** **Oldtown (0)** **Polish Town (0)**	**East Canal (0)** **Railroad (0)** **Towpath (0)**

CHART II.   Dwelling Area and Income (Inherited and earned wealth)
(Inherited and earned wealth are ranks 1 and 2)

nonrespectable or immoral sources of income. These compose the seven points in the scale for income sources.

Inherited and earned wealth (rated 1 and 2) are concentrated in Top and North Circles; profits and fees (3) in the West Side, Top Circle, and Business Area. North Circle has the highest proportion of salaried people (42 percent). In nine of the seventeen areas, over half of the people live on wages (5), East Canal leading all others (89 percent). Well over half of the families of Towpath live on public and private aid. One of the quickest ways to get the salient points of the whole story is to examine Chart II. The

two top-ranking incomes are combined and charted according to
the way they are distributed in the several areas. (The detailed
evidence on the relation of area and source of income are presented
in Table 2.)

The three highest levels of the seven on the occupational scale
[professionals and proprietors of large businesses (1), semi-

Percent
of High   The Areas
Occupation

	Percent of High Occupation	The Areas
I	60	Top Circle (60%)
II	35	West Side (33%) Southeastern (30%) North Circle (42%)
III	21	Featherton (18%) Mill Town (20%) Newtown (17%) Town Center (33%) Business Area (19%)
IV	10	East Side (12%) Northwestern (8%) Oldtown (9%)
V	3	Creek (6%) Polish Town (4%) East Canal (3%) Railroad (5%) Towpath (0%)

CHART III. Where the People with Superior Occupations Live
(Proportion of occupational ranks 1, 2, and 3 within an area)

professionals and lesser officials (2), clerks and kindred workers
(3)] were combined and the totals for each dwelling area placed
on Chart III. The shaded area in each square in the left-hand
column shows what proportion of the families in an area have
these high occupations. The percentages show that over half the
occupations of Top Circle are the highly rated ones. This drops
off rapidly until only six percent or less of the occupations in the

Area	1	2	3	4	5	6	7	Unknown	Total
Top Circle	8.21 11	11.19 15	28.36 38	33.58 45	18.66 25	-	-	-	6.40 134
West Side	3.76 5	3.01 4	31.58 42	24.81 33	36.84 49	-	-	-	6.35 133
Southeastern	0.79 2	3.94 10	21.65 55	34.25 87	39.37 100			-	12.12 254
North Circle	2.33 1	13.95 6	16.28 7	41.86 18	25.58 11	-	-	-	2.05 43
Mill Town	-	1.75 8	16.89 77	24.34 111	56.16 256	0.44 2	0.44 2	-	21.77 456
Featherton	-	-	23.53 4	35.29 6	41.18 7	-	-	-	0.81 17
Newtown	-	0.96 2	15.38 32	16.83 35	66.35 138	-	0.48 1	-	9.93 208
East Side	-	-	5.88 3	11.76 6	78.43 40	1.96 1	1.96 1	-	2.43 51
Town Center	-	1.67 2	19.17 23	32.50 39	45.83 55	-	0.83 1	-	5.73 120

TABLE 2. Source of Income

									Total
Business Area	0.76 / 1	1.53 / 2	30.53 / 40	25.19 / 33	41.98 / 55	-	-	-	6.25 / 131
Northwestern	-	0.82 / 2	15.16 / 37	17.21 / 42	65.57 / 160	1.23 / 3	-	-	11.65 / 244
Oldtown	-	-	16.85 / 15	19.10 / 17	61.80 / 55	1.12 / 1	1.12 / 1	-	4.25 / 89
Creek	-	3.23 / 1	-	9.68 / 3	87.10 / 27	-	-	-	1.48 / 31
Polish Town	-	-	6.09 / 7	6.96 / 8	79.13 / 91	0.87 / 1	6.96 / 8	-	5.49 / 115
East Canal	-	-	5.41 / 2	2.70 / 1	89.19 / 33	-	2.70 / 1	-	1.77 / 37
Railroad	-	-	-	4.76 / 1	80.95 / 17	4.76 / 1	9.52 / 2	-	1.00 / 21
Towpath	-	-	-	-	36.36 / 4	9.09 / 1	54.55 / 6	-	0.53 / 11
Total	0.95 / 20	2.48 / 52	18.23 / 382	23.15 / 485	53.60 / 1123	0.48 / 10	1.10 / 23	-	2,095

Area	1	2	3	4	5	6	7	Unknown	Total
Top Circle	32.09 / 43	15.67 / 21	11.94 / 16	14.18 / 19	5.97 / 8	4.48 / 6	8.96 / 12	6.72 / 9	6.40 / 134
West Side	12.78 / 17	5.26 / 7	15.04 / 20	22.56 / 30	14.29 / 19	14.29 / 19	12.03 / 16	3.76 / 5	6.35 / 133
Southeastern	7.48 / 19	7.09 / 18	15.75 / 40	21.65 / 55	20.87 / 53	15.35 / 39	6.69 / 17	5.12 / 13	12.12 / 254
North Circle	13.95 / 6	11.63 / 5	16.28 / 7	23.26 / 10	4.65 / 2	18.60 / 8	6.98 / 3	4.65 / 2	2.05 / 43
Mill Town	3.95 / 18	4.17 / 19	12.28 / 56	27.63 / 126	15.13 / 69	19.08 / 87	15.57 / 71	2.19 / 10	21.77 / 456
Featherton	5.88 / 1	11.76 / 2	- / -	35.29 / 6	17.65 / 3	17.65 / 3	5.88 / 1	5.88 / 1	0.81 / 17
Newtown	0.48 / 1	9.62 / 20	7.21 / 15	28.85 / 60	13.46 / 28	24.52 / 51	15.38 / 32	0.48 / 1	9.93 / 208
Town Center	5.00 / 6	12.50 / 15	15.83 / 19	23.33 / 28	9.17 / 11	24.17 / 29	7.50 / 9	2.50 / 3	5.73 / 120
East Side	- / -	1.96 / 1	9.80 / 5	17.65 / 9	5.88 / 3	37.25 / 19	25.49 / 13	1.96 / 1	2.43 / 51

TABLE 3. Occupation

Area									Total
Business Area	1.53 / 2	7.63 / 10	9.92 / 13	23.66 / 31	25.95 / 34	18.32 / 24	9.16 / 12	3.82 / 5	6.25 / 131
Northwestern	0.41 / 1	1.64 / 4	5.74 / 14	21.72 / 53	17.62 / 43	29.92 / 73	19.67 / 48	3.28 / 8	11.65 / 244
Oldtown	–	3.37 / 3	5.62 / 5	21.35 / 19	19.10 / 17	24.72 / 22	23.60 / 21	2.25 / 2	4.25 / 89
Creek	–	–	6.45 / 2	25.81 / 8	9.68 / 3	32.26 / 10	22.58 / 7	3.23 / 1	1.48 / 31
Polish Town	–	1.74 / 2	2.61 / 3	12.17 / 14	12.17 / 14	38.26 / 44	33.04 / 38	–	5.49 / 115
East Canal	–	2.70 / 1	–	13.51 / 5	10.81 / 4	37.84 / 14	32.43 / 12	2.70 / 1	1.77 / 37
Railroad	–	–	4.76 / 1	9.52 / 2	19.05 / 4	23.81 / 5	38.10 / 8	4.76 / 1	1.00 / 21
Towpath	–	–	–	–	9.09 / 1	36.36 / 4	45.45 / 5	9.09 / 1	0.53 / 11
Total	5.44 / 114	6.11 / 128	10.31 / 216	2.67 / 475	15.08 / 316	21.81 / 457	15.51 / 325	3.05 / 64	2,095

47

lower areas are in this category. Had we taken the lowest occupations, to illustrate the relationship to dwelling area, the situation would have reversed itself. (See Table 3 for all the percentages.)

Let us now see how the five social classes are distributed through the several areas of Jonesville. A simplified explanation is easily given by reducing the seven-point scale, for ranking the 17 areas and sub-areas, to one of five points and then plotting the areas on a two-dimensional chart. The vertical and horizontal dimensions of Chart IV have five squares, the horizontal representing the five classes, and the vertical, the several regions. The comparative size of the lined area in each square approximates the proportions of each class at each of the five points in the scale, and the numbers give the percent. The upper-class families are heavily concentrated in the top region (68 percent), and families of the lower-lower class in Rank V (46 percent).

Of considerable importance to those interested in the dynamics of class is the fact that the classes which are socially contiguous to each other—for instance, upper-middle to upper and lower-middle —ordinarily show the largest percentages of people whose dwelling areas overlap. For example, the upper-middle class has the largest concentration of its families in the areas ranked II (44 percent), and these areas have the second largest concentration of upper-class people (30 percent). On the other hand, the second largest concentration of lower-middle-class families (28 percent) are in Rank II and overlap the high concentration of upper-middle people. (See Chart IV for this patterning and for the exceptions, such as the two lower classes.)

The vast majority of the upper-class people, as we have seen, cluster in Top Circle, the area which ranks higher than any other in Jonesville. The remainder are distributed within the narrow limits of but four of the remaining sixteen dwelling areas, and the great majority of this remainder, in but two areas immediately adjacent to Top Circle. The top crowd cling together socially and herd together in physical space. (See percentages for the upper class in Table 4.)

The families of the upper-middle class are far more generally distributed through Jonesville. They are in 12 of the 17 areas, but one-third of them are concentrated in Top Circle and West Side, their homes and gardens intermingled with those of the upper class. (See percentages for upper-middle, Table 4.)

The lower-middle class are in all areas but Railroad and Towpath, being more widely distributed than any other class except upper-lower, which has representative families in all of the 17 areas. Very few of them are in the poorest and best areas. The largest concentration of lower-middle and upper-lower are in Mill Town.

The lowest-class families are distributed through 13 areas. Three of the neighborhoods they are not in are Top Circle, West Side, and North Circle, places favored by the two levels Above the

The Top Regions	Upper Class	Upper-Middle Class	Lower-Middle Class	Upper-Lower Class	Lower-Lower Class
I	68	24	(4)	(1)	
II	30	44	28	(13)	(1)
III	(2)	28	47	43	(17)
IV		(4)	(17)	25	35
V		(1)	(4)	(19)	46
The Bottom Regions					

CHART IV. The Highest Class Dwells on High, the Lowest in the Lower Depths, the Others in Between

Common Man. The area of highest concentration is Northwestern (22 percent) followed by Polish Town (15 percent).

A rating for any one of the four characteristics tells much about a family's status in Jonesville; it was soon apparent that when the ratings of the four characteristics for a family were combined they would furnish an Index of Status Characteristics (I.S.C.) which would be a highly reliable indicator of the family's social level. When we learned later to give the rating of each characteristic the weighting it needed, it was possible, before inquiring about the family's social-class level, to predict with high certainty what the position would be. We will examine a few cases.

Area	Upper	Upper-Middle	Lower-Middle	Upper-Lower	Lower-Lower	Total
Top Circle	29.10 / 39	44.03 / 59	22.39 / 30	4.48 / 6	— / —	6.40 / 134
West Side	6.77 / 9	24.81 / 33	41.35 / 55	27.07 / 36	— / —	6.35 / 133
Southeastern	1.18 / 3	25.20 / 64	46.46 / 118	25.98 / 66	1.18 / 3	12.12 / 254
North Circle	11.63 / 5	30.23 / 13	34.88 / 15	23.26 / 10	— / —	2.05 / 43
Mill Town	0.22 / 1	8.55 / 39	43.20 / 197	42.76 / 195	5.26 / 24	21.77 / 456
Featherton	— / —	17.65 / 3	17.65 / 3	64.71 / 11	— / —	0.81 / 17
Newtown	— / —	3.85 / 8	32.69 / 68	54.81 / 114	8.65 / 18	9.93 / 208
East Side	— / —	— / —	7.84 / 4	50.98 / 26	41.18 / 21	2.43 / 51

Dwelling Area						Total
Town Center	–	16.67 / 20	42.50 / 51	39.17 / 47	1.67 / 2	5.73 / 120
Business Area	–	3.82 / 5	33.59 / 44	53.44 / 70	9.16 / 12	6.25 / 131
Northwestern	–	2.05 / 5	26.23 / 64	48.77 / 119	22.95 / 56	11.65 / 244
Oldtown	–	–	19.10 / 17	53.93 / 48	26.97 / 24	4.25 / 89
Creek	–	3.23 / 1	12.90 / 4	51.61 / 16	32.26 / 10	1.48 / 31
Polish Town	–	–	3.48 / 4	63.48 / 73	33.04 / 38	5.49 / 115
East Canal	–	2.70 / 1	2.70 / 1	21.62 / 8	72.97 / 27	1.77 / 37
Railroad	–	–	–	61.90 / 13	38.10 / 8	1.00 / 21
Towpath	–	–	–	9.09 / 1	90.91 / 10	0.53 / 11
Total	2.72 / 57	11.98 / 251	32.22 / 675	41.00 / 869	12.08 / 253	2,095

TABLE 4. Social Class and Dwelling Area

The Meaning of a Family's Index of Status

Mr. and Mrs. William Taylor live in Top Circle. They inherited their old mansion with its lovely garden from Will's father, who inherited it from his father. Will's grandfather built it to make his wife happy. She wanted a house to fit their status in life and to provide them with surroundings where they might entertain those few who were their intimates. She and old Will had arrived at this decision after she had lost her bid to move to Chicago where she could do the things people of her kind did. Young Will, like his grandfather, wants to be near his farms, permitting him to visit them frequently and allowing his farm managers to report on the crops and his tenants and to confer with him about decisions of importance.

Will, lineal descendant of old Will who had established a dynasty, is at the top of Jonesville's upper class. Everyone says so, and his I.S.C. is a straight 12, for he rates a 1 for occupation, a 1 for source of income, a 1 for house type, and for living in Top Circle. Each rating must be first multiplied by its proper weight:

	Rating		Weight		
Occupation	1	×	4	=	4
Source of Income	1	×	3	=	3
House Type	1	×	3	=	3
Area	1	×	2	=	2
					12

The total score is 12, the highest on the range of I.S.C.'s. If Will had scored all 7's, his score would have been 84, the lowest in the social scale.[2]

The I.S.C. of the upper class, as an index of human living and family life, is easy to demonstrate, particularly among those whose place is assured and where there are no dangers of downward mobility. The story of the status problems of families in the upper-middle class, as revealed by the I.S.C., is more complex.

Mr. George Hill has an index of 29. He is the owner of a rather profitable business, which gives him a 2 for occupation and a 3 for source of income. He lives in a very good house over in the Southeastern Area. His index puts him about in the middle of the

[2] The whole process, with instructions for its use, is described in *Social Class in America: A Manual for the Measurement of Social Status, op. cit.*

upper-middle class. Our interviews show that's where his status reputation places him.

The families of Henry Johnson and Fred Brown are both lower-middle-class. The Johnson family has an I.S.C. of 44, and the Browns, 42. They know many of the members of the Methodist Church and see each other at lodge and club meetings. Their children play together at school. Although their participation is very similar, the factors in their I.S.C.'s are quite different. An analysis of their characteristics tells the investigator much about them and about their pattern of ambition. Henry is a clerk in a haberdashery (3) for which he receives a salary (rated 4). They live in an ordinary bungalow (4) in Newtown (4). Henry's boss says he's a nice fellow but not very ambitious. The members of the Women's Club say Hanna Johnson's the kind of person that doesn't have "much get-up to her."

Fred and Nancy Brown's reputations are quite different. Their friends say they do such nice things and Nancy has everything so nice. "I don't see how she does it."

Fred is only a skilled worker (rated 4) who punches a clock every day and receives a wage every week. When they came to Jonesville Nancy drove all over town and consulted everyone about a nice place to live. Several of her better-placed friends wrote notes to their friends in Jonesville and asked them to be nice to Nancy and Fred. Nancy says, "If you want something hard enough you can always get it. That's how I got our house and met the nice friends we have here in Jonesville." Whatever the cause, the Fred Browns, with only a wage and skilled worker classification, live in a house rated by us as above average (3) in Top Circle (1). Their social equipment, their comparative youth, and their friendships with people who are better-placed than they, make it possible that Fred may move into a higher occupational and income bracket. The chances are better than even that Fred and Nancy will move into the upper-middle class. That's what they want, and they want it hard.

Joe Bird and his family of five God-fearing Protestants, who regularly attend the Baptist Church, came up from the South years ago. Joe got a skilled job at The Mill, which gives him occupational and income ratings equal to Fred Brown's, but the Birds live in a house that is less than average (5) in Northwestern (5). Their I.S.C. is 56, and their social level, upper-lower class. The

Birds are good, respectable people. Joe, they feel, has a good job, and they're satisfied with everything.

Down across The Canal in Towpath, in a ramshackle house, live the Dows. When Tom Dow works he does odd jobs (7), but his principal source of income has been from public relief (7). The Dow family rates an I.S.C. of 84. Many informants placed this family in "the lulu class" (at the bottom). Their I.S.C. confirms the placement.

Each family in Jonesville must face the facts of life, the hard economic factors that mold and limit their actions, but society does not fix their entire status by their economic position. There is flexibility and there is oportunity to fashion a life that rises above or sinks below the average level of others who are occupationally like them. The skeleton of the American Dream may be the hard structure of economic determinism, but the flesh that makes it human is composed of an infinite number of social and cultural factors. The social classes of Jonesville are not fixed; families and individuals rise and fall from level to level, for the open class system of America, foundation of the American Dream, must and does provide for social mobility.

Chapter 4

SOCIAL MOBILITY: THE RISE AND FALL OF FAMILIES

In Jonesville, as in all American communities, there is a process which keeps the class structure fluid. Families may not remain in one social class; or an individual may leave his family and, by one means or another, establish a new position in Jonesville or in some other community. There has been, in America, a tradition of "from shirtsleeves to shirtsleeves in three generations." While the boy "from across the tracks" does not often reach the mansion on the west side, he frequently ends up with a small business on Main Street. Of course, there is still the reality of "shirtsleeves to shirtsleeves to shirtsleeves."*

The process of changing social-class position is known as social mobility. Mobility may be up or down. This chapter describes some aspects of the mobility process in Jonesville. Two case studies, "From Across the Tracks" and "Old Family Moving Down," are used to describe characteristic patterns of upward and downward mobility. It is probable that similar cases may be found in most towns in America. Following the case studies, some ways of identifying social mobility are described. Then an attempt is made to answer the question, "What makes people mobile?" In so far as possible, the people of Jonesville are allowed to tell their own story.

* By Carson McGuire. See List of Authors.

From Across the Tracks

"You know, I was born on the wrong side of the railroad tracks. When I was in high school, my dad told me to get out of Jonesville to find work because I couldn't cross over in this town. But I've showed him."

Mr. Little was in one of his rare moments of relaxation as he talked that day in his office. In the interviewer's mind were the remarks of a doctor: "Paul Little is a self-made man. His father never cut much ice around here. He was just a clerk. Paul's mother was a good lady. Paul started as scrub-boy and office boy, car washer and that kind of thing. He never had more than a high school education but he built himself up to be one of the top men over there. I believe he handles all the business side of the plant."

The man behind the desk went on. "I've lived here all my life. I started out with nothing, and I didn't have so much of an education. I've worked hard and I've done pretty well, I think. My folks were poor. They didn't have a thing. I went through high school, and came down here, and I've been working here ever since.

"I think there's one man in every man's life that molds him for better or worse. When I was in high school, I was just a playboy. For the first two or three years, I just fooled around. I didn't have any ambition. Two or three times I thought I'd quit school. Then we got a new principal. He was a man I really respected. He taught me one guiding principle. Always in life if you have to do a thing, if it's necessary and you consider it honorable, do it, and don't worry about the consequences.

"Later, I realized I lived by another principle. It seems to drive me and guide me. Now, I've never been jealous of anyone. But, when I've seen someone I respected, I've always wanted to be like that person. When I've seen someone with something that I wanted, I've always strived to get that thing.

"Now, I'm just like Ray Caldwell." The speaker looked up to a picture of the managing director. "I like to organize things, to see them go. There's nothing I've ever been in that failed. The fact of the matter is, there's no definite limits to my job. I just don't have any title. The way the thing is organized, I do the work that's necessary, and if I have to come back here at nights

I do, or on Saturday afternoons or Sunday. The job has got to be done.

"Yes, I've learned how to raise money in campaigns and run things just by watching Ray. You know, some years ago, when I took hold of our civic club, it had only a few members. It was ready to close its doors. Well, I rustled around and got people interested, and we've really organized that club. We decorated it and rebuilt it. Now we have one of the finest organizations in town. I really got a kick out of that.

"There's one thing, though, that I really miss in my life. I'm feeling it more as I grow older. That's the fact that I didn't get an education. I couldn't afford to go away to school. Anyway, at the time, I didn't see the need to. But now I really can.

"You know, when you look at this town there are three kinds of people here." The interviewer wondered where Mr. Little would place himself in the social-class framework. "I've lived here all my life and I know it pretty well. There's a group around here that think they're *society*. The fact of the matter is, I won't pay any attention to that society stuff. Ray just laughs at it now. Then there's *the great mass of people*. They are from people like myself, well, down to the workers down here in the plant. That's practically everybody in town. Then there's the worthless *don't-give-a-hoots*. They won't work and just live from hand to mouth."

Mr. Little was placing himself in what the social analyst would call the upper-middle class, looking down upon, yet identifying himself with, the lower-middle and upper-lower classes.

"Take myself, for instance, I'm in the great mass. I've always been and I always will be. I know they call me a self-made man. I remember they used to call me 'Paul' and now it's 'Mr. Little' out here at the plant. That's because we're getting farther and farther apart from the workers since this place has grown so big. But you can't separate the great mass. You see, the society group more or less runs around together. The great mass of people can't do that. There's too many of them so they are broken up into groups.

"Ray is my closest friend. I know he goes with the society crowd whenever he wants to. Yet, often my wife and I will go over to Ray's house, and we'll play some bridge. We'll have a few drinks, and we'll really have a nice time. Then, again, we'll go out and play bridge with the Howard Johnsons. Howard works right out here in the plant. Yes, I move up and down the scale."

Mr. Little recognizes four levels in the town of Jonesville. Explicitly, he distinguishes "society," "the great mass of people," and the "worthless don't-give-a-hoots." Implicitly, he sees himself in a fourth level below the Caldwells of the "society crowd" and above the Howard Johnsons who belong to "the great mass." Moreover, earlier in the interview, he speaks of being "born on the wrong side of the tracks" of working parents who did not participate much in community life. Thus he indicates the five social-class levels and the extent to which he has moved in them. Paul Little's mobility has been from the lowest level of "the great mass of people" (upper-lower class) to the top level of that grouping as he sees it (upper-middle class).

Paul Little, in his upward mobility, is a living example of the American Dream. Belief in social mobility is rooted deep in our idea of democracy. People don't explicitly admit that there are different classes; yet through their words and actions they place themselves and each other in social class. Everybody seems to recognize that Mr. Little has moved up in the ranking system.

OLD FAMILY MOVING DOWN

Efforts at concealment make downward mobility more difficult to observe. One family in a rural village near Jonesville, however, underwent a noticeable downward shift in social status during the course of the research. Our first information about the Wells family had come from a well-known doctor: "The Wellses are an old family around here. They're not in the top group now, but they're good substantial people. They've been around for a long time. The old grandfather Wells used to own a lot of land in Abraham County. They were really landed gentry. Grandmother Wells was a real belle of that part of the country when he married her. But they lost their land. Even the house in town is heavily mortgaged."

Three generations are now residing in a home built during the Civil War: Grandfather Wells' son and his wife, their son, Fred Wells, and his two children. Fred Wells, at the time of the first interview, was about forty years old. "He isn't living with his wife. She's back East some place. His father and mother are old. I suppose they have some income which has helped in the family's support. Fred sings in the church choir. He's also a member of the Masons, and he's active in some other organizations. Fred is a large man and capable. Not really capable, maybe, but he's not the kind you could feel sorry for. He's very well thought of."

But during the next year, the interviews began to give another picture. We heard: "Wells is not coming to church very much. You know, his wife left him years ago. They say he's running around with a lot of women who don't amount to much."

From the village school came corroborating evidence. "Wells says that he thinks Harold is just a natural bad boy. We feel sorry for the father. His wife ran away and left him years ago, and now Harold has turned out bad. Wells has quit going to church, quit singing in the church choir, and so far as we know he doesn't go anywhere with nice people since Harold has begun acting up so much. It's pretty bad."

The community verdict placing the family in a lower class was expressed by an upper-middle-class woman: "Well, there's a family that really amounted to something around here at one time, but they just lost out. People just don't understand it."

A year later, an eloquent postscript was added. It came from an interview with an upper-middle-class boy. "My folks don't want me to go with Johnny Wells—his brother was sent to reform school. He's boisterous, he's lazy, and he's for himself. But, he can be very nice. Anyway, I'm sure my family wouldn't want me to be with roustabouts, kids that walk the streets, people that don't have any families or reputations. You really shouldn't be that way, but you wouldn't want your family's reputation to suffer."

Downward mobility happens all the time although ordinarily we don't see it so clearly. It's hard to place people when they move down, but the people in Jonesville were talking of Mr. Wells just as they talked about the lowest class—Mr. Little's "worthless don't-give-a-hoots."

The Wells family no longer belong. The middle classes have "de-classed" them. They are downward mobile.

WHAT SOCIAL MOBILITY MEANS

The cases of Mr. Little and Mr. Wells are only two of many analyzed in the study of social mobility in Jonesville. From interviews supplied by the field workers, supplemented by observations, subjects' reports, and various specialized techniques, a wealth of data was available. The problem of the social analyst is to order those data, to give them meaning so that patterns of mobility will emerge. To understand social mobility is to understand the basic process that keeps the class system fluid in the modern American community.

No two cases are the same but, despite the differences, common patterns are formed. Broadly speaking, social mobility is recognized when there is a change in the social behavior and relationships of an individual. It is marked by acceptance or rejection in terms of a new evaluation of the individual's social reputation by others in the community.

The clearest examples of social mobility are those in which a person is put in a higher or a lower social class by the explicit references of other people. In the case of Mr. Little there is clear reference to movement upward to the upper-middle class, presumably from the upper-lower class. His sister and brother have moved, but they are still placed below him. On the other hand, Mr. Wells is no longer regarded as an accepted and respectable member of the lower-middle class to which his family has dropped. His exact status is difficult to determine, but the references to him clearly indicate a change in social position.

In talking about people moving "up" or "down," "in" or "out" of social groups, it seems that reference is almost always made to the social position of the family in which the particular individual concerned grew up. The social class of a person's family is the starting point for indicating a change in status. Both Mr. Little and those who appraise his rise in Jonesville speak of his father as a grocery clerk "from the wrong side of the tracks." Almost every interview having to do with Mr. Fred Wells points to the previous status of the Wells family.

WAYS OF IDENTIFYING SOCIAL MOBILITY

From these two cases and many others like them, it is possible to make certain generalizations about the signs of social mobility. Patterns that tend to occur over and over again may be identified. These patterns provide the social analyst with categories for evaluating the presence or absence of social mobility. Of course, one can infer from what is said by people in the community whether a person is moving up or down. But the scientist wants to know the factors involved and how much of each is present. For this reason, categories for comparison are set up after working over a large number of cases. Each category is in reality an area of change; within each area are varying degrees or kinds of change.

First, there tends to be a difference in the amount of education of a mobile person compared with that of his parents, a category called *educational difference*. Mr. Little completed high school; his father left school at the end of the eighth grade. Of course, this factor of educational difference does not always lead to social mobility. Edith Kraig graduated from Jonesville high school in 1944; her father left school at the end of grade four, and her mother completed grade eight. The father is known as "a typical W.P.A. worker" and the mother "works between children born at home." Upon graduation, instead of becoming a cadet nurse Edith went to work packing egg cartons at The Mill and continued to live at home. She says, "I belong to no clubs. I'm not interested now. My sister and I go with a bunch of girls to the dances." There is a strong bond between mother and daughter. Although she is the only one of the children to go through high school so far, this dependency tie to a hard-working mother overruled her desire to break away from her lower-lower-class home. Nevertheless, a difference in education between parent and child strongly indicates the possibility of social mobility. Today education is almost a prerequisite for mobility into, or through, the middle classes. A boy or girl has to stay in school to be mobile.

Closely allied to educational difference is a second category of change, *occupational variance*. A person engaged in an occupation which is evaluated as different, positively or negatively, from that of the status of parent (usually the father) is said to be occupationally mobile. Occupation is basic to socio-economic status. This may be translated into outward behavior and inner valuations, a way of life that brings about a change in social class through general acceptance or rejection by others in the community. Mr. Little moved into a "white collar job" and finally became "one of the top men down at the plant"; his father was "just a grocery clerk." Mr. Little has climbed to the top of the middle class but, although he has a higher income than many members of the upper class, he is not considered their social equal. High position in a segmental hierarchy, such as a business or an institution like the school system, does not necessarily mean high position in the social hierarchy of the total community.

Like other communities, Jonesville has differentially evaluated church and other formal associations. This points to a third pattern of change, *membership transference*. If a wife moves from the Women's Club to the Monday Club, and if her husband becomes a member of the Rotary Club, the new memberships will be indicators of a movement into upper-middle-class status. The Littles, over the years, have become members of more and "higher" organizations. Moreover, Mr. Little is highly visible in them, especially as the most important man in his church.

This introduces a fourth area of change which we call *activity deviation*. The Littles have held their tie to their church, evaluated as of lower rank in Jonesville than the Federated. In fact, the Federated minister remarks, "I guess he is about the only person of consequence in that church." For the Littles, failure to deviate in their religious affiliation is one factor putting an end to upward mobility. To move up or down in status, a person must consolidate his social position at the new level, establish new formal and informal relations, and change his modes of behavior. In general, a mobile individual tends to move his center of activity out from the church and family center into a new kind of participation. Similarly, the interests and activities of mobile families usually assume a new configuration in the community. The nonmobile person tends to adhere to a stable family pattern, including its religious participation. The downward-mobile person generally presents a negative picture. Mr. Wells' home life has changed, and he has withdrawn from his activities in the church and the Masons.

Observations of *clique change* mark a fifth pattern of mobility up and down. The mobile individual will tend to associate in cliques with other individuals who have a different status from the one he or his family originally held. Naturally, the average status of the new clique in which he participates will be modified by the presence of other mobile individuals. Cliques, as a whole, are differentially evaluated. People in Jonesville, as in other communities, place persons by the cliques to which they belong and correct that placement from time to time.

Related to clique change is a sixth factor, *role revision*. To move upward in status, an individual must be accepted and evaluated positively by others. Mr. Little, in the roles he plays as a successful business executive in Jonesville, is an example of the upward-mobile person adapting his activity to his new social position. On the other hand, the loss of social position involves nonparticipation and negative evaluation. Mr. Wells was "declassed" on both counts. Mr. Little is accepted as a "leader"; Mr. Wells is isolated as a "rejected" individual. But the factors involved in playing a social role in group relationships—one's relations with, and reputation among, others in the community on the interpersonal level—go deeper than the surface. There are persons who are mobile because they have the capacity to isolate themselves from their fellows (and from the family in which they grew up). However, that self isolation must retain a favorable relation to others. And a person's role may be revised without his realization of what is happening to him. The dominant individual who lacks warmth for others, who manipulates people without emotional involvement, may be successful in influencing, or stimulating, or appealing to, a majority of his fellows. But his manipulative energy may reach a point where it arouses a feeling of unpleasantness in others which will prevent further mobility. Sometimes this kind of a mobile person becomes a tool of other people.

A seventh aspect of mobility is concerned with *interclass marriage*. Such a marriage, however, is only the observable result of more complex interpersonal relationships between men and women of different social classes. Personal appearance and heterosexual appeal often are critical factors in bringing about interclass marriages, operating more frequently in the cases of women than of men. Positively evaluated, these factors induce upward mobility through marriage into a higher class; negatively evaluated, they may bring marriage to a partner of lower status.

Interclass marriage more often results in a change of social status for the woman than it does for the man. However, a woman who marries a man of a higher status does not always meet with immediate acceptance. Her behavior is watched and related to her background.

"Hell, that's just the way that woman would do. I suppose she thought you didn't belong here, that that wasn't your social position. Damn her! When I think of her background! Her father was a school teacher. She thinks she has an intellectual background. The way that woman acts makes me so damned mad. She's against everything and resents the fact that her sister-in-law is prominent.

Those two hate each other's guts. She gets in a lot of women's hair around here. She wants to move in a higher social group than the one she's in. They won't let her in. She resents it and takes her grudges out on her sister-in-law and her friends."

The upper-class man who appraised this woman clearly saw her striving for upward mobility and indicated the frustrations experienced when the upward movement ceased.

An eighth category of mobility is *residential movement*. Type and area of residence form one of the material status symbols of our society. The house and its grounds become ordered symbols of one's place in a community. Because of their social importance, "house type" and "area lived in" have been used as factors in the Index of Status Characteristics. One reliable sign of mobility in adults is a change in these factors. The upward-mobile person tends to acquire a house and live in an area placed higher in the scale of community valuation than his previous dwelling. Conversely, there tends to be a negative change in one or both of these factors when an individual or family is downward-mobile. In some cases, the home is allowed to deteriorate, or it is broken into sub-dwellings; in others, there is a move to a poorer area.

There are, then, a number of categories by which mobility, upward and downward, may be recognized and perhaps measured. Some are merely signs; others are patterns. They tell what kind of change is being made, in what direction, and how far it has gone. The several areas—educational difference, occupational variance, membership transference, activity deviation, clique change, role revision, interclass marriage, and residential movement—are interrelated and interdependent. A change in one is not present without some degree of change in the other factors.

For many mobile persons, though, what has been called *activity deviation* is the preliminary step. One has to be different from his family, or a whole family has to be different from what it previously was. Mobility for Paul Little did not extend beyond the top of the middle class because he did not move his activities into the constellation of social structures of the class above. He moved only through a grouping of classes which tend to hold common values and similar beliefs—the upper-lower, the lower-middle, and the upper-middle classes in the "Old American" culture. For persons not belonging to the dominant culture, the problem is complicated if they wish to move out of their subculture.

WHAT MAKES PEOPLE MOBILE?

Manifest mobility, movement out of a social position and up or down into another social class, is a phenomenon that may be observed and evaluated without too much difficulty. In a community, people note it and comment upon it. The social analyst may describe the forms it takes, point out the signs, and set up a frame of reference for measuring, in one way or another, the kind, the direction, and the amount of change. He can mark the beginning, the processes, the areas of change, and the end of a social movement. But what makes people mobile?

Two kinds of answers can be given to this question. One set has to do with the necessary *conditions* both within the individual and in his relationships to the outer world of reality. The other kind of answer refers to the possible areas of *motivation* that may be present. Taken together, they describe the dynamics of social mobility in terms of forces or pressures within the person concerned and his situation.

There are certain conditions or factors that mark *potential mobility* in a person. These factors may be present in varying degrees and indicate a positive or negative direction in different persons. They represent forces that tend to make a person move up or down or limit the changes he can make. Moreover, they have different effects according to the social position from which the person starts a mobility movement, if he moves at all. In many cases, they are latent or hidden forces that may never come into play.

In general, a prime condition for upward mobility is a high *achievement level.* In Jonesville, as in most American communities, the achievement drive that produces change has to do with the socially expected employment for the person's age level. Traditionally, there are two basic areas for achievement: obtaining an education and finding a place in the occupational hierarchy. Success in one or both of these areas is almost a basis for achievement in other aspects of living. It is an expression of the ambition drive of an individual.

As in other communities, the school system in Jonesville operates to select and encourage the pupil who functions at a high level in terms of teacher expectations, whose performance is equal to, or better than, his ability. A high school senior puts the distinctions felt by the average middle-class student into words in speaking about three lower-class boys from "north of the tracks."

"Those three boys don't go downtown at night, they never mix with anybody, they never play pool. They get that way because they devote all their ability and most of their time to that single thing, studying. They give their all to it and the teachers think they're good. We snob them and they snob us. We make fun of them, and I myself feel I'm above them, even though I don't shine as brilliantly as they do in class. I feel I have the potentialities if I wish to do it, and I feel I will wish to do it, sometime in my life.

"You know, there are different kinds of kids in school. First of all, there's a group that comes to school and goes home again, an inoffensive group. In school, they're just a name. Then there's *the ones that study hard* in school and take their books home and study hard. They're the ones that make it tough for us. Then there's the ones that come to school, *the wild ones,* who nobody knows why they come, *they're mostly weeded out by the senior year.* Finally, there's the group that seems to try to get the most out of everything, but don't succeed in getting a lot out of a single thing. They do the most things in school. I belong to the last, as I see it.

"Kids in class, some are like characters in a book, but you don't know it. There's one bunch that get in every night at nine o'clock, and they have no idea how many others stay out till early morning. When a nine o'clock boy tries to imitate the late crowd, an issue is made over his conduct, where the habitual conduct of others is overlooked. If you start out with one rule of conduct, you are expected to stay there permanently. Boy! wouldn't the teachers make a fuss if those three fellows started to stay out late and fall down in their work!"

The three boys, to whom the senior refers, were not upward-mobile at the time *but they were potentially so*. Whether or not they measure up to the implied teacher expectancies depends upon the fulfillment of other conditions. However, unlike many other lower-class boys, they were staying in school and planning to go on to university.

Related to achievement level is a second factor, *personal talent.* Certain personal talents make it possible for an individual to establish new formal and informal relationships and to learn new ways of behaving. When held in high esteem, these talents give an individual prestige among others. They may be observed in a person or reputed to him by others. They may range all the way from personal attractiveness to uncommon artistic, creative, scientific, or athletic abilities.

The value placed upon athletic ability in school is indicated by what happened to an upper-lower-class boy whose "gang" had been in trouble. "Last year there was no go for Jack Raymond. The upper kids just wouldn't let him in to anything. This year, though, he's gone out for football and he's going up. *He's working his way in.* Football and athletics, though, is the way he's doing it. By the time he reaches his senior year, the upper kids will let him in. That's what most of the athletes do—they work up—they go out and play on the team and the upper girls want to go with them. They get to running around with that group of girls and they more or less climb into positions of prestige that way."

In general, potential talents have to be related to varying probabilities of utilization and evaluation in later adult life. Some "talents" are of bad repute in the community and are marks of potential downward mobility.

A third factor in potential social mobility concerns a person's *social techniques.* When an individual is capable of changing the ways he thinks and feels and acts, he may select behaviors which "fit" the particular patterned situation and by-pass others. On the other hand, the person who moves downward often does so because he fails to conform. His behavior does not dovetail into what is expected at his status. He goes beyond the limits of tolerance. Tendencies in this direction range all the way from the restless, disturbing, or "sissyish" person who arouses negative feelings in others, to the individual who adopts the "I don't care" or "tough guy" role along with crude behavior, emotional outbursts, or physical aggression. In most cases of inferior social technique there is a lack of ability to relate oneself to others. One of the patterns might be summed up this way:

"I am passive and must avoid attacking. Most people are against me—except some who will occasionally protect me. I can be comfortable when left alone with my own thoughts. There I can hit out safely without making anyone else angry with me. I secure nothing from most people so they don't enter into my thoughts. But sometimes this becomes very confused, and I get restless and afraid. I need affection and care but I don't know how to go about it. I would give everything if I could have it but I'm afraid of being burnt."

The boy concerned is a social isolate. The teachers say, "he doesn't get on with his age-mates." Now he is a truant from school. Without looking further into his case history, one could predict a sorry road ahead for this boy.

Individuals with superior social techniques, the kind that lead to upward mobility, range all the way from the warm, friendly, sensitive person, whose charm and good manners are not overdone, to the driving individual who succeeds in managing people without arousing hostility, despite a certain amount of crudeness. Sometimes there is a spontaneous and accepting attitude which marks the tactful outer conformity of a person who is basically self-centered but quite aware of reality demands. Sometimes there is a sensitive friendliness mixed with a rough male exterior, seeming contradictions in a boy who consciously restrains his impulses and is quite concerned with social success. These and many more patterns occur in Jonesville as they do in other American communities. Their counterparts are found in adults.

One of the effective techniques for upward mobility is found in the man who has a degree of competence in manipulating others despite a certain amount of self-centeredness and lack of warmth. Mr. Little seems to have this ability. However, this same technique may lead to hostility against the person who uses it, especially when there is a strong drive to manipulate other people. Positive social techniques, those that have potentiality for mobility, must "fit" into the pattern of behavior acceptable in the social class into which the individual is moving.

In most upward-mobile persons there is a fourth condition—namely, concern about getting ahead in the world. The term, *status anxiety,* refers to the balance between the satisfactions an individual is seeking and those his status provides. The person who places a value upon status symbols, who seeks recognition from those in superior positions, who strives for roles which may bring prestige, is the one who is overtly characterized by status anxiety. In others it is hidden and takes the form of reconciliation of behavior to the demands of the situation and a positive awareness of social hierarchies.

A fifth factor in evaluating potential mobility has been called *situational responses.* Other people evaluate the ways each individual behaves. Some people are looked upon as "getting ahead in the world," as "knowing how to behave," as being "able to do the right thing." Comparable with these more socially aggressive individuals are the passive but highly conforming persons who are reported to be "a fine fellow," "a good student," or "a pleasant personality." If there is agreement, especially at the individual's own status and in the one above him, one may infer the possibility of mobility of a person so evaluated. On the other hand, an individual's overt behavior may be regarded as nonadaptive or abnormal at his class level. Mr. Wells and his son were declassed on this count. When sanctions are imposed, or a person is actively rejected because his responses are not acceptable, there is a strong possibility of downward social mobility.

There appears to be rather a high degree of awareness among girls in the high school as to what happens to those who follow nonacceptable patterns. A few years back, there was a group of girls who were rejected by most students and particularly by the upper clique in the school. They skipped classes frequently, bringing them into conflict with the faculty. They were reputed to go out with town boys and boys who had left school. They were associated with undesirable spots in town, particularly as a part of the "skating rink crowd." A certain member of the group was referred to as a "brazen little hussy" and "jailbait." A high school senior, some years later, referred to her in terms of downward mobility as an outcome.

But a member of that particular group of girls gives a different report of the situation from that given by members of higher cliques. Her report brings out the factor of *emotional deprivation*—the same condition which influenced the three boys from "north of the tracks" to be good students and which led them to seek companionship and satisfaction of emotional needs outside the school.

These factors—achievement level, personal talents, social techniques, status anxiety, situational responses, and emotional deprivation—are present in some combination in each mobile person studied. They represent forces that are found in many individuals who move out of one social position and change their status either upward or downward. But these same factors are also found in persons who do not seem to be moving at all. According to the signs of mobility described earlier, such persons are not manifestly mobile but only potentially so. On the other hand, some persons who were judged to be mobile under the criteria set up for identifying social mobility were rated low in some of these factors.

PATTERNS OF MOTIVATION

The second set of answers to the problem of what makes people mobile refers to the possible areas of motivation that may be present. These may be classified under five headings—self motivation, family motivation, self-family constellation, response to school and teacher, and situational pressures.

Mr. Little's movement from the upper-lower to the upper-middle class is a clear case of mobility striving. He expressed it in these words: "When I've seen someone I respected, I've always wanted to be like that person. When I've seen someone with something I wanted, I've always striven to get that thing." Despite his father's warning he stayed in Jonesville and worked his way up. Not all cases of *self-motivation* are as clear-cut as this, but they all have certain common characteristics. Usually there is in the person an ability to make, and to follow out, decisions about behavior and about goals that are socially evaluated as different from those of the family in which the individual was raised.

If mobility arises out of *family motivation,* the individual tends to be much less consistent in his behaviors. The daughter of a lower-middle-class merchant, Donna McNeill, falls into this category.

"The McNeills," we were told, "have a lot of anxieties about their social position, about Donna's popularity, and financial worries and so on. The first year we were here they were pushing Donna pretty hard. They came and talked to us. They wanted Donna to go only with the boys of the best families, and they wanted her to associate only with the right group of girls. They wanted her to have dates, but only date with the boys from what they called prominent and good families. They were worried about Donna's popularity. They wanted her to make good grades, to be prominent in music, to go to all the parties and be a good girl. They had her so that she didn't know which way she was turning. The poor kid ran around the school in a fog. They've just put too much pressure on the girl. I don't think it's been good for Donna at all."

As a result of the urging and guidance of her parents, Donna made full use of her intelligence to be an honor student and undertook a wide range of activities. She became a member of the Sub-Deb Club, the upper-class girls' clique, for a time.

"Donna McNeill is a Sub-Deb all right but she's pulling away from them. She doesn't really belong in that crowd. She's developing into a lone duck. She's just getting away from the group. That's about all one can say. She is a nice girl but she has a peculiar personality. She's pretty moody at times and at other times she's very friendly with people."

Part of Donna's troubles may be explained by one student's observation. "She's our musical leader and she's hated for it, to tell the truth. She's good all right but she thinks she's good and she knows she's good and the kids just don't like it."

People seemed to think, too, that Donna was aware of her mother's trying "to work around socially," and they also said that her father had "such a shaky foundation" because of financial difficulties in connection with his business. Nevertheless, Donna held on to a fringe position in the upper group, graduated with honors, and went on to the Prairie State University to study music.

At the university, Donna wrote her mother that she was "unsettled and unhappy." It appeared that she wanted to drop the music curriculum which her parents wished her to follow and that her interpersonal relationships were not too happy. The mother, for the first time, decided to let the girl work out her own troubles.

"You know, I never learned to keep my hands off. This time, I've kept still—for four months now. In high school, I had to keep pushing Donna to do the things she did. Otherwise, I knew, she would go off on a tangent. Well, last week end, she wrote me, 'But, Mother, when I do find myself, find my place, I'll be so much stronger for having gone through all this.' She's probably right. I'm glad she was able to see it in that light."

Donna had, in varying degrees, certain of the attributes of potential mobility—high achievement level, outstanding musical talent which she used in high school, status anxiety inculcated by her mother. She is still learning techniques of relating herself to people and self-directed responses that will meet with approval. In high school, she was manifestly mobile. At the university, the die will be cast as to whether she can develop for herself the motivation and the guidance that her mother supplied. On the other hand, the fact that she has a university education will give her opportunity for higher status in Jonesville.

A third kind of motivating situation operates rather smoothly when upward mobility is involved. In the *self-family constellation* there is usually evidence of a change in participation and reputation of both the family and the individual concerned. Moreover, there is a parallel reorientation of beliefs and valuations of both parents and children without the strain found in the two previous circumstances. There is no need to break away from the family as there often is in self-motivated mobility striving. There is an absence of the pushing and constant direction from parents often found in family motivated social movement. At least other members of the family supply examples of behaviors to be followed.

A secondary motivating situation, *response to school and teachers,* is often coupled with self-motivation. Paul Little gave a clue to its nature when he emphasized the influence a new principal had upon his remaining in school and in shaping his later career. Usually this motivation is involved in movement of lower-class children into the middle class. A number of factors are present. In the first place, a good proportion of teachers in communities like Jonesville are themselves mobile from the upper-lower and lower-middle to a special kind of "middle-middle" status. This mobility, together with the teacher's dependence upon the active, influential upper-middle class in the community, leads to a compulsion to conform. They reflect the codes, customs, and values of the middle class. They enforce upper-middle and professional standards of language. This leads to clashes with children from the lower classes—a lowering of the value of children following the lower-class patterns, especially where peer group and family influences conflict with school demands. Thus a boy or girl who is "ambitious," i.e., mobile, is prized. Teachers tend to devote time and energy to them.

Secondly, success is measured by school achievement. Teachers project their own self-realization and frustrations upon their pupils. Their success was measured in terms of the acquisition of knowledge and skills. They tend to project this in the teacher-pupil relationship, to rationalize any failure of interaction by placing the blame upon the pupil for nonachievement, without looking behind the façade. In the third place, absolute conformity to the school code for conduct and the teacher's own moral code is stressed. The middle-class virtues—honesty, promptness, reliability, hard work, to name a few—determine right and wrong. Pressure from the administration and other teachers tempers any inclination to modify these absolutes in the understanding of particular cases.

Finally, in the case of many lower-class children who fulfill the requirements of being "ambitious," a "good student," and a "fine person," an interpersonal factor is involved. Many of these children establish an emotional identification with one or more teachers. Some seem to have a sympathy-winning power which the teacher is able to relate to his or her background. Of course, for every case where this occurs, there are a number of rejections of lower-class children. These are the ones who are "weeded out by the senior year."

Since such selective processes as these are present in the high school, it tends to operate as an agency which picks out certain lower-class children for mobility into the middle class and to encourage certain lower-class and many middle-class children to go on to college. On the other hand, it operates to restrict the mobility of individuals who do not conform to its middle-class standards, especially those from the lower classes. The high school in Jonesville, like secondary schools in other communities, is a selecting and controlling agency for mobility between the social classes.

MOBILITY BETWEEN DIFFERENT SOCIAL GROUPINGS

When one studies a large number of individuals in terms of the several signs which identify manifest mobility, the forces within a person and the situation which make for potential mobility, and the areas of motivation, several distinct patterns appear. There is a change of emphasis upon the factors which operate at the various class levels and in the case of the mobile ethnic individual.

First, it was noted repeatedly that movement from the lower-lower to the upper-lower class or higher is a matter of attaining a social reputation. The summary of one case study points up neatly a lower-lower-class girl's feelings in the process.

"Squarely in the middle of a family set-up that provides virtually no real personal protection or affection, with a young mother who has been pregnant or attending to a baby a good share of the time, the world is not a particularly friendly or attentive place. Life would be so much more pleasant if people were kind to one another. It helps to be physically attractive and cute, for the boys don't overlook you entirely; but you don't know where you stand, when you can't even point to your own father. People are pretty casual with you. Of course, you can build a world of your own but, although fantasy and fancy provide delightful excursions, the world is a real one; and you must live in it. The way you talk and dress must conform with the standards of the girls in your class; and the typical high school girl should be your model. Your morals 'are probably like the majority,' though it doesn't seem a good idea to smoke and drink. They'll criticize you very quickly if you do or if you don't do what the teachers want in school."

Although Rita Kelly's fantasies took her into a world which she never had had an opportunity to know, they were neither excessive nor beyond the range of attainment. Her touch with reality remained sure. She was aware of the demands for social conformity, of establishing a "belongingness," while using her physical attractions to the best advantage. To be a nurse was an acceptable and possible ambition. As an ideal it represented the emotional responses lacking in her own life. As a practical aim it carried her upward in the system of social rank.

At the opposite pole, in order to achieve mobility between the upper-middle and the upper class, family symbols and a relative independence from community affairs seem to become extremely important. When Mrs. Goodspeed belonged to the "social register" she was marked as a daughter of "a wealthy land-owning family." Now that the Barkers are in the upper groupings, Mrs. Barker's "old influential family of pioneers" is being remembered. One neat summation of a move into the "real 400" appears in this extract:

"George Manning's father had some money. He had a business down south of here. George made some money himself. He is a strange person—went away to university to study law and gave it up when he came back here. He went into business. He started with a shoestring and then he made a pile. He and his wife were trying hard to get in the 400 and hadn't quite made it, so they went in for thoroughbred horses and *galloped into society*. Now they also raise thoroughbred cattle. He makes fun of the crowd he is in to their face. His wife has the best figure in town and she wears marvelous clothes. Now she's in, she feels pretty sure of herself."

In between, for movement between the Common Man Level (upper-lower and lower-middle) and the upper-middle class, mobility seems to be related to evaluated social participation and material status symbols. Participation is evaluated by association memberships, clique status, relationships within groupings, successful or inappropriate marriage, as well as changes in the various activities. Material status symbols are rated in terms of education, occupation, and area and type of residence. A majority of the cases presented belong in this area of social mobility, either in adult life or in the adolescent period. The realities of the differences are pointed up by a newcomer to Jonesville:

"I like Jonesville, but I call it clannish. Take kids in senior high one by one and they're very nice. It's just when they're in a group they take that high attitude. They won't snob you, they'll be very nice to you, but *if you ever sit in their group* at the drugstore, or bowling alley, *their conversation won't include you.* It seems they are always the ones the teachers choose to do anything toward entertaining. Take the operetta for example. . . ."

As one boy said, "You have to go along with your group or you're too far apart, and *if you're too far apart it's not so good.*"

Finally, the ethnic may follow one of two patterns. If he stays in his group he may be mobile within its limits. If he wishes to move outside, there is a question of changing one's behavior and participation to the socially approved modes of the dominant culture. Unless the family moves with the individual, the move is dangerous. One loses the support of a group which has formalized its life around a religious belief. Too often the person is regarded as a "backslider" and fails to find a satisfactory place in the community structures.

One beautiful Polish Catholic girl showed many of the characteristics of potential mobility, including academic achievement in high school. Her activities were restricted by the sort of sentiments expressed by one high school senior:

"It seems as though there is an invisible barrier between us. If I dated her it would be an exception to the rule because of the opinion of others. If I knew she wasn't Polish, well, I'd think she's pretty. I just haven't entered her into my thoughts and I wouldn't know how to enter her in, if you know what I mean. There's too much attention paid to what other people have to say about that sort of thing. I wish I could be above such things, but if you try to do it, it appears as though you were peculiar."

For the most part, the social mobility of a member of an ethnic group is limited to the highest class within the group.

In Jonesville, as in every American community, social mobility is the process that permits movements between class levels. One of the explicit beliefs of American democracy is the tenet that an ambitious person may rise to the top. Coupled with this belief is a denial of the existence of systems of social rank. But people do rank each other. Moreover, they can tell you what people are moving and, indirectly, the factors involved. The scientist merely puts together what they say about each other with the data that his techniques of study uncover. Out of this combination he derives the categories and explains the processes and forces involved in the individual and his social situation. Whether one looks at it as a scientist or a layman, social mobility goes on in its own peculiar patterns in every community. It is the dynamic, living process that keeps the class lines fluid.

The best place to see the beginnings of mobility is in the life of the child. All people who become aware of status and class in American life wonder how this affects children and how soon such values appear in the life of our young people. The next chapter will give some of the answers to these important questions.

Chapter 5

THE DEMOCRACY OF CHILDHOOD

The belief that American society is a classless society has been one of our most cherished illusions. Even more unshakable has been our faith that children—children, especially—are democratic. It is often said that the child, "unspoiled as he is," recognizes no social distinctions. He evaluates individuals as individuals, and knows no other way.*

As we studied Jonesville, and as it became clear that a class system is operative in the lives of all its adult members, we began to study also the ways in which the class system is operative in the children's lives. Differences among social classes in techniques of child training, and in attitudes and value systems taught to children, were soon apparent. But we were interested also in the extent to which social status is operative in the child's own society. Is the social-class position of his parents a contributing factor in determining, for instance, a child's choice of friends, or the child's reputation among his age-mates?

The children of Jonesville are like the children of any similar community in America. They play the same games, they learn the same things in their schoolrooms, they see the same movies, they hear the same radio programs. At successive ages, they become more and more engrossed in their relationships with their peers. As a group, they are no less intelligent and no more self-conscious than the same aged children in any other American town.

To the casual observer, the children of Jonesville live democratically. The overwhelming majority attend public school, "that

* By Bernice Neugarten. See List of Authors.

great leveling agency of our American society"; they mingle freely on the playgrounds and on the streets; their friendship groupings seem flexible and self-initiated. Of course, certain children are more popular than others; but these differences appeared to us at first to be the natural correlates of differences in appearance, personality, and ability.

As our observations multiplied, however, we began to feel certain doubts. Friendship groupings seemed to follow a pattern in which children of a given social class tended to associate with others of the same class. The child who was socially isolated from the other members of his school group was usually the child of a lower-class family. The hostilities expressed among children seemed often to reflect the adult social values. For instance, such remarks were frequently encountered: "Aw, I don't like him—he's got a big brother who steals"; "My mom says I shouldn't have anything to do with kids like that"; "She lives up there on X Street, and they think they're important or something"; "He's dirty!" "He doesn't know how to behave nice in school."

To check our observations, a systematic study was undertaken of all the children in the fifth and sixth grades of the public school— a number totaling 174, ranging in age from ten to twelve years. In Jonesville, beginning with the fifth grade, all public school children are in one building and have the same teachers. From the fifth grade on, the child comes into daily contact with all the other children of his age in the community (with the exception of those few who attend parochial school).

After several months of the school year had passed, allowing time for the children to become well acquainted, they were asked for their evaluations of each other. They were told, first, to name their best friends, and then to name the boys and girls with whom they did not want to associate. They were then asked to name those children who they thought were well dressed and those who were not well dressed; those who were good-looking and those not good-looking; those who were fighters; those who were popular and those who were unpopular; those who seemed to like school and those who seemed to dislike school; those who were leaders; those who always were clean and those who were dirty; those who seemed always to have a good time and those who never had a good time; those who had good manners and those who were not well-mannered; those who always played fair and those who did not play fair.

The children wrote this information in prepared booklets, under circumstances which insured the greatest possible freedom from restraint—in their regular classrooms, with the investigator the only adult present; with the assurance that no person in Jonesville would have access to the booklets; and with the instruction not to sign their names to their papers.

On the basis of previous research, each child's family had been class-typed. The investigator could thus group the names of the boys and girls according to the five social classes of Jonesville and could find what proportion of the votes went to children of each social class. Furthermore, the booklets had been coded beforehand in such a way that the authorship of each was known, and the investigator could study how children of each social class cast their votes.

In a few instances, children wrote their own names in response to certain descriptive statements. Such self-mentions were excluded from the data.[1]

It happened that there were no children of upper-class families in the fifth or sixth grades; six percent of the group came from upper-middle-class families; 17 percent, from lower-middle; 62 percent, from upper-lower; and 15 percent, from lower-lower.

If social status were *not* influencing the way in which the votes were distributed, then it was to be expected that each group would receive approximately the same percentage of votes as the proportionate size of the group in the total population of the fifth and sixth grades.

The percentages actually obtained, however, were markedly different from these proportions. On the ten positive, or favorable, items ("best friend," "well-dressed," "good-looking," "popular," and so on) the upper-middle-class children, with 6 percent of the total population of the two grades, received from 11 percent to 29 percent of the total vote for each item, or an average of 19 percent. On the ten negative, or unfavorable, items ("don't like," "not well-dressed," and so on) the upper-middle-class group received less than three percent of all votes.

The lower-middle-class group, constituting 17 percent of the popu-

1 For a detailed description of the research techniques used in this study, see Bernice L. Neugarten, "Family Social Position and the Social Development of the Child," Ph.D. Dissertation, University of Chicago, 1943.

lation, received 27 percent of all favorable votes and only 6 percent of all unfavorable.

The upper-lower class, 62 percent of the population, received approximately 50 percent of all votes on both favorable and unfavorable items.

Table 5

HOW CHILDREN OF DIFFERENT SOCIAL CLASSES ARE RATED
BY THEIR AGE-MATES

	UM	LM	UL	LL
"best friend"	64	37	18	15
"well dressed"	93	33	14	3
"good-looking"	43	27	11	1
"popular"	39	15	8	1
"likes school"	45	15	9	3
"clean"	44	16	8	2
"has good time"	27	14	5	5
"good manners"	41	15	5	3
"plays fair"	28	11	7	4
"leader"	41	12	5	1
"don't like"	9	5	11	37
"not well dressed"	0	1	11	55
"not good-looking"	2	3	10	27
"unpopular"	1	2	6	21
"doesn't like school"	3	3	9	28
"dirty"	0	1	7	34
"never has good time"	3	5	4	8
"bad manners"	5	6	5	19
"doesn't play fair"	4	4	5	11
"fights a lot"	20	8	9	21

The lower-lower-class children, 15 percent of the population, received less than four percent of all favorable votes, but received an overwhelming share of all unfavorable votes—over 40 percent.

These data, recomputed to take account of differences in the size of each group, are presented in Table 5. The figures shown there may be interpreted as the series of ratios which would obtain if there were an equal number of children in each of the four social classes.

For instance, for every fifteen votes obtained by lower-lower-class children on the item "best friend," 64 votes went to upper-middle-class children—a ratio of more than four-to-one. On the item "good-looking," for every vote which went to a lower-lower-class child, 43 votes went to upper-middle-class children.

Looking at the first pair of items in Table 5, we find a striking degree of relationship between social status and social participation. The lower the social class of the child, the fewer times he is mentioned as a "best friend" and the more times he is mentioned as "don't like to be with."

Perhaps the most significant fact about the data is the consistency of the ratings given to children of the four social classes. Without exception, upper-middle-class children are ranked highest on every favorable item; lower-middle-class children are ranked second; upper-lower-class, third; and lower-lower-class children are given the lowest ranking. Similarly, without exception, lower-lower-class chil-

Table 6

HOW CHILDREN OF DIFFERENT SOCIAL CLASSES CAST THEIR
VOTES ON "BEST FRIEND"

	UM	LM	UL	LL	Average Rating
UM	120	67	47	22	64
LM	40	53	34	19	37
UL	12	15	29	20	18
LL	7	1	10	40	15

dren receive the largest proportion of votes on every unfavorable item.

There is a mirror-like relationship between the positive and negative characteristics being rated: as status decreases, the number of votes on positive characteristics decreases, and the number of votes on negative characteristics increases. The obvious contrast is between the child who comes from an upper-middle-class family, the Level Above the Common Man, and the child who comes from a lower-lower-class family, the Level Below the Common Man.

Social-status factors seem to determine not only which children receive favorable and unfavorable mention but also the way in which each child casts his votes. Returning to the data on "best friend," Table 6 shows the way in which each class group distributed its votes on this item.

The vertical columns show that upper-middle-class children voted 120 times for upper-middle-class children, as compared with 40 times for lower-middle-class children, 12 times for upper-lower-class children, and 7 times for lower-lower-class children.[2] To put it another way, the odds are 19 to 1 that an upper-middle-class child will mention as his best friend another upper-middle-class child rather than a lower-lower-class child.

These data show, furthermore, that, with the exception of the lowest-status group, children tend to mention as their friends, first, boys and girls of higher social status than their own, and second, boys and girls of their own social status. Lower-middle-class judges cast their votes in the proportion of 67 for upper-middle-class children and 53 for their own class; upper-lower children cast their votes in the proportion of 47 for upper-middle class, 34 for lower-middle, and 29 for children of their own class; and lower-lower-class children, on the contrary, vote for their own group more often than for any other. (The average rating of 15 obtained by lower-lower-class children is comprised largely of the votes of lower-lower-class children.) Perhaps in mentioning as his best friends other boys and girls of his own social level, the lower-class child is exhibiting a greater awareness of social realities than the child of other classes.

Whatever interpretation is put upon this finding, the fact is that seldom does a child of higher status mention a lower-lower-class child as his friend, and seldom does a lower-lower-class child mention a child of higher status. This is evidence of the social distance which exists between children Below the Level of the Common Man and all other children of Jonesville.

When data on reputation were studied in the same manner, it was found that, contrary to the data on friendship groupings, *all* groups of judges cast their votes in about the same way. Let us look, for example, at the item "good-looking." As shown in Table 7, each group of children—including lower-lower-class children—gave the largest proportion of their votes to upper-middle-class boys and girls and successively smaller proportions of their votes to boys and girls of other social classes. With one exception, the pattern of voting was the same for every item. (This exception occurred on the statement, "fights a lot," where children of upper status received a large share of the votes, but where these votes were cast *by* children of upper status.)

Thus, while the lower-class child stands apart from other children in the manner in which he selects his friends, he agrees with all the

2 These figures do not represent the actual number of votes cast, but rather the *proportions* of votes cast.

other judges that children Above the Common Man rank highest on all the positive characteristics; that children of the Common Man Level rank second; that children of his own level are at the bottom of the list.

To sum up, these data show that, by the time children reach the ages of ten and eleven, they make clear-cut differentiations along social-class lines. The class system of Jonesville operates in the child society much as it does in the adult society, both in its effects upon the child's social participations and in its effects upon the child's reputation.

Table 7

HOW CHILDREN OF DIFFERENT SOCIAL CLASSES CAST
THEIR VOTES ON "GOOD-LOOKING"

	UM	LM	UL	LL	Average Rating
UM	40	43	43	44	43
LM	23	30	21	28	27
UL	6	12	12	15	11
LL	0	0	3	1	1

Regarding friendships, the child from the upper-middle-class family is the one who occupies the enviable position: many of his classmates consider him their friend, and few of his classmates mention him as a person they would not want for a friend. The child from the lower-lower class faces the opposite situation: he is seldom mentioned as a friend (and then only by children of his own social position), but he is often mentioned as a person his classmates do not like.

As to reputation, all children, whatever their own social status, agree that the upper-middle-class child is the most attractive, the most popular, and so on; that the lower-middle class ranks second on all these traits; that the upper-lower class ranks third; and that the lower-lower class ranks fourth.

The consistency of these rankings is even more remarkable when one considers the fact that the characteristics being rated are of different levels of objectivity. For instance, "dirty—clean" can be more objectively rated than "good-looking—not good-looking"; and "good-looking" can probably be more objectively rated than "likes school."

It may well be that lower-class children, because they *are* lower-class, are not so well groomed as middle-class children; they are more likely to be "dirty" and certainly more likely to be "not well dressed."

It is also likely that lower-class children actually do not like school as much as do middle-class children. The degree to which a child of this age enjoys the school situation is determined to a large extent by how well he gets along with his teachers. The teachers of Jonesville, like most public school teachers in America, are themselves middle-class, and they express middle-class values and attitudes in dealing with their pupils. As a consequence, the lower-class child often finds his relationship with the teacher somewhat less pleasant, and the school situation much less rewarding, than does the middle-class child.

It is less probable, however, that lower-class children are actually less good-looking than middle-class children. Certainly, the adult who steps into a fifth-grade classroom in Jonesville, knowing nothing of the social background of the children, would rate these boys and girls differently on this attribute from the way in which they rate each other.

It is also improbable that leadership, fair play, spontaneity, and some of the other qualities implied in the original descriptive statements are, in actuality, so closely related to social class.

The fact is that fifth- and sixth-grade children make judgments about each other along stereotyped lines. A group of children rated high on one positive trait is rated high on all the others, and vice versa. When it also turns out that the group rated highest is always the group of highest social status, and that the two intermediate groups occupy intermediate ranks, the conclusion seems inescapable that a class bias is operating in the minds of the judges.

This does not mean that young children are conscious of the class structure of their community. On the contrary, the very concept of "class" is but vaguely understood, to say nothing of being accepted as true, even by many of the adults of Jonesville. The child selects his friends and evaluates his age-mates not on the basis of social class itself, but on the basis of a whole configuration of factors: whether or not the child is well groomed, the kind of clothes he wears, the playthings he owns, the language he uses, his manners, where he lives, his attitude toward school, and a host of similar factors. The ten-year-old bases his judgments upon such criteria without the accompanying awareness that cleanliness, clothing, manners, and language are themselves reflections of social-class differences.

The child applies such criteria uncritically; and, in doing so, he is merely expressing the social-class stereotypes as he has learned them from his parents and teachers. The attitude of ten-year-old Mary Richards toward ten-year-old Bill Smith is influenced to a great degree by the things Mrs. Richards says about Bill and Bill's family and by the way her teacher behaves toward Bill in the classroom.

Mary may be told not to play with "that Smith boy—his family's no good," or "he lives down by the tracks," or "he swears." She may relate to her parents that her teacher, Miss Colby, "made Bill go wash his face and hands before she'd let him sit down at his desk this morning. And she really lectured him about the way he always comes to school dirty!"

Bill Smith may have it pointed out to him that "that Richards girl—her father's rich," or "she thinks she's too good for the likes of you," or "she's not your kind." And Bill also may have stories to tell about school. "Mary Richards is teacher's pet. Miss Colby always calls on her first, and she acts as if she's so wonderful. Mary spilled ink today all over everything—but Miss Colby didn't even say a word. Oh, no—not to her darling Mary!"

Consider the position of the lower-class child in Jonesville. He has the reputation of being poorly dressed, unattractive, unpopular, aggressive; of not liking school; of being dirty and bad-mannered; of never having a good time; and of not playing fair. Few lower-class boys and girls are exceptions to this rule.

It is safe to assume that a child of this age soon becomes aware of his position in the group and makes his adjustment to a psychological climate which he recognizes as cold and unfriendly. There is a circular relationship between the psychological environment of an individual and the behavior he exhibits. The child's behavior has an effect upon his reputation, of course; but his reputation also has an effect upon his behavior. Many lower-class children, facing so difficult a situation, become increasingly hostile and aggressive; and many welcome the first opportunity to drop out of school and limit their associations to members of their own social class.

In our society, education offers the best route to social mobility. But the frustrations experienced by most lower-class children in their daily school situations force them to give up the struggle for advancement. In the literal sense, they know what the score is. And with the bitter poignancy of children who have been deeply hurt by the rebuffs and veiled insults of their playmates, they are trying to put their feelings into words the adult might understand. They are learning, the hard way, that "this is the way it is," and "life is like that."

A few lower-class children fare somewhat better. A few equipped with hard enough exteriors continue to push their way on through school and into college, despite all obstacles. These are probably the individuals who have learned how to take on the behavior and the value patterns of their social betters and who have learned thereby how to gain the approval of their teachers and fellows.

What happens by the time boys and girls reach high school? When all the sophomores and juniors in the Jonesville high school (over two hundred, averaging sixteen years old) were asked to evaluate their age-mates, we obtained data similar to those obtained from fifth- and sixth-graders. Adolescents select their friends largely from the same social class as their own. The boy or girl from an upper-status family is mentioned most often on the "best friend" item; the lower-class boy or girl, least often. Regarding reputation, the upper-middle-class adolescent is ranked highest on every favorable item; the lower-middle-class, second; the upper-lower, third; and the lower-lower, fourth.

There was one major difference, however, between the high school and elementary school responses. At the high school age, there was no clear-cut relationship between social-class position and the number of votes received on the *un*favorable items. While the upper-status group received an overwhelming share of the votes on every positive characteristic, they also received approximately their share of the votes on the negative characteristics. The lower-class group received few favorable votes; but neither did they receive more than their share of unfavorable votes. The middle-class group continues to occupy its enviable position; but the lower-class group is now less conspicuous. It is a relatively ignored group.

If we consider this finding in the light of certain other data concerning the high school population, it seems to bear out our earlier interpretation—that it is only those lower-class boys and girls who succeed in adopting middle-class attitudes and behavior who go on through high school.

In the first place, there is evidence which shows that, of the boys and girls who drop out of school from the eighth grade on, the great majority are lower-class. There is a heavier weighting of lower-status groups in the elementary school of Jonesville than in the high school. At the fifth and sixth grades, 62 percent of the children are upper-lower-class; 15 percent are lower-lower. At the tenth and eleventh grades, these proportions drop to 46 percent and 6 percent, respectively. Thus, the high school population in Jonesville is selective in relation to not only academic ability but also social status.

If a boy or girl whose family occupies the lowest social position in the community has continued in school to the tenth or eleventh grade, he is likely to have certain characteristics which set him apart from other lower-class boys and girls. He is probably more studious, more ambitious, more persistent. He may have certain special abilities—prowess on the athletic field, or unusual academic aptitude, or a talent for art or music. He is sure to have greater social adaptability than the average boy or girl of his age. He is, in brief, the mobile member of his social class; and, as such, his appearance and behavior do not differentiate him markedly from the boys and girls with whom he is trying to "make the grade."

Such a lower-class boy or girl wins a certain measure of acceptance. He is not selected by his middle-class associates as their friend, nor does he receive favorable mention. But neither does he serve as the target for unfavorable mention, as is the case with the lower-class child in the elementary school.

It happens occasionally in Jonesville that a high school boy or girl of a lower-class family goes even further in winning acceptance for himself. Jennie Stone, a girl from a lower-lower-class family, was a member of a clique which, besides herself, included only boys and girls of upper-middle class. In addition to being mentioned by her clique members as "best friend," she received a large number of votes from all her age-mates on "good-looking," "popular," "leader," and other favorable reputational items.

It happened that Jennie was one of those rarely gifted creatures—beautiful, intelligent, charming. She had learned how to handle social situations, and she was a great favorite with her teachers as well as with her peers. She knew how to put her best foot forward, and how to keep it there.

But for every Jennie, there are scores of Priscillas and Penelopes who retreat into the safety of the social level where they were born.

The number of lower-class boys and girls who manage to force their way up the social ladder are few; and the price they pay is usually dear. For in a society in which middle-class values are dominant, the lower-class child, if he is to be successful, must manage to discard the pattern of living and the pattern of thinking that he has learned from his family. He must fight the social-class stereotypes which operate so forcefully against him from earliest childhood. He must win the favor of his social superiors, and, in doing so, he must establish a reputation for himself different from that of the rest of his class. He is expected to accomplish all this, in most cases, unaided. It is little wonder that, faced with so formidable a task, few are successful.

The next chapter shows how the forces of social status and class, generally described and qualified here for all children, actually operate in the life of a lower-class child and her family.

Chapter 6

ROOM AT THE TOP

To Him That Hath Shall Be Given

Mr. Sellers, usually a heavy sleeper, was sitting straight up in bed, wide awake, listening. A strange sound had awakened him. It was like someone crying, someone in the back bedroom. He felt anxious and a little frightened, for none of the family should be home now. It was early in the afternoon, and his wife was down at the Volmers' doing the weekly washing for the boss's wife. Maggie and Bill were at work, too, and Priscilla should still be at high school. He continued to listen but could hear nothing. He lay down again and wondered if he could get a couple of hours' more sleep before he went on night shift.*

Then he heard the sound again. It was like the way the kids used to cry when they had been badly hurt and had run home to him and their mother for help. The sobbing increased and suddenly became unrestrained. Something certainly was wrong. He hurried out of bed, pulled some clothes on, and came out of the darkness of his room into the light of the small hallway which connected the girls' room with his. The door to the girls' room was shut. No sound could be heard. He knocked, but there was no answer. He waited a moment, wondering if he had been dreaming, started to go back to bed, when he heard the crying again. It sounded like Priscilla.

He opened the door and looked around. There was no one there. He looked in the closet and looked out the window into the yard, but could see no one. This frightened him even more. He was sure now that something was wrong. He heard a suppressed sob. It

---

* By W. Lloyd Warner. See List of Authors.

seemed to come from under the bed. In the dark beneath it he saw Priscilla's body, knees pulled up against her, head buried in her two arms, and all of her squeezed against the farthest and darkest corner.

"Priscilla, are you all right? What's the matter with you?" he asked. "Are you sick? What's the matter with you—have you been hurt?"

"No."

"Well, what's wrong?"

"Nothing."

"Priscilla, you come out from under that bed. You're acting like a baby. You used to get under there to cry when you were a little kid. Come on out now and tell me what's wrong."

After considerable coaxing, Priscilla came out. Her face was smudged, her eyes red, and her tears had made little marks like small dry pools on the powdered surface of her face. The sweater which covered her well-formed figure was smeared with spider webs, and her short, white socks were covered with a gray dust. She held her head down and would not look at her father.

"Now, tell me what's wrong. What's happened to you? Maybe I can help you."

"No, you can't, papa—no one can. I'm in the dog house again, and this time it's an awful big dog house. I can't stand it any longer. I'm going to quit that terrible high school. I want to get a job and go to work."

"Priscilla, I can't understand you any more. Why you used to love grammar school. You always had all A's on your report card, and now you're flunking and getting in trouble with your teachers. I just can't understand it, Priscilla. You used to be such a nice kid, and I believe you still are. You liked school and had all those nice friends. What's happened? You don't want to quit school."

"Yes, I do, and I am."

"Look, Priscilla, I'd planned on your sister and brother going through school, but they quit and went to work. They had plenty of brains, but I let them quit because I thought they lacked ambition. I know it's hard to stick it. I remember how my sister and I quit school, too. But you're the last, and I wish you would go on and give it a try."

"No, I'm never—absolutely never—going back to school again."

Her father put his arm around her. Priscilla started crying again. After a while she said, "You and Mother just got to let me quit. I can't take it any more. Everyone up there hates me. No one likes me. The teachers hate me, and the kids won't have anything to do with me."

"That can't be true, Priscilla. Our family is okay in this town. We ain't rich, but I earn an honest living, and everybody thinks we are okay. No one can point the finger at us. Now, tell me what happened today. What did you do?"

"Well, I got caught playing hookey again. That old Swenson caught us. He's always snooping. He thought we were going down by the river to meet some boys, but honest we weren't. Florence, Ruth, Carol, and I just wanted to have a little fun. Just wanted to get away from all those snooty kids. And I'm not going back." Her voice became shrill and harsh. "I'm not going back. None of us is going back. We're all through with that school from now on.

"The way a lot of us girls are treated at school no one can blame us for the way we feel. There's nothing there for a lot of us but just coming to classes, listening to the teacher, reciting our lessons, and studying, and going home again. We're just pushed out of things.

"There are a group of girls there who think they're higher than us. They're a group of girls from the wealthier families. They look down on us. They have a club that's supposed to be outside the school, but it's really in the school. They can do things we can't afford, and they just go from one club to another and hog all the offices, and are in all the activities. They just talk about what they're doing and what they're going to do, and they ignore us. They won't pay any attention to us. I've almost quit going to church because the same girls go to our church. I just don't feel like I want to go to church any more.

"I used to like to go to church, but I don't any more now. I don't like the kids there any more, and I don't like our Sunday School class. Those kids make you feel just like you don't belong there. They think they're better than me, and they just talk about the things they do and sit there and they just ignore us kids. All of us kids have dropped out. June dropped out first. That was about a year ago. Then Ruth and Florence dropped next, and now I've quit. We quit because we just don't go around with those kids, and they don't go around with us. And so we just didn't want to go there any more.

"The same thing happened to the Senior Sunday School as happened with us. They're ahead of us. Those kids in the Senior class, they made Florence feel so bad that she quit going." She named the children who had made her sister feel bad, and they were upper-middle-class kids. "Those kids are all snobbish, and they snub us. That Laura Madison makes me sick, the way she gets into everything. Now that she's got that new flute she stands up there in front of the Sunday School class, toodle-dee toodle-dee, and toodles away just like she was somebody really big."

Mr. Sellers said, "Priscilla, you shouldn't say that." Priscilla said, "Well, that's just what she does.

"And I don't feel like I want to go to school. They snub us, and they won't talk to us. Some of them will speak to us sometimes, but most of the time they just ignore us. Now I know we're not rich. We're really poor people. I don't want the kids in high school to know that Mother takes in washing to get a little extra money to get some of the things that she needs. A lot of women take in washing here in town. There's nothing wrong with that. But they'd look down on me if they knew it.

"And we can't do the things they do. We have a large family, and I know, Dad, you're only a working man, and we can't afford to do a lot of things.

"But us girls would like to be in the school activities and school games—to go to the dances and things like that. We could do that without money. But they just make us feel like we're not wanted. I went to some of the activities when I first started to high school. But they just ignored us. Last year I was in home-making and in the Pep Club, but this year I'm not in anything.

"You know I don't go with the boys in the high school. I just don't care to. I'd like to go with them, but most of the boys that I'd want to go with, they wouldn't ask me. I guess they just don't want to go with me. If you go to the high school dances, nobody will dance with you. They just dance among themselves and have a good time, and you're just nobody. If you go to the football games, it's just the same way. Now, those Pep Club girls are supposed to sit together at a game and root together, and if you're not in one of the groups, you're left out. That's just the way it is."

Priscilla turned up both her palms and shrugged her shoulders and said, "Well, why go? We're made to feel out of place, and that's just the way it is.

"I want to graduate from high school, but I'll have to have English if I do. I flunked it last year. And I've been cutting it again this year—because there are just little kids in there, and they make me feel ashamed. I'm so much older and bigger than they are. Miss Jacobsen bawled me out for cutting right in front of the class the other day because I didn't know the questions because I hadn't been there the day before. Well, that made me mad; so I cut the next day."

While Priscilla spoke, Mr. Sellers looked at the floor. He said nothing. He knew what she said was true. His two older children had told him the same thing when they quit. He and the Missus had gone up to school and raised hell, but it didn't do any good. Now it was Priscilla's turn.

By God! It wasn't going to happen to her. But what to do? It wouldn't get him to first base to talk to Swenson or Lawson, those dirty so-and-so's. He'd go to see Oldham, the lawyer. He liked to raise hell. The big guys hadn't got a hold on George Oldham yet.

He gently patted Priscilla on the shoulder and kissed her on the forehead. "Look, honey, Daddy's going to try to help. We ain't going to take this without no fight. Mama will be home in a little while. Fix yourself up, Priscilla. Mama and I are going to do something about this. You'll see, we're going to help you."

He washed up and put on his coat. When his wife returned they went down to Oldham's office.

Before Priscilla entered high school she was well liked by her teachers and classmates. She had had an outstanding record ever since she had been in grammar school. She had a reputation for being a nice child and for being intelligent and diligent as a student. All her playmates said she was a good sport. She went around with all the girls in her room, particularly "those nice girls who belonged to the best families" and who live over in the "Top Circle." Florence, Ruth, and Carol were also in that group. All of them came from Mill Town. Everyone knew it, but it didn't seem to make any difference. Their grammar school teachers said it showed what a good character, nice personality, and brains could do for anyone who really tried.

Now it was all different. She, Florence, Ruth, and Carol, and some of the others were no longer friends with the girls who came from The Circle. Only that morning Priscilla had put on her new pink sweater and plaid dress and gone to school almost happy. She looked just as good as anybody else. She had actually spoken to Sylvia Volmers, but Sylvia had turned her head and said something to Jane Eberhart and Judith Morrison and all three of them had laughed. Priscilla blushed, for she knew that they were laughing at her—particularly because they had been her friends in grammar school, and she had never learned why they had dropped her. When she got to her seat in the assembly hall, Mr. Scott had asked her to come to his office. When she got there he told her he was sorry but she could no longer be a majorette in the band, an honor that all the girls competed for, because she had been skipping school and was behind in her studies. She knew when she walked into his office what he was going to tell her, for one of the girls who belonged to the corps said that the others were trying to force her out and get the Madison girl in. She went back to her seat. She saw Ruth and Carol and the others sneaking out. They had had a row with old lady Kennedy because they had been caught passing notes to the Gear boys. She decided to go with them.

Swenson had caught all of them. He brought them back to his office. They all attempted to lie out of it.

"I've had enough lies from you girls. Now just cut it out; get your story straight; I want the truth. I know that all of you are lying. And you're all trying to hide where you were. Do you want me to get your mothers down here again?

"I suppose I'll have to go out here and get a baseball bat and come in here and beat some brains into your heads. No, I guess that wouldn't do any good. Just nothing in you, nothing at all. Now I'm trying to save you girls, and you're just too dumb to know it. I think you're worth being saved, but if you won't let me save you, well, that's your own fault. I'm going to get your mothers in here, and we're going to try to save you."

"Can't Win, Can't Place, Can't Show"

It was late afternoon when Mr. and Mrs. Sellers arrived at Oldham's office. Oldham was alone.

"What can I do for you, Tom? You haven't robbed a bank, have you?"

"No, Mr. Oldham, but I wish I had. My little Priscilla has got into trouble at school with Lawson and Swenson. My wife and I thought you might help us."

"You see," said Mrs. Sellers, "it's like this, Mr. Oldham. We know her skipping school is serious. We realize that, and I think she realizes it. But the seriousness is not skipping so much as it is the situation in the high school. I'm referring to the discrimination among the students, by the superintendent, the principal, and the teachers. We noticed this same thing when my older daughter was in high school, and we saw the same thing when my son was in school. And now it's going on with the younger girls. Ever since we've been here, we have known that the sons and daughters of the members of the school board have an inside track. The same is true of the wealthy people here in town. The good grades seem to be given to the people that think they're a better class and have more money than we have. The same thing seems to be true of the class offices, parts in the plays, and things like that. Of course, it doesn't happen in every case, but that seems to be the way it works out most of the time. We're a large family. We have to watch the pennies to get along. Mr. Sellers is a workingman, and there are seven children in the family; so we have to be careful with our money. But this shouldn't make any difference in the school. But it actually does.

"The latest thing that has hurt Priscilla the most, but it's just like all the other things that have happened before, it's this majorette business. All the boys and girls pay for that course, and Priscilla was selected to be one of the majorettes. Her father and I thought she did as well as anyone else. At first, she did better, I think. But they did a dirty trick on her. Priscilla told me that band leader, Mr. Scott, told them to practice as much as they could outside of the school time. Well, the other girls used to get together and practice, but they would never tell her until it was all over. The only way she'd find out was when they all met at school, and the others had worked on one of the routines, and she couldn't do it. And then someone would say that was the way they did it at such and such a time.

"I think they were actually working to get Priscilla out of that group. Mr. Scott didn't find out what was going on until Lawson told Priscilla that she couldn't twirl any more. She came home and cried all afternoon and almost all night. I found it very difficult to get her to go back to school. Mr. Scott didn't want them to take Priscilla out. He felt that she could do as well as the rest if she only had the chance to practice. I'm pretty sure that Mr. Lawson told Mr. Scott that he had to take her out of there. I believe the girls had a lot to do with Priscilla's being taken out."

While Mrs. Sellers spoke, Mr. Oldham looked out the window.

When she stopped he said, "It all sounds familiar, but I didn't think the kids were as class-conscious as their parents. Tom, I'd like to have you talk. What do you think about it? What do you think was back of all this?"

"Well, a number of things, Mr. Oldham. I can't say all of it. Swenson said she was dropped because she skipped school, but that isn't the whole thing. On my job I run into a lot of things and talk to people a lot, and I hear a number of things. A lot of kids skip down there, and Swenson overlooks it. He just seems to land on certain ones. But if he gets it in for a boy or girl, he's very hard on them, and he always rides them. The school board's children and prominent people around town who have children there in the high school, their children always have the inside track. They seem to be in everything, and it's difficult for other students to get into activities and offices and grades and things like that.

"A number of the teachers over there give the good grades to the students whose parents are influential. I guess they keep their jobs that way. I can't understand it, and I never could, but it's been that way ever since we came to town. It doesn't seem to make any difference who the principal is or who the teachers are. The school board and the prominent people's children have the good grades and get into the activities." He looked at his watch and said, "Well, I guess we'd getter be going now.

"I still can't understand," Mr. Sellers continued, "what has come over Priscilla. She used to be such a sweet girl, cooperative, and worked with everyone. But just this fall she's become stubborn and bitter. I can't understand her any more. She used to come to me and discuss things with me far more than she ever would with her mother. But now she holds everything back. Today's the first time she's talked. When she was in grammar school, she ran around with that group of girls who think they are somebody, the ones that run the high school. But when she went into high school they quit going with her, and that hurt Priscilla. She kept working, and her interest continued in school, and she made very good grades. And then last year she was in the majorettes, and the girls really like doing that. She was satisfied with it and would look forward to practicing and to the performances. Then, when she got dropped out of that she just turned bitter, and I can't get anything out of her any more."

When Mr. and Mrs. Sellers left, Mr. Oldham stood up and looked out the window. He stood there a moment, then pulled the shades down, walked over to the door and locked it. He removed two large law books from his library shelves. The opening revealed a number of objects of sentimental value and private utility which he kept hidden from every one in Jonesville. From among them, he pulled out a pint bottle of good Bourbon. He took several long drafts from it; he felt better. He replaced the bottle and reached behind an adjoining legal volume and brought out a small badly worn book. He had treasured it since his father had given it to him on his tenth birthday. Its title was *Strive and Win, A Book for Boys*. The leaves fell open to a marked passage.

"There is always room at the top, my boy, for a young man of ambition to climb the ladder of success. All it takes is good character, hard work, a few brains, and a will to do."

"Thank you for your good advice, Mr. Stevens," said David. "Some day I will be at the top like you."

Oldham re-read the passage. "Well, that's what happened to me any way. I made it. This goddamned town!" He shook his head, replaced the book, had another drink, and returned the legal volumes to their proper place among the several hundred which stood on his shelves. He put several peppermints into his mouth. He pulled the shades up and unlocked the door.

"Don't be a goddamned fool, Robert, my boy. Why can't you learn to keep your nose clean? So you want to put on the big white plume and the shiny armor and go out to attack privilege and power and save little girls in distress all because your heart aches for the downtrodden. For Christ's sake, you could get a whole new school board and what the hell difference would it make? They'd go on acting the same way. Charlie McCarthys for the big land-owners and Jonesville's 400 and what the hell could you do about the kids? Could you get Louise, your own daughter, to change her ways and go with the Sellers kid? The hell you could!" Anyway he could find out from Louise about what was going on, and maybe he could do something.

That evening Louise seemed very communicative, so he brought the subject up. "Louise, do they have a snooty crowd at high school?"

"I'll say we do. The upper gang in my class is the PFP's. You see, I'm in the PFP's, but I don't run around with the PFP's all the time. I'm kind of in between them and the other kids. I was out of the PFP's for a while because they made me mad. They drew the social line too fine. You see, Marie is a very good friend of mine. When she came up here to visit me, I introduced her around to all the girls in the PFP's. And I'd go down the street, and they'd say 'Hi, Jane,' and just ignore Marie. I couldn't stand that; it hurt me so. So I pulled out of there. But now I've more or less started to go back with them."

"The PFP's sound like the Monday Club you mother belongs to."

"It's just the same, Daddy."

"And who's the lowest bunch at high school?"

"Right now, those kids like Florence, Priscilla and Ruth are the lowest-ranking bunch in high school, but they're not as bad as we had last year." Louise confirmed the story of Mr. and Mrs. Sellers. Then she added, "Nobody, I don't think, around here will tell their parents this. But this happened in the eighth grade. Maybe I shouldn't tell you, but I just want you to know the way that they do things around here and the way the upper kids and the poor kids are treated. This is very confidential. When we were in the eighth grade, all of us kids ran around together. There were us girls who later were in the PFP's and then there were the other kids, and there were a couple of boys' gangs. Now, the boys got to stealing things. They went all over town stealing merchandise— candy and cigarettes and things they wanted. They used to store them in their clubhouse. There was another gang of the upper kids, and they were doing the same thing. They stole just as much and maybe more than the others." She named boys from several upper-class families.

"Well, the cops got wise to these kids' stealing and rounded them all up and made them tell. Both gangs were caught. And the police took the merchandise that they had stolen. But they hauled Marco and his bunch up before the judge and put them on six months' probation. The upper kids didn't have anything done to them. Now everybody's forgot the upper kids were doing that. They haven't forgot that Marco and his kids were in that. They just cut Marco out of everything and all the rest of them. That's the way it is for all of us at high school."

On the way to his office next day, Mr. Oldham was stopped by Mr. Lawson.

"News travels fast around here, Mr. Oldham. A little bird told me that the Sellers were in to see you last night. I was wondering if they said anything about the majorette business?"

Oldham said, "Oh, a little, I think. It is still eating on Priscilla from what her mother said."

Lawson chuckled to himself and went on. "You know, she is so clumsy it was pitiful with her out there trying to throw the baton around. She just made the other girls look ludicrous. My, it was a sight to see her clumping down the street like an old truck horse. We just couldn't have her there, as it ruined the whole show for the other girls and made the band look bad. Scott did not want to take her out, as he thought she was doing a good job. The other girls did not like her in there. Don't you believe a word of it. Nice to have seen you. By the way, Louise's a remarkable girl. She's doing a fine job. Well, good-by."

After a few telephone calls, Mr. Oldham asked for Swenson. "Hello, Dick. Mr. and Mrs. Sellers were in. They're considerably distressed about their daughter's quitting school. I guess the other parents are too. Could I see you? Why don't you come down to the house and have a drink?"

Their second drink was almost consumed. They had been talking about Priscilla's and the other girls' difficulties. Mr. Swenson said, "Hell, that's an old story. The Sellers, the Conways, and the Grunds were skipping school last year, and the year before, and I suppose they'll be skipping this year. I used to think that the Sellers girls, when they were in grammar school, were the sweetest little kids in town. But they've changed so much in the last year. The problem there with all those girls is lack of parental control. The Sellers let those kids run around like rabbits and never pay any attention to what the children do. The Conways are the same way. There's no parental control there, and so what can you expect from those kids?

"Old Tom Sellers just doesn't understand. He's just one of those sweet, loving souls who doesn't know what the hell it's all about. You know, I think that the only appeal you can use on that girl is to take her down in the basement and beat the hell out of her. Of course, you hate to do that with a girl that old. But I've tried to reason with that girl; I've tried to threaten her; I've tried to talk to her; I've tried everything. But, hell, there's no way to appeal to her. The only thing left is to beat the hell out of her. I think if she had the hell beat out of her a time or two, then she'd begin to see things.

"I think Priscilla and the other girls were both out with boys this morning. They were up town fooling around."

"But what about the majorette business? It sounds like that raised hell with the kid."

Swenson said, "Yes, I'm sure of that. That's what I gathered when I talked to her a few days ago. Her mother talked to me on the street the other day. I've almost reached the decision to put her back in there. If the other girls will let her come in, and if Scott will let her in. I'm pretty sure that Scott will, but I just want to be sure that she can make her grades and that she doesn't cut school any more. Really, the big thing, though, is that the girls are objecting to her being in there. The truth is that. Her skipping school was more or less an excuse to get her out of there. Lawson didn't want her in there because the other girls had been kicking about having her in there. The first time she did something, the heat was put on by some of the old families to get Priscilla out of there. Some of these old families around here really put on the pressure."

A few days later, Mr. Oldham saw Mr. Sellers on the street.

"It's no use, Mr. Oldham. She's quit. She's got a job over in Alexandria. She seems happy now and I guess that's what counts. I did hope, though, she'd go on to school and amount to something. I never had an education, and I wanted her to have a better chance in life than I had. Now she isn't going to get no place either. Nobody in my family ever wins. We don't have a chance. My sister and I tried for a good education but we dropped out; my two older kids came along and I sort of bet on them to come through, but they didn't. Then Priscilla, now she's out. It's like when I bet on the horses. I haven't got a chance. I can't win, can't place, can't show. I guess that's the way it goes in Jonesville."

Mr. Oldham looked at him, "Yes, that's exactly the way it goes here in Jonesville."

Chapter 7

THE MILL: ITS ECONOMY AND MORAL STRUCTURE

WORKERS AND MANAGERS

The Mill, a series of squat buildings stretching awkwardly across the prairie at the meeting place of the town and corn lands, dominates the industrial life of Jonesville. A large part of the city's income is earned within the high steel fences which surround it; 700 of the city's 2,000 urban employees work there. When the citizens of the town talk about The Mill, they rarely refer to it in economic terms but speak in moral terms of its place in the life of the town. They are forever concerned with its power for good and evil in the lives of Jonesville.*

The economic and social force of The Mill affects every part of the life of the community. Everyone recognizes its power. Politicians, hat in hand, wait upon Mr. Waddell, manager of The Mill, to find out what he thinks. Civic leaders seek out the manager of The Mill for the answers to such important questions as "Shall the tax rate be increased to improve the education our young people are getting?"—"Shall the new minister be Mr. Jones or Mr. Smith?"—"Should the city support various civic and moral enterprises?"—"Should new industries enter the town and possibly compete with The Mill for the town's available labor supply?" They want to know what Mr. Waddell thinks. Mr. Waddell usually lets them know.

Young men and women go to school in Jonesville until they grad-

* By W. Lloyd Warner and Marchia Meeker. See List of Authors.

uate from high school; then many of them enter The Mill as workers. They spend the rest of their lives there. Boys from the farms, no longer needed in a tractor economy, seek their fortunes there. They, their friends, and kinspeople wonder if it is a good place to be and if a man can get ahead in a place like that. Young wives say their husbands get little pay, and there is no chance for advancement. "When you work in The Mill you can't get ahead, you stay where you are," they say. The wives of older workers speak of the boss's constant solicitude for the workers' health and happiness. They tell how Mr. Waddell acts just like a father to all his workers. Maybe their husbands don't get very far, but they had jobs and were looked out for "even in the depression." In Jonesville people choose sides and take moral positions when they talk about The Mill, its owners, and what it does, or does not do, to and for Jonesville.

A few vital statistics about The Mill are necessary before we can examine what it does to the city and learn how it operates as a social force in the lives of the people and as a power for social mobility. Until Mr. Waddell reorganized The Mill shortly before World War I it had not been much of a success. There had been several reorganizations, a few failures, and incorporations under a succession of new names, each of which testified to the continuing manufacture of electrical appliances and to the fact that a new ownership had taken over. Waddell interested Chicago capital in The Mill; the major part of the ownership is still in their hands. The present worth of the enterprise amounts to several million dollars. As a manufacturing and financial concern, The Mill is in every way a success. It competes on equal terms with other important companies in the United States which manufacture the same appliances.

Since its last incorporation, The Mill has been under the same management. It grew rapidly in the twenties and in ten years' time had about 500 employees. There was a slight recession during the depression, but The Mill stayed open continuously. Since then it has expanded and increased the number of employees and the amount of production. It secured war contracts so that it was not forced to curtail production during World War II.

The job hierarchy is divided into managers and workers. Like many small town factories, most of the top executives do not live in Jonesville; the owners, including the president, all vice-presidents other than Mr. Waddell, and the secretary, are in Chicago. Less than ten people belonging to the top management live in Jonesville. On the other hand, almost all of the workers are members of the community. About 20 percent are skilled workers; 31 percent, medium-skilled; 46 percent belong to the low-skilled category; and the remaining 3 percent are shipping clerks.

The Mill management is said to be opposed to other industries' coming into the town and to have taken steps to prevent new plants' opening up and creating competition in the labor market. Several informants reaffirmed the following statement of a person who knows the town intimately: "The people out at The Mill are very strong politically. I suppose you have been here long enough to know how important The Mill is in this town. They seem to see to it that things go along the way they want. Now I have heard of several cases, and I know of some myself, where business tried to come into this town. They get just so far and then nothing happens. Any kind of new activity just can't get started in this town. There is the Johnson factory building. Several people have been interested in getting it started, but nothing ever seems to happen. The people at The Mill bought up the plant and started something there, but after a while it folded up and the building just sits there. It seems an awful waste; but The Mill group owns it so nobody else can get in there."

A banker refers to this same situation: "Waddell and some of the owners out at The Mill own the Johnson factory—you can't blame Waddell for not wanting someone else to come in and operate that plant. The towns down The River are making it difficult enough to get an adequate labor supply. If someone started a company to fill that building they would need about 100 men, and that would make a serious situation for The Mill. After all, if you had come in here and taken over a worn-out, run-down mill and built it up to a point where you employed six or seven hundred men, you would see to it, if you could, that some other company didn't come in and take over your workers from you."

Thus the policy of The Mill not only influences the employees but directly affects the economy of the whole community.

Those who complain about Mill policies far outnumber those in favor, but some people feel that Jonesville is fortunate to have The Mill since it contributes to the prosperity of the community. They feel that Mr. Waddell "has been a good influence" and "has helped the community." A well-informed woman made the following criticism: "The Mill does a lot for this town, and they kept open all during the depression, but they don't pay living wages. They had men working just a few hours a day just a few days a week, and a man couldn't live on that kind of pay and support a family too. What really kept the town going during the depression was the government's work on the waterways."

Other people express a different kind of hostility toward The Mill. While it is often spoken of as "Waddell's Mill," it is generally known that The Mill is owned by people outside the community, that Waddell is not the owner but "just a paid employee and just like anybody else." It is also known that the Chicago people who own it are Jewish and, since many people in the town are anti-Semitic, it is often said that The Mill is "owned by Jew money" or "run by a bunch of Jews." The resentment seems to be less because they are outsiders than because they are "a Jewish corporation."

THE MILL IS JUST LIKE A FATHER

The Mill has adopted a paternalistic attitude toward its workers; until recently there was no union and there had never been a strike. The relations between the few workers who composed the original working force and the managers were intimate and close; first names were used by both levels. But now there are too many men employed to maintain these close personal relations. Foremen have taken the place of top management in relations with the workers; as the organization has become more complex, the relations between the top and bottom levels of the hierarchy have been increasingly remote and impersonal. The older workers who have stayed on more often speak well of management, and when they get into trouble they go to Mr. Waddell or one of his immediate aides to ask for help.

Jim Davidson has been with The Mill for twenty years. He knows everybody in management, and they all know him. He has a reputation for sobriety, being a good father and husband, and a faithful worker. During the research he was having trouble at home. A friend of Mrs. Davidson had told her that Jim was chasing around and that Jim was having woman trouble and a lot of it.

By this time Jim knew he needed help and needed it badly. He had been trying to work up his courage for over a week before he finally got enough nerve to walk into the main office of The Mill to ask to see Al Waddell, the boss. "Al," he said, "I've got to talk something over with you. It's a family matter, but if you've got the time I'd appreciate it if you'd let me talk."

"Sure, I've got lots of time. Go ahead."

"Well, I'll tell you, Al, you've got to remember you've known me for a long time. I wouldn't be in here if you hadn't."

"Yeah, I have. I must have known you almost since the plant started. What's the matter?"

"Well, I'm behind the eight ball now. My wife has been sick. She's been sick now for pretty near a year. We can't have intercourse, and goddamn it, she's blaming me for running around with women in town, and I tell you, Al, I'm not. I'm not that kind of a guy."

"No, Jim, you're not. I've known you a long time, and you're not that kind of a guy."

"The doctor says she's got to have an operation before we can do it again. And it's going to take a lot of dough, $175, and I just haven't got that kind of money."

Al said, "Okay, Jim, now I'm going to tell you what you can do. I know you're a good workman, and I'm going to see that you get the money. You just go back to work and stop worrying. I'll tell you what I'm going to do. I'm going to fix it up down at the bank and up at the hospital so that you can get the money to pay the hospital bill, and we'll take it out of your wages, $5 a week. And say, Jim, I know goddamn well you're not running around with any women."

When Davidson left the office, the boss called his friend, Dean Keating, president of the bank, and arranged for the loan. He said, "Davidson's okay. If I'd said so, he could have stood $10 a week instead of $5 because he's just that kind of fellow. We'll stand back of him." Mr. Keating called the hospital and spoke to Dr. Cartwright, a friend of his, and told him that Jim and his wife would be by to see him and that the money for the operation was okay. Shortly after this, the wife was operated upon, and in five or six weeks, Jim's work began to improve. Al said afterwards, "Why, hell, Jim's happy as a bird now. He's back and working, and he's paying off that loan. That's just the kind of thing we do whenever we can."

A woman whose husband had worked at The Mill for a good many years and enjoyed a close relationship with Mr. Waddell and the other members of the management said that they had always taken a personal interest in the welfare of her family and had been particularly kind when her husband had died. "The afternoon my husband was stricken, Mr. Waddell came to the house to see how I was getting along. Everybody at The Mill was always awfully nice to us. When we were building our house Mr. Waddell said, 'I am glad you're building your own little home. Be sure to let me know if you are ever hard up and are afraid of losing the place because I'll help you out on that. I like to see you and your family have a little home.' Whenever I get into trouble I always go to see Mr. Waddell. You know, when people are so good to you like they were when my husband had his accident, you feel like you owe them something and you're always under obligation to them. So whenever I go to do anything I feel like I ought to ask them about it before I do it and see what the men at The Mill think."

The older men in management and the older workers have a closer relationship than the younger ones do. A number of workers and all of management feel that no matter to what extent the close feeling existed in the past, with the increase in the size of the plant, the relationship is breaking down. A man who knows The Mill well says, "The plant has grown so big, and Mr. Waddell has become so busy, that they have lost contact with the workers. Back in the old days, when they first got started out there, Waddell used to be out in the shop with the boys, and they called him 'Al'; it was none of this Mr. Waddell stuff. But now they're getting farther and farther apart from the workers. Hell, workers want appreciation, they want to be recognized, and they want to have their work recognized."

Mr. Johnson, a member of top management, says, "We've got so damned many new employees, fellows who have come in in the last year or so. They don't know me, and I don't know them. There's a gulf between us, and there's a gulf between them and the older workers. Now I'd really like to know more about these people and the way they think and the way they act. I think some of our problems could be ironed out if we knew a little more about our workers and their problems."

Many people believe The Mill wages are too low. One woman said, "The only reason The Mill is a success is that they pay their employees so little." A minister who had close contact with the workers believes the pay rate is low. He said, "The Mill has never paid high wages. They started here because the wages are lower here than in the city."

The wage rate extends from 45 cents an hour to $1.07½ an hour. Most women employees are paid 45 cents an hour. The scale for men is from 57½ cents to the maximum limit. Two-thirds of the employees receive 62½ cents an hour or less. The average rate for all employees, men and women, is 70 cents an hour.

During the depression, lines of men formed outside The Mill looking for jobs which The Mill could not supply. The men who had jobs were paid at such a low rate that they had to work long hours to make sufficient money. A worker who was out of a job during the depression said, "When things were toughest around here, there were more than 350 men looking for jobs. Let me tell you, you couldn't find them. Every morning you would see men lined up—40 or 50 of them—in front of The Mill. The fellows down at The Mill who were working wouldn't lay off. They were working 60 and 70 hours a week for 20 and 30 cents an hour. Then the N.R.A. came in and they had to work shorter hours, and they put on 150 men, and that eased things up quite a bit."

The union came in during the depression. Management strongly opposed it. The first president of the union said, "Waddell was very strong against having a union. He had to be careful because the National Labor Relations Board forbids employers to influence workers' decisions concerning unions. He called our committee into his office one day. We hadn't organized, but we had a temporary committee and were going around to sign up the boys. He talked to us for three and a half hours straight—all afternoon practically— trying to get us to give up the idea. He'd build up to what he wanted to say and then he'd stop just short of it and start in all over again. That happened about six times. It was really sort of pathetic. Finally, he said, 'Well, boys, you know what I want to say, and you know I can't say it, but you know what I am trying to say.' "

Mr. Waddell's attitude has not changed since the union was formed. One field worker reports: "Waddell spent forty-five minutes on the New Deal, berating Roosevelt, Hillman, Green and Lewis. Since the union came into the plant, Waddell said that 60 cents out of every dollar given to the union goes outside the city. Waddell said, 'I really don't matter around the plant any more since the union came in. The union has changed the attitudes of the men. They think I am an economic royalist living off of what I take away from them. That's what the New Deal has taught them to think.' "

Generally speaking, the workers believe that they are better off with the union. Most of them believe that the principle of seniority is the fairest way of assuring equal advancement for all, that it gives men security and offers less chance of showing favoritism. The members of the union list the number of benefits they have received because they are unionized.

During the last three years there have been a number of disagreements with management, and there was a strike in the spring of 1945. A lawyer who lives near Jonesville and comes there frequently said, "You remember that strike they had in April. That was really a wildcat. They didn't have any sort of decent union set-up. It's supposed to be an A.F. of L. union, but of course it's really a company union. There was one good fellow who used to be president of the union, but he was one of the first fellows to be drafted. Everyone always felt that that looked a little suspicious—I thought so at the time. All the fellows say he was a real union man. He seems to have been the life of the whole thing as far as the workers were concerned. But take this wildcat strike. They just walked out because they knew the union wouldn't take any action. . . . I asked some of the men about it, but they just said that since this fellow who used to be president left there wasn't anybody to take the lead. I think there will be another strike out there for sure."

In its dealings with the workers, the company recognizes the difference between the office and mill employees. It is clear too that both the workers and the community make a similar discrimination. For example, when management holds annual mill picnics for the employees, both the office and mill forces are invited. The picnic is held in the public park. Later in the year the office forces are invited for an outing at the Jonesville Country Club. The mill workers are not invited.

The Workers' Place and the Managers' Social Position

The people of the town fit the mill workers and their managers into the Jonesville scheme of things and assign them their place in the life of the community. Everyone in the town knows the relative status of the mill hands and the office employees. Their evaluations show up in the social score the workers receive and the place they and their families are permitted to occupy in the life of the town. All the subtle gradations of prestige known and valued in the plant are not made by the people of the town; but the larger stratifications in the job hierarchy of The Mill are recognized by

the town and reflected in the social position assigned to the families
or the workers. The mill workers are usually referred to as "the
working class" or "the good, solid people who live right but never
get any place."

On the basis of such evaluations, it would be expected that
workers in The Mill have a low status in the community. The
townspeople place mill employees at the lower end of the system,
below the level of most tradesmen, craftsmen, and many small shop-

Table 8

SOCIAL STATUS OF THE MILL WORKERS

Class	I.S.C. Score	Frequency	No. in Each Class	Percent in Each Class
UM	36	1	1	less than 1%
	40	1		
	42	5		
LM	46	19	70	14
	48	29		
	52	33		
	54	80		
UL	58	67	316	65
	60	59		
	64	65		
	66	56		
	70	47		
LL	72	17	95	20
	76	3		

keepers. A well-informed professional man, while discussing social
status in Jonesville, assigned the mill workers to one of the lower
social levels. He said, "There are several social strata around here.
The top stratum is made up of people with money. Below this is
the one composed of the prominent business and professional families. The small businessmen and foremen out at The Mill are in
a lower, but middle, stratum. I mean a lower stratum than the one
we have just been talking about (professional and business people).
I don't know much about their social life, but that's about where
they fit in here in town. The ordinary workmen in The Mill are
mostly ranked as lower-class around here, but they are not as low
as the older Poles, The Canal renters, and the people back of the

tannery." He has placed the foremen and skilled workers in the lower-middle-class position and the bulk of the workers in an upper-lower-class position. He has excluded members of the lowest class from the ranks of the workers.

The relation of the workers to their social class is presented in Table 8.

There are seventy individual mill workers in the lower-middle class. More than half are skilled workers, and most of the others are semi-skilled or clerks. There are only five low-skilled workers, and three of these are women. The I.S.C. or status of women workers is more likely a function of their husbands' or fathers' occupa-

Table 9

OCCUPATION AND CLASS POSITION

Job Classification	Total No.	Upper-Middle No.	%	Lower-Middle No.	%	Upper-Lower No.	%	Lower-Lower No.	%	Unknown No.	%
Skilled Workers	121	1	1	42	35	60	50	..	..	18	15
Semi-Skilled	183	..	..	14	8	119	65	27	15	23	13
Unskilled	270	..	..	5	2	132	49	68	25	65	24
Clerks (Shipping)	15	..	..	9	60	5	33	..	..	1	6
Total	589	1		70		316		95		107	

tions than of their own and is, therefore, higher than their own jobs would indicate. In general, there is a greater discrepancy between women's occupation and status than between men's occupation and status.

There are 316 mill workers in the upper-lower class. They range from skilled to low-skilled, but the majority are in the semi-skilled and low-skilled categories. There are 95 individuals in the lower-lower class; none of these is skilled, and the majority are low-skilled, but none falls in the very bottom of the lower-lower class or in the range from 77 to 84.

The I.S.C. scores for the office workers place them, on the whole, above the industrial workers. None is below lower-middle class. Furthermore, the great majority are at the top of the lower-middle-class range, while the industrial workers in the lower-middle class fall at the bottom of that level. In the table below the scores for office workers and management are given. On the basis of this material it can be seen that management falls into the upper and upper-middle classes; office workers, in the lower-middle; and industrial workers tend to be in the lower-middle and upper-lower classes.

The range for office workers and management is as follows:

Table 10

SOCIAL STATUS OF OFFICE WORKERS AND MANAGEMENT

I.S.C. Score	Frequency	Class	Rank
16	1	Upper	
18	1	(2)	Management
28	2		
30	1	Upper-	
34	1	Middle	
36	1	(5)	
40	7		
42	21	Lower-	Office
46	9	Middle	Workers
48	4	(42)	
52	1		

(Unknown—3)

Comparison of these scores with those for industrial workers shows that only 88 industrial workers, or 18 percent of those with an I.S.C., overlap with the office workers.

Table 11

JOB CLASSIFICATION OF CLERKS AND FACTORY WORKERS

Class Position	Total No.	Skilled No.	Skilled %	Semi-Skilled No.	Semi-Skilled %	Unskilled No.	Unskilled %	Shipping Clerks No.	Shipping Clerks %
Upper-Middle	1	1	100	..	..	..	..	..	..
Lower-Middle	70	42	60	14	20	5	7	9	13
Upper-Lower	316	60	19	119	38	132	42	5	2
Lower-Lower	95	..	..	27	28	68	72	..	..
Unknown	107	18	17	23	22	65	61	1	1
Total	589	121		183		270		15	

It is clear that mill hands do not enjoy a very high place in Jonesville. On the other hand, it is also clear that few of them rank below the Level of the Common Man. Most of the workers are at the Common Man Level, but the great mass of these are in the upper-lower class and at the lower level of the Common Man stratum. If an ambitious young man is realistic when he leaves high school and enters The Mill, he must not fix his level of aspiration above that of the skilled worker, and if he stays in The Mill he cannot hope to attain a higher social position than lower-middle class. Most likely he and his children will stay in the upper-lower class from which he came. A few men and women become foremen, but no foreman was ranked in the community above the Common Man Level. The social limitations of the workers, the top ceiling for their aspirations, is lower-middle class, and very few workers ever achieve this position.

Mobility in the Factory for Managers and Workers

A complaint that is constantly heard in Jonesville about The Mill is this lack of opportunity for advancement; the attitude sometimes heard about American industry that "you can work all your life and still not become a foreman" is frequently expressed. A prominent minister said, "The trouble with The Mill is that though the men get paid all right there is no future in it because they never advance into top positions in the company. Sometimes I think we are developing into a class society. Where in this town can a man start to work and be able to work himself up to a really good job? There isn't any future for anyone who is working at The Mill. It is that kind of thing, I think, which is turning us into a class society."

There are a number of processes which operate to prevent mobility in the plant. All the men in positions of importance have sons who they hope will take their positions, and some are being trained for them. The son of one of the managers said, "The really good jobs in The Mill aren't so easy for most guys to get because Mahoney and Waddell and Jones and even my dad have all got kids who are after those jobs. There are two Waddell kids. Jean is down at The Mill now, and the other one will soon be there. Then there are two Mahoneys and three Jones boys, and I am working to take Dad's place. It doesn't help morale one bit to have us boys taken in. It seems you can't get into the side with good jobs unless you have someone pulling for you, that is, someone to help you. Of course, I can't complain because it is not every place where my dad could give me the advantages that I have had. I am really being trained to take his place in The Mill. Of course I never really worked at The Mill. I've been studying under my dad how to run The Mill department."

The necessity of increased specialization limits the opportunity for advancement. Most of the positions at the top require special skills and must be filled by men who are trained for those jobs. For example, the chief scientist came from the East, the engineer came from Detroit, one of the accountants, from Alabama, and all of the people in a managerial position with the exception of one were brought in from the outside. The Mill has done very little to train men for the better jobs. One of the members of management said, "It is true that there isn't much room for advancement in The Mill, and it is difficult under any circumstances. That is, you can't take, let us say, a finisher and move him all around the plant and try to fit him into something else. If a guy makes good as a finisher then you have just got to leave him a finisher. Then there are other positions like the chemist's place because no one has got the training, and if the chemist should leave and there should be an opening they would have to bring someone in from the outside. It is pretty hard to advance a person into that job because you can't train a guy to do it."

Some members of management admit that the situation exists but blame the condition on union organization and the increase of labor legislation. One of them said, "The situation for a young man who is starting out now is very different than it was before the New Deal. It has been quite different around here since The Mill was unionized. The union won't let people rise according to their ability. From our point of view we want to advance the people who are the most capable and have the most ability. That is the only thing we care about. But the union won't let us do that. Our advancement has to be on the basis of seniority. There aren't any opportunities like there was before. Nobody can tell me that these days a young fellow has as much opportunity to get places as they used to. Ever since Roosevelt came in most of the opportunities are gone."

Closely related to the lack of mobility in The Mill is the lack of enthusiasm for the work. One of the younger members of management said, "It is true that the workers aren't very enthusiastic about working in The Mill, and they aren't very proud of it. They seem to feel that their jobs are dead-end jobs without much future. I know how the fellows feel because I have heard mill talk all my life. It was really different over at the auto plant where I used to work. You find a good many fellows there who have been with the company a long time, and they were proud they worked for Studebaker. They show off their buttons that they get every five years, and they are proud of them. It doesn't matter whether a fellow was particularly good or not. I admit that the fellows in The Mill just don't seem to feel that way. I guess things could be better in The Mill all right, but I don't known how it could be done."

It might be asked, "What about those who climb beyond the factory and push up into the higher realms of top management?" Only one of the members of top management came from the ranks of the workers. He rose socially from an upper-lower to an upper-middle-class position. It might be thought that when the present generation of managers retires capable men with experience in The Mill would be lifted to take their place. This, too, is impossible, for we learned earlier that all the men in top management have their sons well placed in managerial positions. The positions they now occupy assure the members of the younger generation of managers that they will inherit the occupational and social positions of their fathers.

The workers' "stairway to the stars" in Jonesville and America is no longer an open highway. The royal road to success now is by higher education. Many great corporations and small enterprises forbid the sons of managers from moving into the fathers' positions, but many permit it; and, more importantly, all managers help their sons train themselves for high occupational positions. Advanced education and early placement in promising positions give their sons the necessary advantages to assure their futures.

The Lincoln myth and the American Dream of striving to win and getting to the top do not fit the mill worker. To start today in youth as a mill worker in the Jonesvilles of America is usually to end there in old age.

Chapter 8

THE JOINERS—MALE AND FEMALE

Associations and the Community

Americans have sometimes been called a "race of joiners" because of their proclivity for joining and supporting so many clubs and lodges. The man who belongs to six or eight or even ten clubs is not an unusual figure in our society. The tendency is even more pronounced among women, some of whom attend a club meeting every day of the week. This prodigious club activity is now so well recognized that the American club woman has become a national figure, of sufficient importance to be the topic of academic discussion and the subject of many current jokes.*

The people of Jonesville are no exception to this general pattern of American life. One hundred and seventy-six organized clubs were found, roughly one for every thirty-five citizens. These organizations, including among their members over half of the people in the community, vary in kind and function; there are social clubs, secret societies, philanthropic societies, business organizations, and church groups. They vary in size from large groups, with over 300 members, to small ones with less than a dozen members. There are organizations for men, organizations for women, and a few open to members of both sexes. Different organizations have a different place in the social order, for, like people, they are socially evaluated and thought of as possessing high, medium, or low status.

These organizations, so diverse in form and function, are a powerful influence in the life of the community. Touching all major spheres of group life, they bind the community together. As the

* By Marchia Meeker. See List of Authors.

activities of any association overlap those of other associations and other groups, they unify the interests and the aims of discrete elements. They cut across the major divisions which exist, causing individuals from different groups and different segments of the society to meet, talk, and act together. Organizations connected with the church, school, political groups, and business interests draw a large group of people into their activities and allow these institutions, with a limited role, to extend their influence throughout the community.

The strength of the associations reflects the breakdown of the old ways and the changing patterns of American society. The family is declining as a unit of leisure-time pursuits, and the neighborhood is less important as a basis of association. Though people still know their neighbors and others in the block, the relationships are more casual and less likely to develop into permanent friendships than was the case a generation ago. The church and the church circle have declined as an influence in American life and as a means of acquainting the members of the community with each other.

The newcomer particularly finds it difficult to establish contacts in a town. People generally complain of loneliness, of the lack of friends, and the difficulty of getting acquainted. It was found, moreover, that this sense of loneliness is greater among the members of poorer families than among the well-to-do. While the latter may have less difficulty in making friends because they are better known in the community, and often more permanently established, they also belong to a much larger number of clubs through which they may establish new friendships and associations.

Against this background the club takes on new significance; it becomes an antidote against the increasing social isolation of modern living. The individual who has few friends or acquaintances may join a club and, in this way, make friends and establish himself in the community.

Even among the individuals who have lived in Jonesville all of their lives and have friendships lasting from childhood days, club activity plays an important part. This upsurge of club life probably reflects the general trend toward greater organization of leisure-time pursuits. The informal calling and visiting and the spontaneous parties of a generation ago have largely been replaced by planned parties and formal entertainment.

The size of the town appears to be a factor varying the prominence of clubs and associations. Unlike many rural communities, Jonesville is large enough and prosperous enough to support a number of organizations. Many have a sufficiently large membership—and treasury—to plan meetings regularly, arrange programs, and even invite outside speakers. Yet Jonesville cannot support concerts, theaters, and similar forms of entertainment. It has two movie houses, a skating rink, a roadhouse, and an occasional traveling carnival. A number of taverns along the main street have a fairly steady business, but the individual who sometimes visits them runs the risk of losing his respectability, while the habitual customers are generally considered outcasts by the other members of this community in the "Bible belt of America."

Associational participation is greatest at the top of Jonesville's society and decreases on the way down the class hierarchy. The upper class belongs to the greatest number of associations, the upper-middle class next, and so on down to the lower-lower class which belongs to the least. However, it was learned that the lower-middle and lower classes, though they participate least, are most dependent upon their clubs for social life. These classes do less entertaining on their own, while the upper and upper-middle classes, with bigger houses and larger incomes, are better able to entertain their friends at home with dinner parties, bridge parties, and informal get-togethers. The difference, however, is only one of degree. The prevalence of the social hour in all clubs, regardless of the segment of the population that makes up its membership, points conclusively to their essentially social nature and their importance in organizing the leisure time of their members.

DESCRIPTION OF THE ASSOCIATIONS

What are these organizations like that play such an important part in the social life of the community? How are they formed, who are their members, and what role do they play? All of the organizations that were discovered are alike in that they are voluntary organizations, with a formal structure and organization, including officers, rules, and a definite meeting time. They vary in type, in kind of activity they sponsor, and in the characteristics of their membership. The 176 clubs of Jonesville include 133 adult organizations, with members twenty years of age or older, and 43 juvenile organizations whose members are all under twenty years of age. Nine organizations include both adults and sub-adults but since thcy are run by adults and in general resemble the pattern of adult organizations they are included in this category.

The 133 adult organizations were analyzed and classified according to function or type, according to size, and according to certain characteristics of the members, as age, sex, class position, and ethnic affiliation. They vary in size—the smallest is a woman's social club of nine members, and the largest, the P.T.A. with a total of 385 members. Unlike juvenile organizations which are sensitive to age differences and tend to age-grade their members, adult organizations are not strictly organized on an age basis. A considerable age

Table 12

ASSOCIATIONS BY TYPE

Type	Men's Associations	Women's Associations	Mixed Associations	Total
Civic	..	..	6	6
Lodge	6	5	..	11
Patriotic	2	2	..	4
Social (large)	3	11	1	15
Social (small)	..	16	8	24
Professional (or occupational)	9	2	1	12
Political	1	1	2	4
Charity	..	2	1	3
Church	6	28	18	52
Miscellaneous	..	2	..	2
Total	27	69	37	133

(In addition, there are 43 juvenile associations which have not been classified according to type.)

range was found not only in the large organizations, but also in the smaller, more intimate groups. We concluded that age was not a significant factor in determining membership in most adult organizations. However, they tend to divide the population according to sex, with nearly three-fourths of the associations (72 percent) open only to members of one sex and only 28 percent open to both sexes (see Table 12). Some associations open to only one sex, particularly women's organizations, occasionally invite members of the opposite sex, but this is the exception rather than the rule. It was found, moreover, that there was considerable difference in the type of adult organization depending on whether it was open to men, or women, or both sexes.

The principal types of organizations open to the men of the community are lodges, civic or service clubs, and professional or occupational groups. While the old-style lodge still maintains a foothold, it is generally agreed that it is a dying institution. A generation ago every important man in the community was a Mason, and often an Odd Fellow or a Woodman. The prominent men who have maintained their membership take no active part in lodge affairs today and their sons have not joined and express no interest in doing so. The occasional new members and those who continue to take an active part in the lodge are mainly the working-class men, lacking the prestige of the lodge leaders of a generation ago. Many profess to take no interest in the lodge ritual and some are unable to perform the intricate steps that are required. The pomp and ceremony are gone, and nothing has appeared to take their place. An upper-class man says:

"The Masons are pretty much on the downgrade now. They're heavily in debt and having a tough time holding on to their lodge. I rather think they'll lose it [the Masonic Temple]. The time was when the Masons were not only the strongest in town, but they were *the* social group. Every year they had their Knights Templar ball, which was the social event of the year. All the Masons showed up in full dress uniform and it was really quite an affair. If you couldn't get invited to the Knights Templar ball, you just weren't anybody. That was about 30 or 40 years ago when I was a kid, but it's certainly not that way now.

"The real trouble was that no one came to the meetings but the officers, maybe 12 or 15 of them, and we'd go through the ritual over and over again and we weren't taking in any new members. We had to do all the work ourselves. And after all when you've held all the offices and there's no new blood coming in, there's just no point in keeping on going through the ritual just for nothing.

"There are too many other things for the fellows to do. In the old days the Masons put on a vaudeville show two or three times a month and there was always something doing in a social way. But now you have the movies, the radio, and the automobile."

However, two lodges, Moose and Eagles, have managed not only to withstand the loss of popularity, but even to show a slight increase in membership. Like the older lodges, they, too, offer insurance benefits to their members. But unlike the older lodges, they have secularized their behavior to a great degree, minimizing the lodge ritual and its dependent features including the use of pass-words, the wearing of lodge regalia, and the performance of the secret ritual. The president of the Eagles said, "They are going to put on a drill team and ritual in December. . . . I don't keep up with all that bunk. We have a difficult time putting it on ourselves because we have to read it. . . . This is my third term as president and I ought to do better with that kind of stuff than I do, but I've just never been interested in all that ritual."

While the older lodges are mainly concerned with controlling the behavior of the members in terms of the lodge and directing the interest of the members toward the lodge, the Moose and the Eagles turn their interest outward and make their influence felt to a greater extent in the total community. They organize dances, stag parties, and picnics, sometimes limited to the members, but more often as a money-raising device, open to the whole community. Each of these organizations supports a hall, with a bar, slot machines, and gambling tables, open every night. Members can drop in casually and enjoy the benefits of a men's clubroom, with its male solidarity, horse play, and drinking. By sponsoring different behavior and creating new interests, these organizations have managed to survive but retain no more than a superficial resemblance to the older type of lodge.

The decline of the lodge is not limited to the town of Jonesville, but has been a general feature of American society for the past twenty years. One possible explanation is the economic conditions of the times; the decline that began in the twenties was accelerated by the depression of the thirties when many thousands of members were unable to keep up their dues. Coupled with the decrease in dues-paying members was the added financial burdens put on the organizations as time went on. Many of them are insurance societies who gained their members through promises of benefits to be paid to needy members. As the number of older members increased, the organizations had difficulty in meeting their obligations.

A further, and perhaps more important, factor is the loss of status which lodges have suffered in recent years. As few of the important men of the community belong to the lodge, and these few rarely attend the meetings, the lodge is no longer a means of meeting the important men of the community, and membership is no longer a mark of esteem. The Masons, always the most influential and the most exclusive, have managed to retain their edge and to rank somewhat above the other lodges in town, but even the Masons are fast losing ground and the fact of being a high-degree Mason is no longer a sure step to social success.

As the lodges have died out other forms of organization, the service clubs and economic groups, have risen to take their place. Jonesville has a chapter of Rotary International and a chapter of the Lions Club. The 37 members of Rotary represent the most outstanding and prominent businessmen of the community, and Lions, a notch lower than Rotary, includes 30 of the lesser businessmen, assistants in large businesses, owners of smaller stores, and lesser supervisors in the large enterprises of the town.

After-dinner speeches are the highlight of the evening meetings and center around three general topics. In line with the service motives of the organizations they discuss civic and community problems—"Pupil Individualized Training," "History and Care of Tuberculosis," and "Law Enforcement." The various business classifications represented in the membership are discussed: "History and Development of the Telephone," "Wages and Farm Profits," and "Control of the Corn-Borer." Patriotism, undoubtedly stressed during the war, was the central theme in several lectures. Miscellaneous topics also appear sporadically: "An Appreciation and Evaluation of Music," "Photography as a Hobby," "The Joys of Eats," "Electrical Magic," "What Basketball Means to the Athlete," "Life of Mark Twain," and "History of Starved Rock," to mention a few.

The inconsistency in the programs of these weekly meetings is probably an expression of the obvious conflict between the profit motive and the service motive. This suggests that the real importance and purpose of these clubs cannot be gauged merely by examining the content of the weekly speeches; greater insight is gained by considering the spirit of the meetings, the symbols of the clubs, and the informal behavior of their members. Friendliness and informality are the keynotes, yet friendship is not an end in itself, but a device for giving the members a sense of community and an awareness of the common interests and common problems they face. The activities emphasize the need for cooperation and advancement in the business world and charge the members with their collective responsibility, creating a sense of group solidarity among the businessmen of the community.

Somewhat similar to the service clubs are the economic and occupational organizations for members of the various professions—for doctors, dentists, lawyers, and farmers. At the meetings, held sometimes regularly, sometimes sporadically, members get together to read papers and to hear their colleagues discuss the problems of their own business or profession. Less selective than Rotary, and possibly less selective than Lions, they still have a small membership, usually 10 or 15, because of the small number of people available in any profession.

The men's organizations are limited in number and type, and it is unlikely that any of them, with the exception of Rotary and possibly Lions, arouse much enthusiasm among their members. Not so for the women of the community! The zeal with which the women pursue their club activities causes the women's clubs to flourish with ever-increasing success. The profusion of women's clubs, representing more than half of all adult groups in the community, occurs at all levels of the society. Ranging in size from large organizations with over 200 members, to small groups of less than a dozen, these organizations sponsor countless activities which offer the members an escape from the routine of everyday living. The reports on these groups, small and large, high or low in the social hierarchy, contribute the bulk of the material in the society column of the local newspaper. The space allotted to this subject and the diligence with which the minute details are recorded attest to the importance of this form of behavior in the daily life of the community.

The women's clubs are more avowedly social than the men's clubs. Few are directly concerned with the economic activities of the community; the two exceptions are organizations for beauty-shop owners and for graduate nurses. The multitude of their social activities—luncheons, teas, dinners, potluck suppers, dances, card games, quiz contests, and informal get-togethers—make up a large part of the social life of the community.

However, among these social clubs for women it is possible to distinguish between those which are purely social and those which profess a special purpose or aim. In the latter category, some pose as civic clubs, organized to wrestle with a local community problem, a few are political clubs or patriotic organizations, and some have been organized to do charity work, to raise and distribute funds, to support the hospital, and to give aid to needy families. When such a purpose or goal is announced, it is cherished by the members. It would even appear that the more doubtful the accomplishments of the organizations, the more eagerly they proclaim a record of achievement. To say a club never does anything when it has specifically announced that its members are engaged in a worthwhile project brings fire to the eye of many a club lady. One ruffled member complained, "People say we don't do anything, we just meet to have a good time, but we really all work very hard. We have lessons scheduled for each meeting and someone gives a paper on the topic selected. Then we all discuss it. . . . Then we have different money-making projects throughout the year, rummage sales, bake sales, dance raffles, and give the money to different worthwhile organizations."

The special interest or purpose is not in itself a sufficient drawing card and these clubs, however worthy their intentions, must continue to sponsor social events if they wish to retain their membership. The president of the organization formed to aid the local hospital said, "Lots of our members aren't interested in the hospital at all, but they just belong so they can come to the teas we have every month."

The study group, the approved form of woman's organization in the nineties, has largely disappeared, but many clubs still have as their stated aim the "self-improvement" and "mental improvement" of their members. These aims are expressed in the club mottoes: "Be not simply good, but good for something," "Intellectual Improvement and United Effort for the Welfare of Society," or "Self-Advancement and Community Betterment." Many clubs have not only a motto but also a club color and a club flower and a slogan: "No matter what his work or position may be, the lover of books is the richest and happiest of children."

The form of program varies not only from club to club but also from one meeting to the next. It may be a debate, a formal lecture, or an informal talk; the speaker may or may not be a member of the club, and occasionally is an individual from outside the community. The range of subject matter is tremendous; a list of all club programs presented in a year would probably reveal all the current topics of interest and most of the primary values of the community. Except for a few special interest groups, such as the Red Cross and the W.C.T.U., range of subject matter is the rule.

Again this leads one inevitably to the conclusion that the real *raison d'être* of these groups is not to be found in the purpose proudly proclaimed in the annual program, but in the opportunity for social meeting and visiting with friends and neighbors. An informal social hour, following the program, is an integral part of all meetings; refreshments are served and the members gather in groups to discuss the topics of the day and catch up on the latest gossip. The importance for the members of this part of the meeting is reflected in the care taken by the local newspaper in recording it.

There are a number of women's clubs which forego the speech or program and stress no purpose other than that of bringing together the members for an afternoon or evening of visiting. These groups, generally having a small membership, are a far cry from the traditional women's clubs, with their speakers, their programs, and officers equipped with gavel and versed in the art of parliamentary procedure. Yet they have many of the features of the more familiar groups. Beginning usually as cliques, they decide in time to organize and select a name. Then a definite meeting time is set and they elect officers.

The meetings of these groups are little organized compared to those of the large, more formalized clubs. They are held in the various members' houses and follow the same pattern: the business session, games, awards, refreshments, and the social hour. The business session consists of a statement of the club's funds—usually rather small—and a discussion of where the next meeting will be held. On rare occasions a roll call follows, the members responding to such topics as "Handy Kitchen Tools," "Bible Mothers," "Advice to a Bride," "Picnic Suggestions," "Current Events," "A Local Person Who Would Make a Good Movie Star." Generally the games take up most of the afternoon, with pinochle, euchre, bingo, bunco, and "500" the favorites. Toward the close of the meeting the hostess serves refreshments of huge proportions and great elaborateness. Pity the poor husband who comes home hungry that evening looking forward to a large dinner!

The pattern of these meetings varies only in so far as these clubs observe all holidays—Thanksgiving, Halloween, Christmas, St. Patrick's Day, Valentine's Day, and Easter—with decorations and often a roll call to express the spirit of the day. On holidays also the exchange of gifts among members is traditional. Birthdays are observed with cakes and presents.

In contrast to the small intimate groups, the women's auxiliaries, affiliated with the male lodges, have 100 and sometimes 200 members. The auxiliaries have their greatest popularity with the older women of the community and have not been overly successful in attracting the younger women. But in spite of this failure, all available evidence indicates that the auxiliaries have not suffered as great a decline as the lodges. They still manage to arouse the interest of their members and to draw a large attendance at the meetings which are held at regular and frequent intervals. While the Masons have been losing the interest of their members, the auxiliary, Eastern Star, still holds an important place in the community and has even retained the active support of women of high status. Odd Fellows can muster no more than a handful of men on any one night, but its auxiliary, Beulah Rebekah, holds weekly meetings with a large attendance. Royal Neighbors is the largest woman's organization in the community (over 200 members) while its parent organization, Woodmen of America, is now defunct. The only woman's organization which has followed the trend of the male lodges is the Pythian Sisters, which now has barely a dozen members and is little more than a bunco club.

The greater popularity of the women's groups is also mirrored in the relative strength of the American Legion and the Legion Auxiliary.[1] The Legion has so few interested members that they frequently cannot hold regularly scheduled meetings, and it is generally agreed that "the Legion doesn't amount to anything here any more." The Legion and its Auxiliary are both societies which attempt to arouse feelings of patriotism in the community and to preserve the memories of those who died in the First World War (and, now, the Second World War). The peak of their activity comes on national holidays—on Navy Day, Independence Day, Memorial Day, and Armistice Day—when they organize parades, speeches and public banquets. Now most of this work falls on the Auxiliary which is much larger and has much greater strength in the community than does the Legion. The Auxiliary has largely taken over the annual sale of poppies and does most of the work in

1 This refers to the period before veterans of World War II were admitted. It is possible that the great increase in potential membership will increase the strength of the Legion. However, a cursory examination made in the winter of 1945-46 indicated that the Legion had not been too successful—up to that time— in recruiting new members. Most of the young veterans preferred to join the V.F.W., which had recently started a post in Jonesville, believing that the latter would secure more benefits for them and also fearing that the older men would continue to control the Legion.

connection with securing benefits for hospitalized veterans. The Auxiliary manages to have a large attendance at its regular meetings held throughout the year.

There are at least two possible explanations for the relative strength of the men's and women's organizations. If we assume, as suggested here, that the chief purpose of these organizations is to provide satisfactory social relations for their members, then it may be that this function is more important for the women than for the men. The men are out in the community every day and, through their work, inevitably achieve some social contacts, even intimacy, with others. The women, who remain in the home, have less opportunity for establishing such contacts in the course of their everyday living and look to the associations as a means of meeting people and entering into the community.

A second possible explanation, related to the popularity of the male lodges and female auxiliaries, is suggested by comparing the behavior of the two types of organizations. In the past the lodge behavior has consisted largely of the ritual, which gives dramatic expression to the teachings and the principle of the lodge. The ritual is based on a myth or legend, generally taken from one of the familiar Bible stories. At the performance of the ritual the principle participants are dressed in costumes, the lodge room is decorated with special paraphernalia, and there is a constant use of symbols. A simplified version of the ritual is performed at all meetings, and a more elaborate form takes place on special occasions —when new members are initiated into the mysteries of the lodge, when a member rises from one degree or step to another, and at the annual installation of officers. The men's lodges continue to center their activity around the performance of the ritual and hope in this way to provide a rallying point for their members which will give them feelings of loyalty to the lodge and intimacy with other lodge members.

The women's organizations have taken over the ritual, the dogma, and the symbols of the parent organizations with which they are affiliated, but have minimized their importance. All auxiliaries, including the American Legion Auxiliary, have secularized their behavior to a great extent. This shift in behavior, reflecting the general secularization of our society today, may explain the greater popularity of the women's groups over the men's lodges.

The organized social life of the community does not stop here.

There are a great number of voluntary organizations sponsored by the churches and dominated to a greater or lesser extent by the churches with which they are affiliated. Although theoretically open only to members of one particular church, they often include members of other churches and even individuals who have no formal affiliation with any church. These organizations are different from non-church groups in that their existence depends primarily upon the sponsoring institution, the church. A few of these groups, primarily the Sunday School classes, concern themselves with the sacred dogma of the church. For the most part, however, they are social and include activities similar to those of non-church groups. Membership is not regarded as a form of religious behavior but as organized secular behavior.

These organizations are one of the principal means of integrating the church into the larger community. The ministers who sponsor the groups are well aware of their importance to the church today; they recognize that many people take no interest in the ideology of the church nor its formal expression at the Sunday morning services, but that these same people may be attracted to the church through social events. The Catholic Church has apparently not found this technique necessary, for it supports only one subsidiary group for the women members. However, the major Protestant churches of the community have numerous organizations of this type.

On the other hand, the Federated Church has not met with great success in its efforts to organize subsidiary groups. Drawing its members primarily from the elite of the community, who are traditionally little interested in, and even openly scornful of, church participation, the Federated Church has great difficulty in arousing the enthusiasm of its members in church groups. Working to the advantage of the minister in his efforts to increase the strength of his church is the fact that the Federated is known as the "social church" of Jonesville and, consequently, its subsidiary groups have greater prestige than other church groups and are popular with the socially ambitious. However, as the members who give the church its social reputation are lethargic about these activities and irregular in attendance, their social status appears to be of dubious advantage. With the desultory support they receive, most of these organizations are short-lived or exist on a rather precarious basis.

The Methodist and Baptist churches have both met with moderate success. The members of these churches, coming primarily from the middle classes, accept the church as an integral and necessary part of American life. More than that, church membership is a mark of dignity—or at least respectability—within the community. Therefore, while they have not aroused the religious zeal of the Lutheran Church, they have a fair number of active church members who support these groups.

The clubs and associations so far described are all organized in town. They hold their meetings in town and draw their members primarily, though not entirely, from townspeople. There are also a number of social clubs organized mainly for the rural population. Here, as in town, it is the women's clubs that have the greatest popularity. These groups are organized primarily on a geographical basis, with a group formed in each township and drawing its members primarily from those living in that township. Some of these clubs are affiliated with the County Federation of Women's Clubs and discuss the topics parceled out by the county committees. However, the Home Bureaus, which have greater popularity with the farmers' wives than with the women in town, are the most active and stable groups in the rural areas. The Home Bureau is organized on a county-wide basis, with local organizations in each of the townships which carry out the county-wide program. As the name suggests, these groups are concerned primarily with the problems of interest to the homemaker—"Lard and Its Use in Baking," "Slip Cover Lessons," "Consumer Information on Soaps and Washing Powders," "Personal Hygiene," "Use and Cooking of Eggs," "Family Cooperation in Homework," "Footcare and Abuses," and "Accidents in the Home." In addition, these groups work with the 4-H clubs, especially the girls' 4-H clubs, giving assistance and advice on such matters as the production of home-grown foods and the canning and conservation of food products. Much of the social life of the rural people takes place in the community clubs, organized in connection with the rural schools and meeting at the school houses. Every school has its own club and all people living in that particular school district are welcome. The meetings are mainly family affairs, attended by mothers, fathers, and children. The programs are very informal, consisting largely of group singing and refreshments, though occasionally a member leads a discussion on a particular topic and, more frequently, the school children give a musical recital. These groups meet once a month, but also plan special parties on holidays, in which the members all share in bringing supper and afterwards play games together or visit informally.

These are the only clubs which include all members of the family. For the most part the adults and children pursue their associational life independently, the children of the community forming their own clubs independent of their parents.

So the associational life of the community goes on, day after day, week after week, occupying the time and energies of adults and children, men and women alike. Called on from time to time to act in various community affairs, these organizations bring their members into the main channels of activity in the town. The regular meetings, coming at established intervals, give continuity to the organizations and to the relationships of the members. There is a definite cycle of club activity: interest in these clubs is greatest in the fall and winter and reaches its peak around the Christmas holidays. Especially those clubs which observe the holidays show the greatest activity at those times. Interest falls off in the late spring and becomes progressively less during the summer months. Many clubs cease to function at all during the summer when members are away on holidays or occupied with other recreational activities. After Labor Day when members return from vacations, when the schools open, and the normal routine of life once more prevails, the clubs return to their dominant position and proceed with renewed vigor to the programs and meetings of the coming year.

Chapter 9

STATUS ASPIRATIONS AND
THE SOCIAL CLUB

Associations, like people, are evaluated by the community and assigned varying degrees of social prestige, depending upon the characteristics of their members. Those which are patronized and supported by the upper class have high status in the eyes of the community; those which draw their members primarily from the lower levels of the hierarchy are assigned low status in the community. The way in which these associations are ranked and the manner in which the members align themselves within these associations reflect the major cleavages within the social structure.*

Most associations draw their *active* members—the officers, committee members, those who take part in the programs and perform the countless club activities—from a single stratum of society. These individuals who are most intimately associated with the club activities exert a much greater influence than those who hold only nominal membership. As a result the community comes to identify the organization with the class or classes which dominate the activities and contribute the majority of members.

The associations of Jonesville can be ranked in a hierarchy on the basis of community evaluation of their behavior and membership distribution. Different types of organizations are peculiar to different social levels: certain classes tend to belong to one type of organization, others to different types. It is possible, therefore, to distinguish the pattern of associational behavior of the various classes and to

* By Marchia Meeker. See List of Authors.

show how this pattern maintains and strengthens the class structure of the community.

ASSOCIATIONAL BEHAVIOR OF THE UPPER CLASS

A higher proportion of the members of the upper class belong to more associations than the members of any other class. All upper-class families hold membership in at least one organization and the majority (88 percent) in more than one. They average 3.6 memberships per family compared to 1.3 for the total society. They are found most frequently in social clubs and charity clubs, and these are the only organizations in which they take an active part. Some of the women belong to the satellite organizations sponsored by the most socially prominent church, but, as already indicated, they take little interest in these groups. None of the women of this class belongs to an auxiliary. Some of the men belong to the professional and occupational organizations, and, presumably also for business reasons, a few belong to the Masons and Rotary. This is the extent of the associational behavior of the upper class. The women's bridge clubs and men's poker cliques are not formalized or organized and cannot rightly be called associations.

There are four organizations which might be called upper-class associations; they have higher status than any other organization and are most closely identified with the upper class. All American cities possess associations like them. These four are the Country Club and three women's organizations—a charity club organized to support the local hospital, a social club called the Monday Club, and the local chapter of the Daughters of the American Revolution. All but two of the upper-class families in the community belong to at least one of these organizations, three-quarters of them (77 percent) belong to at least two, and half (49 percent) belong to three or all four. Rotary, as the highest ranking male club, might be placed in the top group, but its membership and its values tend to be centered in the upper-middle class.

These clubs are exclusive and have devices for limiting and restricting the membership. Membership is by invitation only, and those who wish to join have to have the approval of the members. Nevertheless, the membership is not limited to the upper class; the largest percentage of the members of the Monday Club and of Rotary are upper-middle and a few are lower-middle. Only the Country Club includes a sizable number of lower-middle-class members, and this situation is deplored by many. An upper-middle-class man said: "The Country Club isn't what it used to be. The trouble is that during the depression they were pretty hard hit so they had to let down the bars and take just about anybody so they could keep going. A lot of people got in then that we wouldn't take usually. Now they are there and nothing can be done about it."

In spite of the spread in membership of the Country Club, the upper class has remained in control, and the majority of the active members are from this class. They hold most of the offices, arrange the programs, and direct the policies of the club.

The upper and upper-middle classes are represented in the four high-status associations in about equal numbers. However, if we consider the relative size of these two classes it is apparent that a much larger proportion of all upper-class individuals are members. For example, the upper-class members in the Monday Club represent less than 40 percent of the members of the club but about half of the adult upper-class women; while the upper-middle-class members represent slightly more than half of the club members but less than a fifth of the adult upper-middle-class women in the community. The same relative proportions apply to other associations. Not only is the upper class more heavily represented in relation to its total size but it contributes the majority of the active or core members.

The presence of so many upper-middle-class individuals in associations dominated by the upper class is due, in part, to the size of the town and, consequently, the small size of the upper class. Since the upper class of Jonesville has only between 50 and 60 families it is difficult to restrict its social interaction exclusively to its own group. In larger towns, which generally have a larger upper class (in actual numbers though not necessarily a larger proportion), organizations are found which are limited to the upper class.

The upper-middle-class members in these associations perform an important function. They admire and envy and emulate the upper-class members and thus express the superiority of the latter group. For the most part the upper-middle-class men and women hold a subordinate position and follow the leadership of the upper class. In their respective roles of leaders and followers the members follow the patterns of behavior which govern the relationships between the two classes and express the dominance of the upper class. As compensation for playing a subservient role, the upper-middle-class members, through affiliation with those of higher status, may gain an increment of repute and thus increase their own prestige in the community.

The four high-status organizations are looked up to by the rest of the community. Not only the members themselves, but those who are not members—some of whom might wish to be included—are aware that these organizations have high status in the community. The three women's clubs are variously referred to as the "oldest club," the "nicest club," or the "most exclusive club." The upper class is frequently referred to as the "Country Club Set," and the upper-class women are frequently spoken of in connection with their activities in the Monday Club. The upper class tends to be possessive about these organizations, discussing "my club" or "the club that we started." Those of lower status often exhibit hostility toward these groups.

The three women's clubs entertain their members with teas, social hours, and occasional luncheons, and they provide the opportunity for informal social relationships among the members. They also have planned programs—lectures, discussions, and musical events—concerned with leisure-time activities.

The special interests and special sentiments of the upper class are reflected in these programs. The members of the upper class profess an interest in travel, a knowledge of foreign lands; they value objects associated with tradition and antiquity; they are preoccupied with leisure-time pursuits, with activities which have dubious economic value, but which are considered worthy, noble, and honorable. The upper-class woman who has both sufficient money and sufficient leisure time (with servants to take care of her home) is expected to become a patron of the arts. The upper class is characterized by its graceful living—collecting objects and goods and learning an elaborate body of social facts to achieve that end. The subjects of the monthly meetings of the high-status women's clubs express these special interests and special achievements and thus give verbal and collective expression to the attitudes and ideologies of the upper class.

Through these associations, the members of the upper class not only express their common interests, but also perform activities of high value to the total society. They preserve relics and other symbols of prestige which are valued by the community. They patronize and sponsor the arts, through lectures and discussions of books, music, and the theater. They perform charitable activities by contributing to needy individuals and institutions. The ability to make charitable contributions is evidence of their wealth, and at the same time it points to their own superior status as compared to the less fortunate people who receive their charity. By performing these activities, which are not only necessary, but also honorable and noble, the superiority of the upper class becomes manifest to the whole community.

It is interesting to observe that the four organizations which function to maintain the distinctness of the upper class in Jonesville are maintained primarily by the women of the upper class. While the Country Club is open to both men and women, the formal activities are entirely social events controlled by the women. With the possible exception of the Rotary Club, there are no high-status organizations for men; the Masons may at one time have filled this role, but they have little prestige today. Throughout associational behavior the separateness of the upper class from other classes is drawn more clearly in the roles of women than of men. The women belong to no auxiliaries or other organizations of low status; the men, belonging to the lodges, have some contact, if not real intimacy, with men of lower status. The organizations controlled by the upper class are devoted to leisure-time pursuits and function to organize the leisure-time activities of the members. The prerogative of leisure is a sign of status and traditionally associated with the upper class. But in modern industrial societies the men of the upper class generally direct their attention to useful employment, and it has fallen on the women of that class to demonstrate the ability of the family as a whole to follow leisure-time pursuits.

ASSOCIATIONAL PATTERN OF THE UPPER-MIDDLE CLASS

The associational behavior of the upper-middle class resembles that of the upper class in many respects. As already said, a large proportion of this class holds membership in associations dominated by the upper class. In addition, the clubs identified with the upper-middle class have programs and policies which imitate the manner of the superior stratum. The members of this class also participate almost as much in associations as do the members of the upper class: every family holds membership in at least one organization and 86 percent in more than one; the average number of memberships per family is 3.5. All but eight upper-middle-class families belong to either an upper or an upper-middle-class association and three quarters (74 percent) belong to more than one.

In spite of these similarities, certain significant differences appear. In general, the associational participation of the upper-middle class is more diffuse than that of the upper class. They are found in the high-status organizations, but they tend to take a less active part in these groups and follow the leadership of the upper class. They are also found in organizations of low status; the men appear more frequently in the lodges and a few of the women even belong to the auxiliaries, though they rarely take an active role. A few women support the satellite organizations of the "social church" and some also take an active part in the Methodist Church which ranks second in the community.

The upper-middle class tends to be most closely identified with the civic and service clubs of the community. Clubs of this type—Rotary, the Woman's Club, and organizations designed to support the schools and the library—frequently have a wide class spread, but they tend to draw the majority of their members from the upper-middle class and to have the officers and other active members come primarily from that group.

Like the top clubs, these organizations are considered among the better associations of Jonesville. The members are said to be the important people or the prominent people of the community. In particular, membership in Rotary is a mark of status and a sign that a man has attained a degree of success in this competitive society. The members of the upper-middle class take pride in their associations and point to the prominent role that they play in the life of the community. These associations are highly regarded by the people of lower-middle or lower-class status, some of whom reveal a desire or hope that they may sometime join them. A woman of the lower-middle class, who had attained her goal of becoming a member of the Woman's Club, said:

"When we first came to Jonesville I didn't think I was going to like it here. I didn't have any friends and at first I didn't meet anybody I liked. But just recently I've joined the Woman's Club and I've met several people there that I would like for friends. They don't let just anybody join. You are supposed to be sponsored by somebody. It is a good way to get acquainted and meet sort of the —the better or the nicer people—I don't know how to say it but they don't let in the lower classes, the sort of common people, I mean.

They are sort of the important people in town. I don't mean that they are always so wealthy, but you do meet the nicer people that way."

The members of the upper class do not reveal the same respect or admiration for these upper-middle-class groups; verbally they subordinate them and they avoid membership in them. Even Rotary, for all its claims of prestige, boasts no more than a handful of upper-class men. Evaluation of these groups is frequently made by way of comparison with the organizations of top status, and the members of the upper-middle as well as the upper class admit that there is a degree of difference, and that those groups dominated by the upper class must be awarded the highest status. Particularly the Woman's Club is compared to those women's groups dominated by the upper class, and it is said to be "not *as* old," "not *as* nice," "not *as* exclusive."

While the upper-class clubs are exclusive clubs and even boast of being exclusive, many upper-middle-class clubs make claims to being "democratic" and "open to everybody." However, close examination indicates that this policy of democracy is fiction rather than fact. The president of the Woman's Club claims they will take in anybody who will be a good member, but the difficulty that the lower-middle-class woman, already quoted, experienced in becoming a member suggests that this is a policy which is not strictly adhered to. One all-male club, in certain respects most selective of all male groups in Jonesville, claims to be democratic and for evidence points to one member of lower status. This man is the son of an immigrant. He had a second-grade education and went to work on The Canal when he was eight years old. In the course of years, he has built up a small business. He is pointed to as an example of the "truly democratic spirit of America." However, the "democratic spirit" has not been extended sufficiently to accept him fully as an equal.

Perhaps the greatest differences between the upper-middle-class organizations and those dominated by the upper class is the emphasis by the former on active participation and accomplishment on the part of the members. The upper-middle-class associations are noted for their activity, achievement, and industry. They put demands upon their members, expecting them to take an active part in club affairs. Not content with arranging an endless round of speakers, the members present the programs, arrange tours, and organize special projects. There is an emphasis throughout on education and self-improvement. By way of contrast it might be said that the upper-class organizations are socially advancing while the upper-middle-class organizations are self-advancing; that the former require only proper family connection, while the latter, in addition, judge performance. The middle-class associations are interested in members with educational talents—musical, literary, dramatic, or artistic—talents which require training which, in turn, require some wealth. They encourage the members to use these talents, and even judge them by their ability to do so. Although the upper-class organizations show some interest in talented members, their primary interest is directed toward artists or speakers who have achieved excellence and fame on a much larger scale.

The upper-middle-class associations extend their influence beyond the immediate circle of members and take an interest in many civic problems. Both Rotary and the Woman's Club give their support to numerous community projects; the P. T. A. exerts its influence on the school system; the Band Parents support and sponsor the high school band; the Red Cross, in addition to raising money, organizes educational courses, influences the local relief office, and gives support to the county health officers. Taking part in these community affairs, the members of these associations perform functions which are necessary to the total community. Whereas upper-class organizations hold meetings on the arts, the theater, and all leisure-time activities, those dominated by the upper-middle class grapple with the problems which face all segments of the community every day. The topics of their meetings include "Public Health and the Prevention of Tuberculosis," "The Future of Our Schools," "Safety in Traffic," "Our Responsibilities and Restrictions as to the War Program," "Personality Adjustment and How to Prevent Juvenile Delinquency," and "Helping Our Children to Be Better Citizens."

A good example of the difference in emphasis is seen in the relative attitude of the various organizations to the problems facing the high school. During the winter of 1941-42 the future of the high school was a critical issue in the community. The school was suffering from insufficient funds, which caused low salaries, poor teaching standards, and old overcrowded buildings, and the North Central Association was threatening to take it off the list of accredited schools. Following the general lecture on the school at the Woman's Club, reports were given by members of the school and members of the club on the conditions and needs of the school, and methods were discussed for raising taxes and building a new school. Groups of club members attended classes and observed the performances of teachers and students so that they would become better acquainted with the school system and the school personnel. In spite of the seriousness of the situation, none of the women's organizations of top status devoted a single meeting to this topic.

Through club activities the women of the upper-middle class come in contact with people of higher status and increase their own prestige in the eyes of the community. On the other hand, in spite of the fact that they deal with problems which affect the whole community, they restrict the membership in their associations, or at least do not permit active participation on the part of individuals of lower status. By this process of exclusion they increase the social distance between themselves and the people who rank below them in the class hierarchy.

Associational Behavior of the Lower-Middle and Upper-Lower Classes

There is, in general, a sharp break between the upper-middle and lower-middle classes with respect to the kind and amount of participation in associations. While the members of the upper and upper-middle classes participate together, there is little participation between the upper-middle and lower-middle classes. The members of the lower-middle and upper-lower classes not only belong to fewer associations than the classes above them, but also appear more frequently in different kinds of associations.

However, while the differences between the upper-middle and lower-middle classes are quite clear, it is difficult to distinguish between the associational behavior of the lower-middle class and that of the upper-lower. There are certain exceptions to this statement; for example, there is a segment of the lower-middle class which deviates from the general pattern of most of the lower-middle and upper classes. We will consider this deviation first.

The lower-middle class has the most heterogeneous associational behavior of any class. While the upper, upper-middle, and (as we shall see) upper-lower classes, each shows a fairly definite pattern of associational behavior the lower-middle class is found in all kinds and all types of associations. Members of this class belong to every organization in town except Rotary and the Monday Club, and they take an active part in all types of associations. Some of the members of this class are the most active "joiners" in Jonesville, belonging to seven or eight associations, and others take no part in associational life. This heterogeneous behavior suggests that the lower-middle class is a sort of "buffer" group within the society. It is subject to both pressure from above and pressure from below. Some lower-middle-class people cling tenuously to the ways of the upper and upper-middle classes; others seek closer affiliation with the lower classes. Thus, they follow all forms of behavior which are found in American society.

The heterogeneity of the associational behavior of the lower-middle class reflects the differences among the social characteristics of this class as a whole. There are the white-collar workers who align themselves much more with the upper and upper-middle classes, and, on the other hand, the manual workers who tend to have closer affiliation with the members of the lower classes. The white-collar workers are a small group, about 110 families, or slightly less than one-sixth of the class. They are clerks, bank tellers, newspaper reporters, minor officials in business, small proprietors, and a few of the lesser professional men such as chiropodists, optometrists, and chiropractors. This group generally belongs to those associations dominated by the well-to-do of the community and also, frequently, to three intermediate groups: Lions, Masons, and Eastern Star.

Most associations have a membership spread from the upper to the lower-middle class or from the lower-middle class to the lower-lower class. But in the Lions, Masons, and Eastern Star, the majority of the members come from the upper-middle and lower-middle classes. These three organizations in many respects correspond to associations found at the top of the society. Lions closely resembles Rotary and, although Masons and Eastern Star follow the auxiliary-lodge pattern and have an elaborate ritual of initiation, Eastern Star frequently has lectures and discussions at meetings similar to the programs of the Woman's Club. The families belonging to these associations resemble the members of the upper-middle class in their tendency to belong to several associations; they average 2.4 memberships per family, compared to 1.1 for the lower-middle class as a whole and 3.5 for the upper-middle class. On the other hand, very few of these individuals belong to lodges, auxiliaries, and other low-status associations where most lower-middle and all upper-lower-class individuals participate.

There is reason to believe that these people are oriented upward and that in many of their basic attitudes and ideals they resemble the members of the upper-middle class more than they resemble the majority of the members of the lower-middle class. Not only do they prefer the kinds of associations identified with the upper-middle class but, as far as income will permit, they pattern their standard of living and social environment after the upper-middle class. For example, they prefer to live in the "right part of town," even if it means a smaller house, in preference to a larger and possibly more comfortable house in a less acceptable part of town.

The remainder of the lower-middle class, about 80 percent, are those who reveal the sharp break between upper-middle and lower-middle. This group, including craftsmen, factory workers, and other manual workers, occasionally appear—but rarely are active—in some of the organizations of higher status already discussed, such as P. T. A., Masons, and even the Woman's Club; they appear most frequently in lodges, auxiliaries and small informal social clubs. In kind and amount of participation they differ radically from the upper-middle class and the small segment of the lower-middle class already discussed, but resemble closely the upper-lower class. In other words, we find a decided break within the lower-middle class, judging by the way the class aligns itself in the associations, but a close resemblance between most of the lower-middle class and the upper-lower class as a whole. For this reason the associational behavior of the lower-middle and upper-lower class is being treated together, though it should be kept in mind that there is a variation within the former group.

The organizations with which these classes are identified have a relatively low rank in the community. The members themselves make few claims to prestige, merely asserting that "We have a nice little club," or "We always have nice times. We're not snobbish the way some people are—it's a friendly group that's there, we just get together and talk and play cards." The members of the upper and upper-middle classes subordinate these groups: "I can't tell you anything about the Rebekahs, I just know they aren't a social group at all," "Odd Fellows doesn't amount to anything now; none of the fellows mean anything in this town," or "That group doesn't count anymore." Members of these various organizations are described as "The fellows who don't amount to much," or "The people that live on the wrong side of the tracks."

The organizations at this level are inclusive, rather than exclusive.

The goal is always for a larger membership with few limiting qualifications. As a result the memberships for the larger organizations
run from the upper-middle to the lower-lower class and, for the
smaller organizations, from the lower-middle to the upper-lower
class. However, those organizations with a wide membership spread
draw most of their members from the lower-middle and upper-lower
classes and almost all the active members from these two classes.
The proportions of the lower-middle and upper-lower classes represented are about equal, and the active members come equally from
both classes. This is in contrast to organizations of top status which
include a much larger proportion of the upper class than of the
upper-middle and draw most of the active members from the upper
class.

There is much less associational participation among the lower
classes. While all upper- and upper-middle-class families belong to
one or more associations, a large proportion of the individuals at
the bottom of the hierarchy belong to no formal groups. Only 55
percent of the lower-middle-class and 50 percent of the upper-lower-
class families hold membership in any association; and the average
number of memberships for a lower-middle-class family is 1.1, and
for an upper-lower-class family, .93.

The chief type of organization for men at this level is the lodge.
The decline of lodges in recent years is not limited to a particular
segment of society, for the working man, as well as the professional
man, has lost interest. But while other organizations have appeared
as a substitute among the well-to-do of the community, the lodge
still remains the chief type of organization for men of lower status
today, whether it be the mystical type, such as Masons and Odd
Fellows, or the type which emphasizes more secular behavior such
as Moose and Eagles. The auxiliaries, affiliated with the lodges, are
supported by the women of the lower-middle and upper-lower
classes, and, as already indicated, have much greater success than the
male or parent organization. Between most of the lodges and the
auxiliaries there is a close relationship—not only the American
Legion, but also some of the lodges, require that the members of
the two organizations be related by marital ties or bonds of kinship.
The parent and auxiliary organizations hold state and national
meetings simultaneously, and many of the local activities are conducted jointly.

For the women of the lower-middle and upper-lower classes there are also the small informal social clubs, called variously the Happy Hour, the Merry Mixers, the Sunshine Club. These range in size from six to twenty, but most have eight, ten, or a dozen members. As might be expected, these organizations are generally short-lived, though frequently the same group of women may reappear as another club with a different name, and following the same kind of behavior.

Church participation rises markedly at this level and here again it is the women who are most active. The Old Americans of the lower-middle and upper-lower classes participate in the organizations sponsored by the Methodist and Baptist churches, and the Norwegians in those affiliated with the Lutheran Church. Some members of these classes belong to the two patriotic organizations, the American Legion and the G. A. R., and their two auxiliaries, and to a few miscellaneous groups such as the W. C. T. U. and the Girl Scout Mothers. It might be added that, in spite of the town's general disapproval of drinking, an attitude undoubtedly reinforced by the strict moral teachings of the Lutheran Church, the W. C. T. U. has few members and has made little headway in its drive for the return of prohibition. The rural people whose class position can be roughly equated with the lower-middle and upper classes belong to a few of these clubs but, for the most part, they belong to the rural community clubs and the Home Bureau. The farmers show much less participation, relatively speaking, within urban organizations among those individuals of lower-middle or upper-lower-class status than among those of high status.

Throughout all these organizations the sex division is more pronounced than at the top of the society. Particularly, the lodges and auxiliaries express the sex differentiation and make use of family configurations to relate themselves to one another. The observance of holidays and the frequent gift exchange among members are characteristic of this level and not of the higher level.

The ideologies of the lower-middle and upper-lower associations express the ideologies of the people—patriotism, brotherhood, democracy, equality—and the symbols are those which provoke common interest on the part of the "common man." This preoccupation with equality gives satisfaction to individuals of low status, for it minimizes, or overlooks, status distinctions and gives them a sense of similarity with other individuals regardless of their position in the community. It reflects the attitudes of those people who are reluctant to accept an inferior status and declare, "We haven't any classes here, we're all equal."

On the whole, these associations fail to relate their members to the community or to define their function in the community. The activities of the lodge and its auxiliary are directed inward and do not affect the lives of the members outside the lodge, nor does the role of the individual within the lodge reflect his role and behavior outside. The symbols of the lodge have no meaning for those who have not been indoctrinated in its dogma and ritual.

Associational Behavior of the Lower-Lower Class

The associational behavior of the lowest stratum of the community is perhaps best described by saying "there isn't much." These people are, in fact, defined partly on the basis of their nonparticipation in most formally organized institutions in the community. This may be because of lack of money for dues, but social facts also enter in. Most of the members of the lower-lower class have feelings of hostility and suspicion toward the members of the other classes, and all are subordinated by the rest of the community. Consequently, they express little overt interest or desire to become a part of these groups. Subordinated and looked down upon, many would find it difficult to join even the least exclusive organizations. Only 30 percent of the families within this class belong to associations: of these, no family belongs to more than two associations, and most belong to only one. The class as a whole average .66 memberships per family.

There is reason to believe that those who do belong to associations are at the top of the lower-lower class and are striving for higher status in the community. The lower-lower class is characterized as a whole by its nonrespectability and immorality, and yet there are a few who may be quite respectable but, because of extreme poverty or living in undesirable neighborhoods, are associated with the nonrespectables. The most notorious families in the community, those with police records, those who are cited most often for their shiftlessness, laziness, dirtiness, immorality, and nonrespectability, belong to no association.

The members of the lower-lower class who are found in associations follow the general pattern of the upper-lower and the majority of the lower-middle classes. They are found primarily in the lodges and auxiliaries and some of the small informal social clubs. Few, if any, take an active part in these organizations, probably because the other members do not wish to have these unfortunate members of the community represent them to the public. We can say, then, that associational participation at this level is like that of the strata immediately above it, but, in general, it is much less both in amount and intensity.

ASSOCIATIONS AND MOBILITY

Associations play an important role in assisting the mobile person to rise in the class system. Movement into a higher class is, in the last analysis, dependent upon association with, and acceptance by, the members of the superior class. In most of the activities of our daily living an individual has little opportunity for intimate contact with those outside his own social *milieu*. In the business world a person may come in contact with people of all walks of life, but for the most part these contacts are casual and impersonal and do not lead to strong ties between the individuals involved. Our most intimate contacts occur in the family and in the clique, the group of close friends; but these institutions tend to have a narrow class spread. The association, however, spreads over at least two, and usually three or more classes, thus permitting the members to have contacts—and even intimate contact—with people of various class positions. An individual may find it impossible to be accepted by a clique dominated by people of high status, but quite possible to join an association dominated by the same people. Through this associational membership he comes in contact with people of higher status and may eventually be fully accepted by them.

Some associations aid mobility more than others: those that are exclusive and limit the membership generally prevent mobility; while those that are inclusive and have a wide membership spread tend to aid mobility. The relationship of the association to mobility is also dependent upon the degree of rigidity of the class structure: if the class lines are not sharply defined then mobility is relatively easy; if the class lines are clearly drawn, mobility becomes more difficult.

Mobility is a slow and gradual process. An individual wishing to become a member of a class other than that into which he was born must move one step at a time: that is, a lower-middle person might move into the upper-middle class (or down into the upper-lower class) but the chances are very slight that he would move directly into the upper class (or down to the lower-lower class). Therefore, the person who attempts to use associations as a means of mobility not only is limited by the restrictions that the association imposes on prospective members—the Monday Club would never permit a lower-class woman to join—but also must consider what associational connections will be most useful in arriving at his goal of higher status, and use those connections which will lead directly to the next higher class.

We can determine which associations in Jonesville aid mobility and also which strata are most affected by them. Associations of high status, generally following a policy of exclusion, tend to prevent mobility. Dominated by and identified with the upper class, they stand as a status symbol of that class. Associational participation is a measure of a person's rank; membership in an upper-class club makes one's high-status position evident to the whole community. However, as these organizations do permit a large number of upper-middle-class women, they are for the latter possible avenues of mobility. The few lower-middle-class women who belong will probably not achieve upper-class status through these organizations: the gap between their status and that of the core members is too great to permit acceptance or equality.

Similarly the Woman's Club, the P. T. A., and the Red Cross are dominated by the upper-middle class but, permitting lower-middle-class members, they offer to the latter opportunity to rise to a higher status. Rotary is the one exception: having almost no lower-middle-class members it prevents mobility between the lower-middle and upper-middle classes.

Low-status associations permit mobility from the upper-lower to the lower-middle or from the lower-lower to the upper-lower class. Joining such a group is particularly important in moving from the lower class into the middle class. The lower class is, on the whole, less organized and less socialized than the middle class. In the lower class relations are on a very personal basis, usually between families and individuals. Club memberships and group relations become prominent with the middle class and cause all relationships to become more formalized. Therefore, the move to join a formal organized group is for the lower-class person a most important step in his bid for middle-class status.

Low-status associations offer little opportunity for the lower-middle-class individual to move into an upper-middle-class position.

In a few cases, if a lower-middle-class person becomes very active and shows an ability for successful organization he may then become known as a "leader" and attract the attention of those above him. But, in general, since there is little opportunity for contact with those of higher status, he has little chance for mobility through these groups.

So far, we have dealt only with vertical mobility, up and down the class hierarchy. While this may be most important in terms of the individual's own strivings and goals, equally important in understanding the dynamics of the social structure is the horizontal mobility which goes on at all levels. Perhaps the single most important horizontal move is that which occurs within the lower-middle class. As already indicated, there appears to be an important cleavage within this class indicated by the way in which the members of this class align themselves within the associations. A small proportion of this class belongs to associations dominated by the upper or upper-middle classes, or to the group of so-called marginal associations. The majority belong to low-status associations which draw their members from the lower-middle and upper-lower classes. The latter are not channels for mobility; but the former are, and a lower-middle-class individual who wishes to move into the upper-middle class must follow this participation pattern if he wishes to be successful. In other words, the average lower-middle-class individual, who wishes to be mobile, must first shift his behavior and move horizontally within his own class before he can expect to move up in the class hierarchy.

Horizontal mobility also takes place when a member of an ethnic group begins to break his ethnic identifications and be accepted by the dominant Old American stock. He will begin to reduce his relations within the ethnic community and increase his relations in the Old American community, thus moving to a different status within the society without necessarily changing his class position. It has generally been found that acquiring membership in a predominantly Old American organization is an important step in the process of assimilation into the native population. While some of the high-status organizations may exclude the members of an ethnic group through their membership requirements, for example the D. A. R., less exclusive organizations, while perhaps not seeking ethnics as members, will at least permit them to join. Except for those few organizations such as the Polish Alliance and the satellite

organizations of the Lutheran Church which are organized specifically for a minority group, the number of ethnics in any association in Jonesville is very small, in some cases no more than one
or two, in no case more than twelve or fifteen.

However, while the associations are not being used extensively
by ethnics as a mechanism for moving into the Old American group,
we cannot ignore the few cases that do occur. Certain Norwegians
who have broken away from their own church have joined an Old
American association and, in so doing, tend to take on the characteristics of the Old American population and to be grouped with
them. Only two members of the Polish group are found in a non-
ethnic association, yet these two are outstanding members of the
Polish group. Participation in the nonethnic group is symptomatic
of their general mobility within the community, and particularly
of their movement away from their own ethnic group.

In addition to the fact that the native group generally resists
assimilating ethnics and that associations, either consciously or
unconsciously, tend to exclude them, other factors also account for
the marked separation and lack of participation of ethnics in
Jonesville's associations. For example, the Norwegians, one of the
two major ethnic groups in the community, are cliquish; also, the
group's mores and the power of the Lutheran Church, with its
subsidiary organizations, tend to strengthen the solidarity of the
group and prevent or retard acculturation.

The other major ethnic group, the Poles, are distinguished by
characteristics which must be attributed to the recency of their
arrival—language, appearance and nationalist customs. Moreover,
they have not had sufficient time to move out of the lower-class
position occupied by most newly arrived ethnic groups; and most
associations attempt to exclude members of the lowest class. The
Polish Alliance, open only to adult Polish men, tends to maintain
the solidarity of the group and to increase national feelings.

The mobile person must not only shift from one association to
another but also change the way he behaves, depending on his own
status and its relationship to the reputation of the association. An
individual who becomes a member of an association dominated by
people of higher status must at first accept a subordinate position;
later when he comes to be more fully accepted he may have an active
role in the association and have a subordinate role in another association of still higher status. Thus an upper-middle-class woman,

seeking an upper-class position, may have an active role in the Woman's Club at the same time that she maintains a passive or subordinate role in the Monday Club.

In general, people who are mobile upward tend to belong to a great many associations of both high and low status because, in the process of moving up, they still maintain some of those connections they made when they had a lower status. But as their higher status becomes more secure and they wish to consolidate their position before taking another step upward, they drop off those memberships which reflect their earlier and lower status. The stable people tend to have less participation in formal associations; and the downward-mobile tend to belong to the fewest associations of all and these within a very restricted class range. Downward-mobile people hold to the memberships commensurate with their former status and refuse participation in lower groups since this might hasten their declining mobility.

The associations of Jonesville and America generally organize the various social classes, expressing their distinguishing attitudes and ideologies and giving to the members a sense of social solidarity. However, the extent to which they organize the classes varies from one level to another. The upper and upper-middle classes are highly organized, well integrated social groups. The lower-middle and lower classes are more loosely organized and have fewer devices for maintaining their own distinctness in the community. This variation is due partly to size: the top strata are small and permit close and intimate interaction among all the members, while the great number of individuals in the lower strata causes diffused interaction. Moreover, the individuals at the top of the society are more ready to identify with their own social strata, while those at the bottom derive little ego satisfaction from such identification. It appears that time may be a vital factor in creating a feeling of solidarity. Particularly the upper class has a feeling of permanence for most of the families in this class have maintained the same status for several generations. There are more movement and shifting of status at the bottom of the hierarchy so the members have less feeling of belonging to a particular social stratum. It appears, though, that as time goes on the class lines will be drawn more clearly and the sense of social solidarity will increase throughout the hierarchy.

Chapter 10

THE SACRED AND PROFANE WORLDS
OF JONESVILLE

THE SACRED WORLD OF JONESVILLE

The concern of men about their relations to the supernatural, with their gods, is an inseparable part of the lives of all tribes and all nations. Although the outward expression of religion is in the form of rituals, symbols, and sacraments, its inner force is extremely deep. The attitudes of most individuals toward society as a whole and its institutions of marriage, family, kinship, economics, and state are often perceived in the light of the central religious experience and the corresponding ideals of that society to which they belong. In other words, religion extends beyond the simple relation of man and God. It adds sanction and defines moral obligations for all situations that are found in daily life. The church is the carrier of the sacred and moral ideology of the community. The influence of religion in Jonesville is both positive and negative; it has an integrating influence binding certain people together, but on the other hand it separates them into opposing factions often deeply antagonistic.*

There are conflicting attitudes on the role that a specific church organization may play in such activity. To many, for the church to lobby for political measures weakens its spiritual position, for such actions violate the American tradition of separatism of church and state. All the churches differ in their doctrines about man's relations with God; all are interested in man's morals but differ in

* By Wilfrid C. Bailey. See List of Authors.

evaluating rules of conduct that are important and should receive their special attention. They condemn their neighbor churches which are more concerned with general social problems as being "sociological" and lacking the true "Gospel."

Churches control the habits of their members through indoctrination. This is accomplished not only by the Sunday morning sermons but through the Sunday School and the activities of church-sponsored organizations. In Jonesville, only the Catholic Church has its own school through which it can control the indoctrination of the child by the educational system.

In actual practice, all of the churches do take direct action in the community. Churches in Jonesville and all over the Middle West cooperated on a drive for reform in the movie industry a number of years ago; some support the W.C.T.U.; some, from time to time, become involved in local issues. The Lutheran Church violently opposes dances held in the high school and the teaching of evolution. One of the high school teachers was accused not only of permitting and teaching such "harmful doctrine" but, in addition, of publicly ridiculing a Lutheran boy for taking an anti-evolutionary stand in class. The Lutheran Church took the matter before the Ministerial Association; and one of the members who was also on the School Board brought the issue to the board. They asked the principal to resign and threatened as taxpayers to have him fired. However, the Ministerial Association and the School Board did not follow their lead and the movement failed.

The daily life of Jonesville is permeated with sacred symbolic behavior and its sanctions. The sacred symbols of the church are a part of the lives of more Jonesville people outside, than inside, the church. The sacred symbol system of the church is used in most community events and in all crises. Public meetings are given sacred sanction by the participation of members of the clergy. The dedication ceremony of the Service Man's Honor Roll was opened by a prayer by a Protestant minister and closed by the Benediction given by the Catholic priest. The Armistice Day Parade is a yearly event. It concludes with a ceremony at the Court House in front of a memorial to World War I men who lost their lives. The ceremony consists of a prayer, a short speech, laying a wreath on the plaque, and the playing of taps. Graduation from high school consists of two ceremonies. On the Sunday preceding the actual commencement exercise a Baccalaureate is held. It takes the form of a religious service with a guest speaker who is customarily a clergyman, either from one of the local churches or from a nearby community. Christian sanction and blessing are thereby given to the act of moving from the formal period of guidance and training by the schools into the adult economic world—a transition which in some ways has the function of a delayed puberty rite.

Organizations and lodges employ sacred symbolism in their ritual and activities; many have a chaplain among their officers.

There is a ceremonial calendar in the community. It is definitely reflected in the religious participation of the people. Some of the key ceremonial dates are based on Christian doctrine, some are quasi-religious in character, and others are related simply to events in American history that are memorialized. The whole cycle has religious, social, and economic significance. Much of it is secular in nature and may represent the general trend from sacred to secular, as seen in the shift from Holyday to Holiday.

The intensity of religious activity in the community follows the calendar cycle. Examination of the attendance records for several churches shows a similar cycle. During the fall and winter months there is an increase in attendance reaching a peak at Christmas; in the next few months there is a slight decrease; but during Lent attendance grows, reaching the high point of the year on Easter Sunday; and then there is a gradual falling off to the low ebb in attendance occurring in midsummer. This general calendar round is found in many aspects of life. There is a cycle of key holidays starting with New Year, then Easter, Memorial Day, Fourth of July, Labor Day, Thanksgiving, and Christmas. Of these, Christmas, Thanksgiving, Memorial Day, and Easter are sacred in their origin, two basic in Christian theology and two peculiar to American history.

In the so-called "primitive" societies certain life crises, including birth, puberty, marriage, and death, are recognized symbolically by *rites de passage*. In Jonesville, as in the rest of America, these periods are recognized in church ceremony which varies in form according to the denomination of the church. The new-born child is officially made a member of society through baptism and christening. According to Catholic theology the child does not receive full status as a human being until baptism, while some Protestant groups do not believe in infant baptism and substitute a blessing and naming ceremony. The child at this time is recognized as an individual, given a name by which it shall be known, and the supernatural is called upon for protection. At the same time the parents and sometimes pseudo-parents, god-parents, assume obligations in respect to the rearing of the child.

Puberty is recognized by another series of rites. Perhaps because in our society puberty does not coincide with the assumption of adult status, the actual ceremony does not take place exactly at puberty but at varying times from eight to fourteen years of age depending upon the group. At this time the individual may be baptized and become a member of the church. In denominations practicing infant baptism the ceremony, at this time, is that of a Confirmation of the individual's faith. For both this marks the beginning of adult participation in the ceremonial life and is in this sense a puberty rite.

Marriage is usually consecrated through a church ceremony. Members of a church may have an elaborate semi-public church wedding; non-church members frequently go to some local minister for a private ceremony; only a minority go to Justices-of-the-Peace for a civil ceremony, which is primarily a simplification of the sacred form. The passing of an individual from the society by death is recognized by sacred ritual. In Jonesville, all but a few of the funerals are conducted in the church. The ritual serves two purposes: to conduct the deceased safely from one existence into another, and to offer condolences to the relatives, friends, and the society as a whole for the loss they have suffered. Even those who almost never go near a church and have skipped the other *rites de passage* will attend this ceremony for those who have died. Although the actual funeral service may be minimal, there follows burial in the cemetery which is "consecrated" ground and filled with religious symbols. Death evokes a series of social interactions. Friends and neighbors visit the family and large numbers of people attend the funeral. A large group of middle-aged and elderly women in Jonesville make it a point to attend every funeral, even those for people they have known only vaguely.

Social Class and the Churches

Although the sacred beliefs of all the seven churches of Jonesville are at war with the secular worlds of social, economic, and political power, with status inequality, and the deterioration of the mores of the community, this hostility is not always apparent in the churches' social actions. The Christian concept of the brotherhood of men is equalitarian and inclusive rather than aristocratic and exclusive; God is a Father and all men are included with no regard for social or racial difference; and His children can know no such distinctions among themselves. Yet, in spite of these strong equalitarian social beliefs, the churches are clearly influenced by social-class attitudes. The upper, middle, and lower classes favor certain churches and avoid others.

The seven churches in Jonesville, in order of the class level of their congregations, are the Federated (Congregational and Presbyterian), Methodist, Lutheran, Catholic, Baptist, Free Methodist, and Gospel Tabernacle. (See Table 13, and Chart V.) The class level of the congregation also indicates approximately the position of the church in prestige. Church memberships are difficult to compare because there is no uniform system for determining membership. Some churches count those baptized, and others only those actually confirmed. Then, there is little pruning of church roles. Some churches continue to carry individuals long after they have left the community, no longer attend, joined other churches, or have died. For this reason, in the research the memberships were counted by families rather than individuals. That is, if one or more members of the family belonged to a church, the family was counted as having one membership in that church. Therefore, the figures in Table 13 and Chart V represent families. The Federated Church is outstanding in that it has 35 of the 45 upper-class families belonging to churches and about one-third of the upper-middle families. Its total distribution lacks the pronounced class concentration of the other churches. The Methodist has a modal level of lower-middle, and all of the others have a modal level of upper-lower. The lower-lower class has members in all churches, but the upper class is concentrated in one, the Federated, with a few members in the Methodist and Catholic churches.

In general, the combined status profile for all the churches closely resembles that of Jonesville as a whole. However, the upper class contributes twice as much to the church group as to the total society while the lower-lower is represented only a little more than half as much in the church group as in the total society. Less than half (46.63 percent) of the families of Jonesville are represented in churches. A total of 44 of the 57 (77.19 percent) upper-class families are found on the church rolls as compared to only 71 out of 253

Table 13

CLASS DISTRIBUTION OF JONESVILLE CHURCHES

Class	Federated		Methodist		Lutheran		Catholic		Baptist		Free Methodist		Gospel Tabernacle		Total for All Churches		Total for Whole Community		Percent of Each Class Belonging to a Church	Class
	No.	%	No.	%	No.	%	No.	%	No.	%	No.	%	No.	%	No.	%	No.	%	%	
U	35	18.32	4	2.15	..	.....	5	1.54	..	.....	..	.....	..	.....	44	4.49	57	2.72	77.19	U
UM	47	24.61	38	20.43	16	10.81	36	11.08	10	8.93	..	.....	..	.....	147	15.02	251	11.98	58.57	UM
LM	67	35.08	74	39.78	54	36.49	89	27.38	40	35.71	2	20.00	2	28.57	328	33.50	675	32.22	48.59	LM
UL	31	16.23	59	31.72	73	49.32	170	52.31	46	41.07	6	60.00	4	57.14	389	39.73	859	41.00	45.29	UL
LL	11	5.76	11	5.91	5	3.38	25	7.69	16	14.29	2	20.00	1	14.29	71	7.25	253	12.08	28.06	LL
Total	191		186		148		325		112		10		7		979					
Mean Class Level	2.66		3.19		3.45		3.53		3.61		4.0		3.86		3.30		3.48			

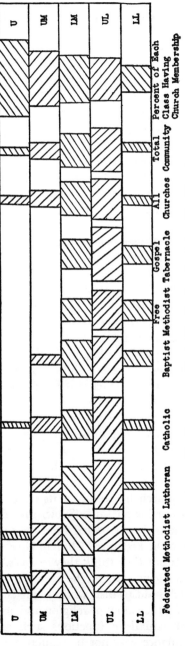

CHART V. Percentage Class Distribution in Jonesville Churches

(28.06 percent) lower-lower class. The mean level, ranking the classes from upper with a value of one to lower-lower with a value of five, for all churches is 3.30 percent compared to 3.48 for the total community. The Federated ranks highest at 2.66 percent and the other churches grade down to the Free Methodist level of 4.00.

The Federated Church in Jonesville was created in 1920 by a semi-union of the Congregational and Presbyterian churches. It is "federated" in the sense that the two congregations have the same minister and hold services together in the same building. However, each group has its own membership roll, maintains its own official structure, and works with its own central organization. All meetings are held together except those of the ladies' missionary societies and the official meetings to take care of strictly Presbyterian or Congregational business.

The Federated Church membership numbers 450, of whom 217 are Presbyterians, 92 Congregationalists, and 141 "Friends of the Church" who belong to neither component denomination but attend services and contribute financially—a common situation in many Protestant churches but particularly strong in the Federated. The Presbyterian group is strongest not only in number but from the point of social status, with the highest number of upper-class leaders in the community and the largest contributors to the church. The Caldwells were Methodists but shifted over to the Federated Church. Evidence points to the fact that when a high-status person joins a church he becomes a member of the Presbyterian Church.

Although the Federated Church is known as the "status church" of Jonesville and is considered upper-class, its membership runs from lower-lower through upper class, with the lower-middle group the largest. It is from the fact that it has the largest group of upper and upper-middle-class members of any of the churches in town that the Federated Church has received its status reputation. An upper-middle professional man said, "Now, the society class here are the 400 and in the main it's rooted right over in the Federated Church. It comes from the Federated Church. Now, frankly, a lot of these people are 398's but they think they're 400's."

Three levels of participation can be seen. At the top are the landed gentry and rich industrialists who use the church as a means of formally recognizing the values of religion and accepted morality, and as a center for ritualistic functions such as marriage and funerals. Their attendance may not be regular except for some of the older individuals, but they make the largest financial contributions to the church. Next, there is a large group of upper-middle and high lower-middle who use the church as a means of attaining mobility and as a symbol of their desired equality with the upper class. These are the active directors of the church—and of the town—and are often called "pushy." At the bottom is a group of lower-status people, predominantly from old Scotch and English families that settled in the area several generations ago but have failed to rise with the church. Some still cling to their old religious tradition but others have drifted off.

Dr. Matthew Carleton, the Federated minister, failed to realize that his troubles, which ultimately led to forcing his resignation, were the result of the great class spread in his church. He tried unsuccessfully to increase attendance and activity in various auxiliaries. He was blocked time after time by the class differences of the members. First, he tried a young people's group. It soon was taken over by a clique of upper-middle and socially mobile lower-middle girls who were also the leading group of the high school. The attendance soon dropped to this group and their boy friends, and Carleton blamed it on the fact that the movies and dances offered too much competition. The attempt to keep a men's club going met with a similar fate. In the Sunday School, the adult classes were mostly from the higher social levels. The adult ladies' class, the Effie McKinley class, became a social club to the exclusion of the lower-status women in the church.

When Dr. Carleton was asked if he thought his church had a larger social spread than the others in town he replied in the negative and expressed the opinion that the Methodists had a greater range. He went on to explain that the Radcliffes (upper) and other families like them had never set foot in the church except for weddings and funerals and that sort of thing. However, when he wanted to get money to fix up the church he went to the Volmers (upper) to get it. He told them that they should contribute because they would need the church sometime. The rest of the members, he concluded, were superior intellectually to most of the community and, because of that, could hold their own with the upper group of people.

Dr. Carleton was the first and only Congregational minister to be called to the Federated Church. He had liberal views and had belonged to several socialist organizations. He believed that "the reason the church has lost a lot of support of recent years is because the church has not faced the problem that our economic system is based on profits for a few and scarcity for many. But what can we do about it? It's obvious that after the war we cannot go back to the old economic order. We have got to have government control of production for the benefit of all. The church should be selling that program to its members, but what can I do? How far could I go in that kind of talk here? I'd get thrown out in five minutes. I can't do a thing actually. Yet, the result is that the church has been able to offer nothing to those who are suffering economically. The church has a very important part that it could play in world affairs, but its hands are tied. The whole trouble with the world today is that, for all the talk about Christianity, our society is not organized on its principles. What we need is an economic order based on the teachings of Christ, not upon the profit motive. But what can I do about it? Nothing! If I did, I'd lose my job."

He was fully aware that this congregation of the socially elite was not interested in this type of theology but in one which would not tread too heavily on their toes and would reaffirm their position in the community. As a result, his sermons were strained and delivered as though under pressure. All too frequently what he did say was over their heads. The lower classes drifted away from the church and attendance dropped to a new low.

Finally, the upper-middle-class Presbyterians forced his resignation. In selecting a successor the upper-class hold on the leadership was re-expressed. At a meeting of two of the members of the Presbyterian official board the problem of nominations of officers came up. After discussing the names, one said, "Well, I guess we really should have some Congregationalist on these boards. We'd better put one of them in one of these vacancies." After a long discussion they failed to find a suitable person of that denomination to fill the post. Finally, Barton (lower-middle) suggested, "What about that Black [upper-class coal mine owner], you know that young Black who is in the men's Sunday School Class. He comes regularly and he appears to be a very able person."

Ralph Trowel (upper-middle businessman) said, "Yes, I know that and every time he comes out I go over to shake hands with him and tell him how glad I am that he comes out and encourage him to come again. Which one of the Blacks is it? It's Harry Black, isn't it?"

They finally decided that it was not Harry but Walter. Then, they couldn't determine whether he was actually a member of the church or not. Norris phoned his wife to check on it, but she wasn't sure either. The meeting closed with the decision that if he were found to be officially a member of the church they would nominate him for the office.

After a young Presbyterian minister was selected by the nominating committee the congregation, both Presbyterian and Congregational, was asked to vote. The voting was to be done by official members only which excluded those on the "Friends" list. The meeting was officiated by one of the upper-middle-class members. Leonard Carter, upper-class and powerful, who attends only on Easter or similar occasions, was there. As soon as he entered the church he was greeted and asked to take part. He reminded them of the fact that he was not a member but was told that they would be glad to have him take a place in front of the congregation beside the chairman of the meeting. The candidate received only one dissenting vote. Immediately a motion was made to make the vote unanimous and was seconded with a short comment by Leonard Carter. The motion carried and the new minister was chosen to carry on the tradition of the Federated Church.

The Methodist Church is the largest Protestant church in Jonesville, its 374 members having a slight edge over the Federated which has a total of 309 official members. It is the middle-class church of the community. The status distribution is distinguished by having its largest group at the lower-middle level with a large number in the adjacent groups above and below and a significantly low number of uppers and lower-lowers.

A prominent Methodist characterizes his church: "We haven't the wealth and the society of the town in our church. Most of our people are Mill and business people." He recognizes the higher social position of the Federated Church and describes its members as "that fancy crowd," the "cold and wealthy group," and "just a bunch of dried-up old rich people." He refers to the Baptists as mostly working class people and to their church as "a notch or two below us." The Lutherans are considered "clannish" and "stand-offish in the matter of church cooperation." The Free Methodists "don't amount to much," and the Gospel Tabernacle is attended by very poor people "with a persecution complex."

One observing citizen of Jonesville says of the Methodist Church: "There are some pretty good contributors in the Methodist Church. Some of them are pretty well-to-do, but there's no really rich people in that church. Some live out in the country, they're pretty well-to-do, but the wealthy people around here don't go to church. The Methodist Church is the largest body in town. I suppose they have more members over there than any other church. The Methodist Church has lots of businessmen around town in it. There're some professional people in there, too, and then you come down and kind of spread out to the people who are poor. There're not so many poor people in the Methodist Church, but there are a few. Most of the people in the Methodist Church are good solid business people, people around town who have a little property and who make a pretty good salary, but they don't go in for social things. You'll see that the people in the Methodist Church are pretty well dressed and they have better cars than the Baptists. Most of them, as I say, are business people."

Thus the Methodist Church, once the most prominent church in the early period of the community, is now solidly in the middle class, while the Federated Church has recently moved into the higher position. Some upper-class, old Methodist families, such as the Caldwells and Radcliffes, have shifted over to the socially more prominent Federated Church. The leadership of the Methodist Church lies in a group of upper-middle-class businessmen.

The Methodists are very much aware of themselves as a separate and distinct group within the Christian Church. They are frequently told of the teachings of John Wesley and have a sense of being a Methodist first and a Christian second. The members have a stock joke that is always good when a group of Methodists gather: "Whenever a bunch of Methodists get together, there is always a collection." The theological emphasis is not on the individual but on the relationship of the church to the world at large as well as to the community. It is the opinion of the members that, if all would work through the leaders of the nation and at the same time pray, the country would be victorious. The war and its social implications were a constant subject of discussion; the men's Bible class studied such things as Fosdick's article on "The Place of the Church in War."

The church accommodates itself to the middle class by many types of organizations. Young people's groups at different age levels provide recreation as well as religious activities. In all auxiliary organizations, religious activities are secondary to social. Many non-members come for the social and recreational advantages and little pressure is put on them to join the church. Young adults are used as leaders for the younger groups to train them for full adult leadership in the church. These activities strengthen the church's position at the middle level in Jonesville. Moreover, with this background of participation at a level that is neither too high nor too low, the Methodist Church attracts a great many people down from the Federated Church and up from the Baptist Church. A recent campaign obtained over 200 new members. It is now the strongest and largest Protestant church in the community, with 500 to 600 members, and it is in the best financial condition of any of the churches.

Many early settlers in Jonesville came from Kentucky and Tennessee. They followed the Ohio and Mississippi rivers and turned up the tributaries to settle the rich prairie lands. For the most part, they were from the group of poor land-hungry people that moved through the Cumberland Gap, settled Tennessee, West Virginia, and Kentucky, and then spread west and north. It was among this group that the Baptist Church was strongest.

The Baptist Church is the outstanding church of the working people in Jonesville: of its 112 families, about 56 percent come from the lower class, none from the upper class, and only a few from the upper-middle class. It has the highest number of lower-lowers of any church in Jonesville and is known as the Church of the Common Man.

Elsie Chase, an upper-lower-class Southern White, says of her church: "Yes, there are a lot of people from the South. You know they call the Baptist Church here the Church of the Common Man, and if you go there and see the people who are there, you know that it is truly the Church of the Common Man. By that I do not mean that we are all poor people. We are all honest, hardworking, good people, and there are not many of the rich, well-to-do people in our church except maybe the Littles. A lot of the people belonged to the Church of Christ in Kentucky. When they came up here, they joined the Baptist Church. My aunt still attempts to follow the old faith. She has been trying to get a branch of the Church of Christ started here but has not had much support."

An important member of the congregation says, "They're mostly the poorer people. I guess you could call them lower-class people. The people in our church mingle quite freely together. Of course, there are some slum people that nobody will associate with, but, of course, that's natural enough. And you'll find that the kind of people we have in our church are accepted for the most part anywhere in Jonesville. That is, they feel perfectly free if they meet a Caldwell on the street to go up and talk with him. There's no great gap between them, and there are some good reasons for that. They are not particularly self-conscious of the differences between themselves and Caldwell. They are not envious of Caldwell's position or desirous of attaining something like it. That is, they don't look up with too much awe or jealousy, and in the same way they don't intend to scorn or sneer at the people beneath them."

In summary, most of the Baptists look upon themselves as the common people of Jonesville. They may be poor but they are hardworking and honest. They believe that they are as good as anyone else and all have an equal chance to make good.

In the old part of town, in a vacant store down from the other churches and facing The Canal, is the Gospel Tabernacle. It is representative of the appeal of religion to the lower class. It is a small group with a core of seven Jonesville families plus several from the rural areas. They come, for the most part, from the upper-lower class with several individuals on the fringes of the lower-middle and lower-lower classes. The Methodist minister calls them "poor people with a persecution complex." Others think they are "a little queer" and say, "they're a pretty shouting, wild crowd down there."

The members of the church all seem to be those who have been frustrated by the society in which they live, and are trying to find their security in a religion that tells them that all are equal in the sight of God and that the only way to salvation is to accept Christ. "It does not matter who you might be, how high or how low—this is the only way." Their doctrine is an escape from their society. The life histories of the two leaders of the church tell the story. One leader is from an old rural family that, by tradition, belongs in the Federated Church but failed to rise in the community from the frontier level to the higher social regions. Long ago, he was on the official board of the Federated Church, but the social pressure from above was too much for his self-respect and in time he became

interested in the Gospel Tabernacle. The other leader of the Tabernacle and his wife come from families that have lived along The
Canal for generations and have become symbols of the lower-lower
class. He is struggling to rise against the pressure above him. He is
using two means to obtain respectability. The first, which attracts
him most, is the religion which tells him that all men are equal.
The second is education. He took home-study courses and was able
to get a better job at The Mill and then pass an intelligence examination and go into the army as a navigation officer.

The core of the Gospel Tabernacle's ideology is that freedom
from sin comes to one as the result of acceptance of Christ as the
master of men's souls. Otherwise one cannot be saved. Salvation
from sin comes suddenly through a conversion experience. It does
not matter "who you are but just that you are saved" and have
"received the Word," been "washed in the blood of the lamb,"
"seen the light," or "come to Christ." This conversion experience
has a profound change in the life of the individual: he is a new
man. The more humble the man's background (more lower-class),
the better his chances for salvation. The upper classes do not have
much of a chance because they have too much (worldly ways) to
give up to be able to humble themselves before God.

The members have an intense religious feeling and say that it is
"their life." They look upon other churches as having gone astray
from the original tenets of Christianity, as having put their trust
in ritual and sociological theology rather than strict Biblical interpretation, and as being duped by a professional clergy. Because of
this they have no formal membership roll and make a point of
stressing their democratic organization. Although they follow the
Moody Bible Institute theologically, they have not become affiliated
with any organization.

Great emphasis is placed on moral character and living a good
clean daily life. Their religion stresses the salvation of the individual; the church serves only as a guide to this end. The final
authority of one's conduct is the dictates of one's conscience. The
rules and commandments of the Old Testament are basic but these
are New Testament days, the Days of Grace. Therefore, it is up to
the individual. If he feels that he cannot do something without
sinning he should not do it. Parents are told that they should set
good examples for their children by keeping a clean house, or holding a steady job.

Although all men are equal in God's sight they have a great suspicion of the rest of the world. They wish to avoid it because of its "worldly" character and because they say that it is in the hands of the devil. For this reason, they feel that participation with the rest of the world through card playing, dancing, movies, and drinking will only lead them astray. The children are cautioned that in school they should be careful not to take as their models the "worldly" men of history and should avoid the "doubtful" sciences.

The lower-class members of the community are faced with a society that is geared to middle-class values. They possess few of the material comforts and luxuries and enjoy little of the prestige that this pattern holds out as desirable achievements. It is possible for them to find escape in their religious beliefs. The conversion to the faith of the Gospel Tabernacle may lessen the frustration of being unable to rise in the social structure through which goods and personal rewards are distributed.

The Free Methodist Church occupies an ancient frame building on the edge of the business section. The building was constructed many years ago by another denomination which has moved up the economic level with the bulk of the community and is now housed in a modern structure. The role of the Free Methodist Church is to care for the residue of people left in the area when the town grew out of its frontier stage. The Methodist, Baptist, Congregationalist, Presbyterian, and other churches had the same function a century ago as the Gospel Tabernacle and Free Methodist churches have today. The membership of the Free Methodist Church is found in a few survivors of old families in the community who have failed to improve their condition. One of the original members is an old woman who clings to the religion of her parents, while her children belong to the Methodist Church. The church, as well as its members, is clinging to the bottom of the church hierarchy. The Ministerial Association recognizes the Free Methodist minister and says it helps him in whatever way it can, although it is not in sympathy with his theology.

The Lutheran Church is the symbol of the Norwegian ethnic minority. Its revivalistic and sectarian character rises out of a nativistic movement of subordinate groups. Up until the past few years, it continued to hold services in the Norwegian language. The Lutheran, Free Methodist, and the Gospel Tabernacle churches have similar approaches to religion and look upon each other as spiritual brothers although they do not actually participate in joint activities (see Chapter 8).

The Catholic Church was the first in the county. It was formed to care for the Irish laborers on The Canal and since has been reinforced by new non-Protestant ethnic groups. The largest of these are the Poles, and there are small groups of Italians, Greeks, and others. The bulk of the Catholics are upper-lower-class ethnics, mostly Poles, Italians, and the lower level of the Irish. It is the only one of the major churches in Jonesville to have more than 50 percent of its membership concentrated in one class. At the top of the social hierarchy in the church are a few old Irish families that have made good in the community. The Catholic priest is continually frustrated in his attempts to keep strong auxiliaries going because of the difficulty in bridging the great social and ethnic differences within the church.

Today the Catholic congregation of 788 is the largest of any church in Jonesville, but it represents a decline from the peak of 1,110 in 1912. As the Irish have become acculturated and amalgamated into the community, they have left the church. Their relative speed of acculturation, as indicated by church membership, can be compared to that of the Lutherans whose church membership has increased from 316 in 1912 to 350 in 1942. The Catholic Church attempts to counteract the effects of religious acculturation by maintaining a separate elementary school and an academy for girls, and by imposing a rather strict endogamy through disapproval of marriage to non-Catholics.

In the strong Republican town of Jonesville, the designations "Democrat" and "Catholic" are often synonymous. This identity goes back a half century to the anti-Catholic, anti-ethnic movement of the American Protective Association. To many people, the A.P.A. meant Anti-Pope Association. The leader of the local Republican machine was also the leader of the A.P.A. In Jonesville, there was an open feud between the A.P.A. and the Clanagails, as the Irish were called. The newspaper office was stormed and one policeman was killed with a brickbat. This open antagonism has now disappeared, but there is still a split between the two parties along a vague religious line. This split has been smoothed over by the fact that one of the leaders of local Republican politics is a high-status Irish Catholic who has teamed up with, among others, the son of the leader of the old A.P.A. movement in the county.

There is a feeling in American society that one of the indicators of respectable behavior is membership in a church. This is particularly true of the middle and upper classes; in the upper class in Jonesville, 77.19 percent of the families have church affiliation. True, many of them attend services only on special occasions, but they contribute financially and use the church as a symbol of their morality. On the other hand, only 28.05 percent of the lower-lower families have church affiliation, a fact which is often used as proof of their immoral behavior.

In choosing his church, the individual, or family, is often motivated by consideration of what is expected of a person in his position. An important public official spoke of joining the Federated Church:

"You see, the people in this church [Federated] are funny. Most of them are, well, they think they're so high and mighty just because they've got a little money. They're not my kind of folks. Those that come, they just come and sit there and after it's over they walk out. They may speak to you, but they're just being nice. You see, they hold you at arm's length and kind of look down on you. You go over to the Baptist Church—they're my kind of folks. You'll notice the spirit there. There's the spirit of friendship and fellowship. They all like one another and they're just common people. But these people over here, well, they're not common people. That's all you can say about it. They really make me mad, but there's not much I can say or do about it. If Penny, my daughter, hadn't started to Sunday School here with the girls [the leading high school clique] and more or less wanted me to come too, I wouldn't have gone here. But I don't know, sometimes when I reflect on it, my job makes demands on me. I seldom go to church, but I've found that Sunday School tended to kind of keep the clan going."

It has been shown that the churches in Jonesville are stratified in the social structure and that each tends to cater to the religious needs of the segment of society at its level. Some owe their origin to the particular needs of a group; others have shifted their emphasis to accommodate to the changing social characteristics of their memberships. The change in the Methodist Church during the past century is an example of the latter, and the emergence of the Gospel Tabernacle, of the former. A few individuals cling to a particular church because of tradition. For most Protestants, theology plays a minor role in selection of a church. They go where they find their own kind of people. During their lifetimes they may belong to several different churches as a result of mobility up or down or because of moving to a new community where the levels of the churches are different.

In Jonesville it is a recognized symbol of upward mobility, or attempted mobility, to shift to the Federated Church, the high-status church, or from the Baptist to the Methodist, or from the Free Methodist or Gospel Tabernacle to the Baptist or Methodist. The reverse is also true. One means by which a member of the lower-lower class may attempt to obtain respectability and upward mobility is to join one of the lower-class churches. It has already been pointed out how the theology of the Gospel Tabernacle and the Free Methodist Church fits the peculiar needs of many individuals in this category by offering also an escape mechanism from the social pressure from above. These churches attract both those attempting to distinguish themselves from their neighbors on the basis of acquired moral respectability and those who feel pushed down out of other churches.

The Lutheran Church is discussed fully in the chapter on the Norwegians as the core about which their ethnic culture is centered. Some of their doctrinal emphasis is the result of their subordinate position in the community. One of the steps in the acculturation of a Norwegian is to lose interest in the Lutheran Church. A Swedish Baptist Church once served the same function for the Swedish group; and as the group became assimilated the church also became assimilated. The Catholic Church is also an ethnic church, not for one group alone but for Irish, Poles, Italians, and Germans. It grew in size as long as foreign-born people from those countries flowed into the community; and when immigration almost stopped and the foreign-born generation began to die off, it slowly lost members through the process of acculturation.

The basic social conflict in the church today, expressed openly in those churches which emphasize "sociological" sermons and symbolically in the churches which stress "other worldliness," is between the equalitarian principles of Christian brotherhood and those which recognize some of the realities of the presence of a class order in Jonesville. The full significance of this conflict is brought into clear focus in the Lutheran Church. It will be dealt with in the chapter on the Norwegians.

Chapter 11

THE NORWEGIANS: SECT AND ETHNIC GROUP

"We Stand Apart"

Every social group within a community is characterized by a set of attitudes, values, and symbols which comprise its ideology and distinguish its members. In the Norwegian group of Jonesville at least two distinctive sets of symbols have been fused: the ethnic Norwegian system of values and the Lutheran religious system. Usually those persons of Norse ancestry who retain some ethnic characteristics and are members of the Lutheran Church are referred to by Jonesville as belonging to this group, which is designated by the compound name symbol, "Norwegian-Lutheran." The social distinctness of the group must be regarded as an expression of religious as well as ethnic differences.*

The Norwegian-Lutherans of Jonesville differ from many ethnic sects in that they have developed their distinctive complex of moral norms since their migration to this country, whereas most ethnic sects have come to America as fully developed and cohesive social units. The Norse sect has developed in Jonesville in the last three or four generations in response to local conditions, though trends toward sectarianism can be traced back to social conditions in Norway a century ago.

Since most of the apparent values and symbols which differentiate the Norwegian-Lutherans from the rest of the community are related to the moral standards of the group rather than to their

* By Donald Wray. See List of Authors.

ethnic background, "religious sect" is used in referring to the group rather than the term "ethnic group." Sumner says that the distinctive mark of the sect is conflict with the established mores. This conflict is clear in the case of the Norwegian-Lutherans; their values are not acceptable to the rest of the community, and, in turn, they reject many of the values common to the other social groups. In some instances the conflict arises through the extension by the Lutherans of moral evaluations to objects and activities which are nonmoral to the rest of the community; in other instances they place negative values on objects and activities which the other groups value positively. Conflict in moral evaluations of activities is the principal basis for the social isolation of the Norwegians, for their lack of participation in many community activities, and their dissension in the conduct of others, such as the school system.

The fact that the Norwegian-Lutherans are here defined as a religious sect does not mean that the ethnic factor is not important. There are many similar cases in which the ethnic minorities are organized as religious groups: for example, the Molokans, the Dukhobors, and the Dunkers. The Irish Catholics represent the same phenomenon on a much larger scale. In each of these instances the organized religious life of the group functions to hold the people together and distinguish them from the larger society, even after the more obvious cultural differences, such as foreign language, have disappeared. After the first or second generation of American-born children have grown up, the only formal bonds which maintain the group are the religious organizations which express the norms peculiar to the group. The religious symbols thus take on increasing importance, and the ethnic symbols *per se* become less obvious. This replacement of ethnic symbols is hastened by the desire of many members of the group to become Americans and lose the stigma of foreignness. The Norse illustrated this point when they changed the name of their church from "Skandinavia," an ethnic symbol, to "Bethlehem," a non-ethnic religious symbol. The shift from Norwegian to English in the church services and Sunday School is in part another expression of this process.

"On This Continent, a New Nation"

The background of the Norse must be understood in order to learn how they have become what they are and the differences between them and the English, Germans, Irish and other peoples who have become a part of the homogeneous population of Jonesville.

The year Will Taylor founded Jonesville, a Norwegian financier, Kleng Peerson, founded the great inland empire of Norsemen in North Prairie in the area north of Abraham County. He had been sent abroad by a group in Stavanger, Norway, to find a place in America where they could improve their lot and find religious freedom. After a false start in the East, Peerson and his followers came west hunting for "the good lands" of the prairie and established the first area of permanent Norse settlement in America.

The original immigrants, called the "Sloopers" because of the small boat in which they came, were extreme pietists motivated, in part, to emigrate by religious persecution. They were also very poor, and the economic motive for migration was apparent. In Norway there was a sharp cleavage between the city dwellers and the official classes, on the one hand, and the rural common people, on the other. The farmers differed from the officials and the clerical group not only in culture but in political and economic interests. The revolt of the lower classes in 1836 against the established order was expressed by an intense religious revival, a new spiritual movement involving numerous sectarian and schismatic doctrines which stressed personal religious and emotional experiences in contrast to the formalism of the state church. After 1836 migration from Norway became organized on a large scale, reaching a peak of 250,000 in 1903. The new immigrants were from many parts of the country and not so radically affected by the struggle for power. They were still much more inclined to accept some form of orthodox Lutheranism.

The area which was selected by Kleng Peerson for settlement was a rich agricultural region where the Norse colonists, as the first settlers, had the opportunity to advance themselves economically and socially. As soon as the Norse had learned to read and speak English fluently, they entered local and then state politics. The great opportunities for improvement of social status led rapidly to differentiation among the North Prairie colonists. The rise of certain families, plus the ill fortune of many farmers during the recurrent agrarian depressions, led to a split among the North Prairie people in religion as well as in political and economic points of view. The well established and prosperous farmers and the business and professional men in the trading towns of the Norse settlement had little sympathy for the evangelical prayer meetings and inclined toward a more formalized type of religion, giving support to the movement which led to the final capitulation of the orthodox Lutheran Church. However, the landless farmers, who constituted a numerous "rural proletariat," continued the tradition of individualized religion and favored the lay preachers who came from their own ranks. All but the extremists accepted the authority of the now established Norwegian Lutheran Church, but they demanded and got certain concessions in regard to simplicity of ritual and holding of prayer meetings. The extremists continued to carry on their own forms of worship autonomously.

The North Prairie settlement, from 1836 to 1900, was extended from the original center near the town of Norway, spreading in all directions to towns with an English-speaking tradition and, finally, into Abraham County in 1846. In the center of this area the Norse were the first permanent settlers and left their imprint in such place names as Norway, Stavanger, and Bergen; but farther out they were increasingly forced to mix with other settlers, usually of Anglo-Saxon or Germanic origin. By replacement of the original Anglo-Saxon settlers, the Norse were able to establish a continuous area of Norwegian occupation across the northern half of Abraham County

THE NORWEGIAN-LUTHERANS IN JONESVILLE

Throughout the principal Norse area the pattern of settlement had been predominantly rural, with farming as the main occupation. Several small trading towns had grown up composed almost entirely of immigrants and their descendants. After 1870, however, the Norse on the edges of the North Prairie colony began to enter larger towns where they were brought into direct and intimate contact with people of other ethnic derivations. Jonesville is the largest town on the eastern edge of the North Prairie region, and the entry of the Norse into Jonesville represents the beginning of a new type of adjustment to the American social structure. For the first time a large group of persons of Norse ancestry from the North Prairie colony were placed in an industrial and commercial town in which they were face-to-face with persons who considered themselves to be more "American" than the Norse and looked down upon them as foreigners.

The details of the Norse movement into Jonesville and other towns are not recorded, but the cause of the migration seems to have been the economic pressure on the farming area. The last available land had been occupied so that the excess population had to find some other means for supporting itself and turned to the industries in the many small towns throughout North Prairie. Jonesville was becoming industrialized at this time. The Norse entered the strange industrial and commercial system as untrained and inexperienced laborers, who had to begin at the bottom of the social and economic hierarchies. They were subordinate not only because of their lack of skill but because they were "foreigners," though many of the Norse had been in America longer than some of the "Americans." The Norse who came to Jonesville soon found that they were socially isolated not only from the "Americans" but from other ethnic groups who were better established in the town.

The lower classes which the Norse first entered (see Chart VI) were composed in 1870 of the Irish and portions of the mixed group of Old Americans. The Irish and the Norse seem to have been in frequent conflict during this early period; informants refer to numerous street fights and tavern brawls. The Norse acquired the reputation of being heavy drinkers, in marked contrast to their present strong opposition to the use of alcohol. Even at this time the Norse were looked upon as different from the other ethnic groups in town.

In the seventy years which have passed since the first Norse entered Jonesville, two types of change have shifted the class positions of the group. One was entry into the commercial and professional activities of the town. This occurred gradually as a reflection of better educational opportunities and the accumulation of wealth by the more successful members of the group. It lifted some into the lower-middle class and a few into the upper-middle. The other change was the increasingly strict observance of the moral rules of North Prairie Lutheranism, and the more rigid enforcement of these rules through both formal and informal sanctions, made more effective by the organization of religious life and the establishment of a large Norse colony which could be autonomous in much of its social life. This enforcement of the rigid moral system of the Norse prevented them from gaining full participation in community affairs, but it also served to end the rough wild behavior for which the Norse were notorious when they first came. They shifted from "disreputable" behavior to "respectability," a distinction which divides the lower-lower class from the upper-lower. And they gained favor in the community because of their conservatism and willingness to work hard at menial jobs.

The Norse compose about 15 to 20 percent of the total population of Jonesville. It is difficult to give an exact figure because many of Norse ancestry have, through marriage and other means, disappeared into the larger population.

A numerical majority of possible Norse membership has been assimilated into the larger community of Jonesville during the last seventy-five years. Not all of these 1,200 persons of Norse ancestry would have been members of the Lutheran Church even if they had remained ethnic because of the numerous denominational factions which split the group at an early date. But it seems probable that most of these assimilated Norse represent a loss of Lutheran Church membership and, certainly, a loss of ethnic membership.

Not all of those who leave the church do so permanently, for many return after marriage when family life has been established. Without exception, the "new" members of the congregation are young adults, married, of Norwegian ancestry. Furthermore, they are introduced with kinship referents, "the nephew of so-and-so," "the brother of so-and-so." The entrance into family life, with the attendant rituals of marriage and baptism of children, causes the aberrant sectarian to recognize the functions of the church in his life. Unless he has been able to achieve a complete emotional break with the church or has established a new religious bond, he must return to the sect, though he may never completely accept the rigid moral code. This re-entrance into the sect means that his children will be trained in the doctrines and will in turn have to face the problem of conformity or revolt when they reach adolescence. The widespread kinship bonds of the Norse serve to reinforce the emotional ties which link the individual to the other church members and offer some degree of security and obligation which becomes more important when the person has taken on the responsibility of a family. The kinship bond becomes doubly strong if the emancipated sectarian happens to marry another member of the Norse group.

THE SECTARIAN IDEOLOGY

The extension and elaboration by the Lutherans of a system of moral values into areas of behavior which the community evaluates on a secular basis form the visible symbol which distinguishes them as a sect. As the negative sacred values are put into operation, they form a system of taboos which prevent the Norse from participating fully in the life of the community. Dancing, card playing, smoking, and movie going are examples of activities which are given negative moral judgment by the Lutherans and regarded with indifference by the rest of the community or as pleasant activities, conducive to good social relationships.

The Norse consider their religious ideals to be those laid down in the Bible and, therefore, the absolute Christian moral values. Other interpretations of Christianity are wrong, so that any compromise with other beliefs is a deviation from the true teaching of Christ. Their tradition of low-church evangelism came from Norway, with the associated dislike of formalism and a trained clergy. This tradition emphasized individual religious conversion and mystic emotional experiences, and made the Bible more important than the Book of Concord, which contains the basic Lutheran doctrine. The final victory of orthodox Lutheranism has forced the Jonesville Norwegians partly to abandon their earlier intransigence, but has left a sizable group of persons who do not fully accept the practices of the established church. Their church has had to yield to this radical movement to some extent, and the effects of this compromise are seen in the retention of the prayer meeting and the encouragment of personal religious conversion.

Most individuals today enter the church through infant baptism, and become full members after confirmation. These rites are associated with age grades, and the individual is expected to pass through these rituals. It is, therefore, possible for a person to become formally initiated into the church by the simple process of attending services and going through the proper ceremonies. However, the more radical members of the church maintain that a person is not fully converted until he has had an emotional experience. A conversion may take place under the stimulus of a sermon or a prayer meeting, but also occurs under what are apparently everyday circumstances. A man who had once been a drunkard but had been converted and is now a Sunday School teacher tells of his experiences:

"You know, I have had the most unusual experiences. I have had many of them. One time I was going down the street. I used to chew tobacco, I never smoked, and I was going to take a bite. I had that plug in my hand when all at once the thought came through my mind, 'How can I tell those little children that this is wrong to use tobacco if I go ahead and use it myself?' Well, sir, I threw that tobacco away and I never touched it since. I have had so many experiences. I remember one time, I was working with a pipe, and I had one of those big wrenches in my hand. I was going to pull on it and all at once I thought what God had done for me. Well, I dropped that wrench and sat down and cried. The other fellows ran over to me and thought I was sick or crazy. The foreman he sent me home and I cried all the way. He didn't understand anything spiritual like that at all. Next day he asked me what was wrong and when I told him he laughed at me. I never try to tell the others about how I feel because they don't understand and just laugh. But I know that is the Lord in my soul and I know I am right. That is what the church is for, to tell us what this means and what God wants us to do. You have to believe in the Bible and do what it tells you to and you will be saved."

The effect of the Norse religious taboos is seen in the way in which the children are kept from many school activities. The sacred negative evaluation of dancing prevents all members of the group from taking part in this phase of social life, but it especially prevents the children from participating in much of the social life of their age grade. Card playing is a significant activity in Jonesville in bringing people into contact with social groups, in forming cliques, and in increasing social interaction. But a true sectarian does not play cards because this may result in gambling, and gambling is bad. Similarly the taboo on drinking prevents the Norse from joining the men's clubs, from establishing clique relations in taverns, or from participating in parties where drinking is part of the expected ritual.

Other citizens of Jonesville feel that the Norwegian-Lutherans are removed from the normal pattern of community life, noncooperative, and unwilling to take part in many community activities. The Norse are blamed for refusing to join social and service organizations, yet there is a definite feeling against admitting them to various associations, especially those which are fairly high in prestige. The fact that only one Norwegian is in the Rotary Club is cited as evidence of the nonparticipation of Norwegians in community affairs; but there are very few Norse who are high enough in business and professional life to be eligible for membership in Rotary.

IDEOLOGY AND CLASS POSITION

Every sectarian or ethnic group faces the problem of holding its members, especially over the span of several generations. As children grow up in contact with the outside world, they tend to become assimilated, depending upon the extent to which the norms of their parental group diverge from those of the larger society, and upon the amount of interaction with outsiders which is possible in the immediate social context. Intermarriage, social, economic, and physical mobility, revolt against the narrow life of the small divergent ethnic or sectarian world, are some of the forces which pull the members out of the smaller group into the larger society.

The methods by which the sect or ethnic minority meets the forces of assimilation are crucial for the life of the group. It must retain the allegiance of at least a core of individuals, in each succeeding generation, who will accept the group norms and transmit them to the oncoming generation.

Social mobility seems to be the greatest threat to the life of the sect. Mobility on a large scale has divided the entire sect into upper-lower and lower-middle class, with implications which have been discussed. Mobility above the lower-middle class means a rejection in large part of the most significant elements of the sectarian ideology. The sect is faced with the problem of providing some form of mobility within the church whereby persons with ambition and ability may improve their social status, yet retain their sectarian behavior. For the upper-lower-class person this is not an important consideration today, for there is a group of lower-middle-class persons in the church who will to some extent help the mobile upper-lower-class individual. Furthermore, the lower-middle class has worked out its own adaptation of sectarian behavior so that there is no necessity for rejection of the sectarian code. The group is large enough to provide its own social life based on its own standards. Within the lower-middle class of Lutherans there are gradations of strictness from the core members to the periphery which provide a choice of interest groups and cliques within which the mobile person may build his social life.

Some provisions are made within the lower-middle class for the social and economic advancement of the lower-middle person which will keep him within the church—for example, scholarships to Lutheran colleges and training schools. During the research period four of the most promising young people of the congregation were assisted in this way: three were given scholarships and loans to permit them to attend a Lutheran college and another was sent to a Lutheran hospital for nurse's training. Neither of these institutions is as rigid morally as the low-church Jonesville congregation would wish them to be; nevertheless, they provide education within Norwegian-Lutheran institutions. As far as we know, these four cases were the only Norse members of the high school graduating class who intended to get more formal education, so that the church had made a successful attempt to combine opportunity for mobility with retention of sectarian allegiance.

At the present time the Norse who are organized in the church are spread through three classes: only a few members are in the upper-middle; about a third of the total are in lower-middle; less than two-thirds in upper-lower. A very few members, who are marginal to the life of the sect, are in lower-lower. The three major class groups display significant differences in their interpretations of the Norwegian-Lutheran ideology and the ways in which they act with reference to it.

Of the seven persons (three percent of the total church membership) who are in the upper-middle class, two are not active in the church and are only formally included in the group, and the others attend occasionally but maintain most of their social life outside the sectarian limits. This is necessary if any individual is to participate on this class level since most of the class is not sectarian, but highly secular in attitude. The mere fact of being upper-middle-class, therefore, indicates that the persons are relatively free from sectarian attitudes and behavior. Since these persons are professional or business men they stand in a special relationship to the sect as a whole. Some of the cases will be presented in detail to show these relationships and the peculiarities of attitude which are associated with the class position and economic functions of the individuals.

The most prominent person socially is Jacob Larson, who comes from an old Norse family and has numerous kinship ties with the group. He began as a clerk in a store and has risen to independent ownership of the business. He is one of the wealthiest members of the church; his assessment for church dues is high and he makes a point of exceeding this tithe every year. He attends services about once a month and goes to the Brotherhood meetings about every second month. These are his only formal contacts with the Lutheran sect. His wife is Scotch-Irish and a Methodist, though she has joined the Lutheran Church and become prominent in the Ladies Aid. She carries the burden of participation in the church group and successfully conforms to the standards of behavior demanded in the sect.

Outside the church, however, the Larsons exhibit another set of attitudes and behavior which contradict the sectarian standards.

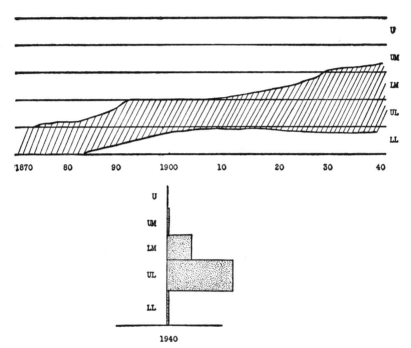

CHART VI.   Class Distribution of Norwegian-Lutherans

They participate socially on the fringe of the upper class and devote most of their leisure time to cultivating social relationships with the upper class. This involves attending and giving bridge parties by Mrs. Larson, and membership in the Country Club and attendance at poker parties by Larson. The Larsons are able to enter these cliques and retain membership in them. His active social life is almost entirely in these groups while she plays a dual role and is active in both the sect and the upper class.

Upper-class behavior is almost entirely secular, and the activities which are considered desirable and necessary for proper social relationships are tabooed by the sacred ideology of the Lutherans. The behavior exhibited by the Larsons toward the upper class is desirable, in the evaluations of the upper class, but bad according to the Lutherans. The behavior shown by the Larsons in Lutheran groups is morally right in the eyes of the Lutherans but bad or at least foolish for the upper class. Larson does not behave in accordance with Lutheran doctrine except in the very superficial matter of attending services and meetings from time to time. He does not hesitate to smoke in public and does not conceal his card playing activities. Mrs. Larson, who participates more actively in church affairs, is aware of the contradiction between her sets of behavior in the two groups, and is constantly trying to keep the two groups apart.

Another upper-middle-class member of the church is Gunnar Johnson. He, however, is Danish and is not identified with the Norse except through formal church membership. He openly violates the taboos on smoking, occasionally he takes a drink, and he states that movies are good entertainment. His occupational position gives him high prestige among the rural Norse and perhaps accounts for his influence in spite of his nonconformity.

John Jensen is a professional man who is more active in the church than the other upper-middle-class members. He is choir director and attends almost every church function. His wife is prominent in the Ladies Aid. Jensen seems to conform closely to the standards demanded of the sectarian, though he does smoke on occasion. His wife once said that smoking was permissible for men but not for women. Jensen is accused by other people of cultivating the friendship of the church members because most of his clients come from this group. This attitude was expressed in connection with his stand on the school tax question and on the issue of high school dances. He upheld the sectarian view on the dance issue and was ridiculed because of this. He is a member of a civic organization but is often criticized by other members of this organization.

The upper-middle-class members of the Lutheran Church have certain characteristics in common. They all show inconsistencies in their behavior with reference to the extended sacred definitions of behavior laid down by the sect. All conform verbally to the sectarian doctrine when they are participating with church members, and all depart from this doctrine in varying degrees when they participate in nonsectarian social life with other members of their class. This violation of Lutheran moral standards is necessary for participation in the upper-middle class, where the sacred dimension in behavior is minimized and secular definitions predominate. There are so few Norse in this class that they could not enforce sectarian standards if they wished and could not create a separate social group of their own at that class level. They must, therefore, accept the standards of social behavior which are set by the other members of the class, none of whom accepts the sacred values of the Lutherans.

The upper-middle-class Lutherans all stand in special relationships to the rest of the church membership. They provide professional services to the Norse, who give preference to these men because they seem to belong to the sect. To retain this support, the upper-middle-class men participate superficially in church activities and act as patrons for various church groups. Such entry into church life requires at least verbal acceptance of the sectarian norms and behavior patterns; but in most of their social and professional life these norms are violated and rejected. They retain their membership in the church because of recent mobility, kinship bonds, and economic advantages.

The lower-middle-class membership of the church amounts to one-fourth of the total congregation. In this class are found some minor professional people, teachers, small businessmen, and a large number of clerical workers. This class group in the church falls into two categories: those who are somewhat marginal to the sect and those who are active leaders in the church.

The first of these represents a partly emancipated group who are church members but do not accept the rigorous sectarian definitions of moral right and wrong. They attend the formal church services and occasionally participate in social activities but do not attend the prayer meetings or other functions which assume a sectarian cast. They tend to regard the church as equivalent to other churches in the community; they may be described as orthodox Lutherans, without the local sectarian elaborations. They participate freely in community life at their class level and violate sectarian taboos in doing so. They are passive as far as the conduct of the church is concerned and participate formally in the orthodox services without attempting to direct or control the church organization. They are quite comparable in this respect to a large segment of the lower-middle-class membership of any other church in the community. They retain little evidence of ethnicity and frequently marry outside the congregation.

Often this group expresses resentment when they are criticized for their violation of sectarian standards; the attempted enforcement of sectarian norms through formal and informal social pressure does not succeed. Those who wish to violate sectarian taboos can do so with no fear of effective punishment since their relationship to the church is formal, and their social life is outside the bounds of the congregation, at least in part. The threat of ostracism and loss of prestige in the church is a mild sanction to this group.

A second group of the lower-middle-class membership is very active in the church and is, in fact, the controlling bloc in the formal church organization. Members of this category hold most of the congregational offices and run the formalized activities of the whole Norwegian-Lutheran group. They have been responsible for the establishment of an orthodox Lutheranism in opposition to the low-church North Prairie tradition and have been the most active in elaborating the associational structure of the church, especially the age grading and educational groups.

The development of the religious education system in the hands of this group is significant because of the ideological variations peculiar to this lower-middle-class group. They accept the extended sacred definitions of behavior which characterize the sect, but overlay the evangelism implied by the sect with an emphasis on formal ritual and automatic entry into the church through the rites of baptism and confirmation. They do not place emphasis on personal conversion, though they accept this form of religious experience in deference to other groups in the church which will be discussed below.

This segment of the lower-middle class stresses the Lutheran elements of church ideology and minimizes the Norwegian elements. They refer to themselves as "Americans" in contrast to the "Norwegians." They were instrumental in bringing about the replacement of Norse by English and are trying to abolish the remaining Norse language services, though without success up to the present time.

The attempt to change the congregation from an ethnic basis to a purely denominational basis is in part a reflection of the intermarriage with outsiders which is so frequent among the lower-middle class. Two of the leaders in the church were Methodists who had married Norwegian women and then entered the Lutheran Church. These men have led in the development of the educational system of the church and in the effort to bring in new members regardless of ethnic background. The fact that they and other members similar to them are in control of church education and formal organization gives them power which far exceeds their numerical importance. If their program continues they will gradually lead the church away from evangelism toward greater orthodoxy and will reduce the significance of ethnicity in the church membership.

Two-thirds of the total congregation are upper-lower-class, the most significant class segment since they form the nucleus of both extreme sectarianism and Norwegian ethnicity. They represent in their class position the socio-economic level of all the Norse after the migration to Jonesville and after the spread of moral standards which were "respectable." They have made no further improvement in their social and economic status since 1900. A few of the church officers are drawn from this class but, for the most part, they are followers, not leaders, in the formal conduct of the church organization.

In the upper-lower class there is present a marginal group comparable to that found in the lower-middle class. These are persons who are sporadic attenders of religious services and do not care to conform to the extensive system of moral rules laid down by the sect. They, too, are Lutherans by formal membership in the church and retain no more ethnic traits than do such persons of the lower-middle class. Much of their social life is outside the Norwegian group. For the most part they depend for economic support on employers who are not Norse; therefore, they have no need to retain the good will of the congregation in order to earn a living, as do the upper-middle-class members. Formal and informal sanctions cannot be applied to this group with any great success by the church.

The core of the upper-lower-class Norse is powerful in the church, not through offices but by constituting a major portion of the congregation. It represents the pietistic tradition in the most extreme form. It emphasizes personal religious conversion rather than formal entry into the church by a ceremony. It enforces adherence and conformity to the extended sacred evaluations of behavior which are the peculiar characteristics of the sectarian. This upper-lower-class core forms the bloc in the congregation which attempts to retain the Norwegian tradition in the church, especially the Norse language service, in opposition to the "Americans" who wish to do away with the stigma of foreignness. All other Lutheran churches in the North Prairie area have abolished the use of Norse in the church, many having made the transition years ago. The church in Jonesville is, therefore, unusual in the maintenance of this ethnic symbol.

The emphasis on the Norwegian tradition is not a result of later migration on the part of lower-class members. They are derived from the same old stock as the middle-class Lutherans. The difference in attitude toward ethnic symbols is in part a function of class position. The middle-class Norse who are upward-mobile find that ethnic identification is unfavorable to them in their business and professional relationships, so they attempt to minimize their Norwegian background. The lower-class Norse have not been mobile and, while they resent the common attitude toward the "dumb Scandinavians," the ethnic identifications do not impress them as a serious detriment to their social position. The common tradition does serve to unify the sect and reinforce the social isolation which goes with sectarian behavior. The kinship bonds among the upper-lower-class Norse are strong and widespread, probably as a result of the emphasis on the ethnic tradition.

The rejection of the narrow sectarian code by persons who are not rising in economic or social position may still be regarded as a form of horizontal mobility; that is, by breaking away from the small social world of the sect, persons can enter many other social groups at the same class level, which would be closed to them as long as they remained sectarian. This process occurs in both the upper-lower and lower-middle classes and has probably accounted for a greater loss of membership than has vertical class mobility. This horizontal movement may take place rapidly, as when a person revolts against the sect and "goes wild," or it may be a gradual process which involves stopping at various stages of emancipation. Slow drift away from the sect produces the type of sectarian, common in the lower-middle class, who, though nominally a member, will still diverge to some extent from the accepted norms of the church. The sect has attempted to prevent this type of mobility by developing numerous associations within the church membership to provide a social life which adheres to sectarian standards. It has extended its religious training program to include adult classes and tries to keep the adults interested in child training. These efforts on the whole do not seem to have succeeded, since the persons who attend are strong believers who would not need such a program to keep them in the church. The marginal persons do not attend these classes except sporadically.

The Church and the School

The first and second generations of American-born descendants of immigrant groups show the effects of contact with American ways of life and ideals, which are usually contrary to the ideals held by the older generation. Every ethnic group is then made aware in many ways that it is in danger of disintegrating and becoming assimilated into American society unless some way is found to indoctrinate the younger generation in the group ideals. The diverse denominational schools, foreign language schools, and folk schools in America are institutionalized expressions of the attempts of religious and cultural minorities to maintain the group in opposition to the forces of assimilation. Such efforts have been more successful than is generally realized. Often such minorities are able to establish national centers of education, especially on the college level, but are unable to do so locally because of their scattered areas of settlement or economic limitations. This latter is the position of the Norse of Jonesville.

Since Jonesville represents a colony of Norse who were in contact with American culture for two or three generations prior to their entry into the town, the issue of public education to maintain the Norse language and culture has never arisen. In the heart of the North Prairie region, the local educational system (also the local political organizations) has been entirely in the hands of the Norse. The replacement of Norse culture began in the days of Elling Eilsen, when that preacher translated the Norse hymnals and prayer books into English. There was a feeling that Norse as a living language would never die out in North Prairie, yet today it is spoken only by a few of the older people and is not used at all by any formal organizations nor in the schools. The Americanization of North Prairie has been accomplished by the Norse themselves—since no persons of other ethnic derivation are in the region—in response to the necessity for carrying on commercial and political relations with the larger American society in which the Norse were submerged. Since this slow indirect acculturation had gone on for forty years before the first Norse entered Jonesville, the colony in the town never felt the crisis of culture conflict in the manner in which so many ethnic groups experience it.

The absence of conflict over language and other overt cultural manifestations does not mean that the Norwegian-Lutherans have found themselves in agreement with the policies of the public school system. Their emphasis on the supernatural world and its implications for worldly life, in addition to their intense concern over moral behavior as they understand it, have brought them into disagreement with the more secularized standards which were incorporated in the public school system. This has been the basis for a battle for political control of the schools in Jonesville by the Norse which has continued down through the time of the research.

The issue which is most emphasized at this time is the practice of holding dances at the high school. The community at large approves since the dances are held in a public building under official supervision. However, the Lutherans oppose dancing anywhere under any circumstances. The pastor said:

"It's not the dance itself that is sinful, it is what the dance leads to. You know that out of many a dance has come a fatherless child. I think that activities that are not sinful in themselves but will lead to sin should be stopped before the temptation of sin is placed before these boys and girls. We talk about chaperoned dances at the high school. There are no chaperoned dances at the high school. After that last dance, the superintendent complained to the whole student body that there was no one left there at the end of the dance. He wanted to know why they left before. I could have told him why they left early. They wanted to be at their own devices. The devil was loose in them."

The pastor used a moral expression typical of the Norse. The sin lies not in the dancing itself but in the consequences. This method of extension of the moral evaluations of the Norse appears in many of their statements and seems to be a kind of apology for their deviation from the evaluations made by the rest of the community; moreover, it usually is so strong that it does make the nonmoral activity take on a moral value.

The Norse try to prevent their young people from attending

these dances by substituting church sponsored parties. They have also brought pressure to bear on the school officials though not through the church council. Two of the members of the Board of Education belonged to the Lutheran Church; they were expected to represent the moral standards of the Norse in the public educational system. However, one of these men was Danish and more liberal than the Norse. The other was a professional man who, although active in church affairs, had often been accused of using his prominence in the church as a means of securing the good will of the Norse, among whom were most of his clients. The pastor had to say of these men:

"If Stassen only had the independence of thought he should have, he would fight for the things the church stands for. Now Jensen does. Jensen tells the Board what the church stands for, but the fellows sit around there and grin at him, and then they insult him with expressions like this, 'Why we can expect this from you.' Then he just keeps still and so they push him around as you would a balloon. You can't trust the members of the School Board."

The pastor hoped to change the school program through the united efforts of the ministers in town but was disappointed in this group as well as in the Board of Education. He accused the other churches of moral weakness and unwillingness to act when important issues arose.

Another conflict between the Lutherans and the policies of the school system arose when the Lutherans challenged the right of a teacher to teach evolution. It is likely that other fundamentalist churches, such as the Free Methodist, may have felt the same way but were either passive in their resistance or did not feel powerful enough to do anything. The Lutherans saw the teaching of evolution as a challenge to all Christianity and a particular threat to their own ideology.

"That Smith should not be in the school system. He'll not be there very long. Maybe he doesn't know it, but he's going. He makes the Bible a public laugh. He stands up in the classroom and teaches that the Bible is untrue. He's been doing that for two years. Oh, I tell you, it is awful, simply awful. Terrible, terrible, terrible."

The Lutherans often appear as a political and economic pressure group which is aware of its strength and ready to use it to enforce its own standards upon the community. They are willing to stand alone but welcome the support of other religious groups, which they are rarely able to secure for reasons which have been mentioned. The Norse resent the defection of the other churches. All of the controversies between the Norwegian-Lutherans and the public educational system have centered around activities in the high school. The grade school seems never to have been the focus of a struggle, probably because the high-school age grade is the one most likely to break away from the rigid standards imposed by the church. Apparently the children do not become aware of the differences which exist between them and the other children until they are brought into contact with the various social activities which begin in the second year of high school. At that time the taboos which the Norwegians place upon their members become very clear, and the children enter a period of personal and social conflict during which some break away from the Lutheran group.

However, the revolts against the Lutheran code are only occasional; the majority of the Lutheran children remain faithful to the standards of behavior which they have learned in the church and in the family. This solidarity, plus the efforts of the church to keep them from participating in disapproved activities such as dancing, forces the Norse students to form their own social group in the high school. Within this group the social pressure is very great; those who do not conform to the behavior patterns of the Lutheran clique face expulsion. One who had been expelled commented:

"She was one of those kids from the Lutheran Church. Those kids gang together except for me. They stick together just like glue. I was ostracized from them because I danced and went to shows and we play bridge. We dance and go to shows and drink beer and play cards, but over there they're against everything. In fact, every time we had a dance at the high school they threw some kind of a party at the church and tried to make the kids come. Those who didn't were ostracized. The Lutherans just wouldn't let us run around with their crowd.

"I quit going to church. The kids over there are all right, but I'm kind of left out of things, and since I   been going out they have left me alone. They are very strict, and they don't want you to go out to dances and out on parties and dates, and they watch what you do."

The result of all this was that a core of the most devout and sectarian young people provided the nucleus of the church-sponsored groups, and a large number of other children who were formal members of the church and attended Sunday School regularly either did not come to the church parties or did so only at times. Some of these marginal persons were so obviously violating the sectarian standards that they were ostracized from the social life of the Lutherans. Others, however, were able to continue in the group as tolerated members, even though they might suffer some disapproval. This whole marginal group, which was unreliable in the eyes of the sectarians, constituted the problem group which might very well escape entirely from the church. The leaders of the church could not afford to censure them too severely for minor lapses from strict morality for fear of driving them completely away from the influence of the church. The marginal or wavering sectarian was, therefore, able to retain formal membership and partial acceptance in the sectarian organizations, while at the same time he enjoyed participation in the forbidden activities of the nonsectarian members of his age grade.

RELIGIOUS REVIVALISM AND ETHNICITY

We have seen that the Norwegian-Lutherans of Jonesville are a sectarian group based upon common ethnic and religious background. They present two distinct problems as far as the study of the community is concerned. What are the conditions under which such a sectarian group can arise? And what are the conditions under which an ethnic minority can retain its identity beyond the life span of the immigrant generation and the first American-born generation?

The Norwegians of Jonesville stand as an exception to the general rule that the degree of assimilation of an ethnic group depends upon the length of time the group has been in this country and upon the degree of divergence from American cultural and racial norms. The Norse have been settled in North Prairie for over a century and are similar in their basic cultural elements and physical type to the Old Americans; yet the Norse in Jonesville stand apart from the rest of the community and retain their identity as an ethnic group, though a great number of individuals have been fully assimilated.

The Norwegian-Lutherans constitute not only a religious but a social group in which all of the interactions necessary to a life career may take place. Within this relatively closed interactive system the factor of ethnicity is important, especially among the upper-lower-class Norse. It is this segment of the congregation which insists upon the retention of the Norse language in the church and stresses the ethnic element in its autonomous revivalist organizations. This emphasis upon the maintenance of ethnic symbols seems to occur only among the Norse of Jonesville, and is not found in the communities of North Prairie which are composed almost entirely of Norse stock. To understand this phenomenon we must compare the process through which the rural North Prairie Norse and the Jonesville Norse came into contact with American society and American cultural norms.

The North Prairie people inhabit an area where all of the population is of Norse extraction; contact with other ethnic groups has been slight and indirect, and there has been no occasion for the erection of distinctions based upon ethnic differences. All segments of the population, whether by class or religion, have a common ethnic heritage. Cultural change in this situation is seen by the people as a conflict between generations, if it is recognized at all. The abandonment of Norse culture and the adoption of American ways have constituted an indirect and gradual process in which the Norse themselves have initiated the changes. The persons who head the local political, economic, and social hierarchies are of Norse ancestry themselves, so they cannot be differentiated from the people below them on an ethnic basis. No group can call itself more American than the others; no group can claim priority in the area; Lutherans are no more Norwegian than are Methodists. While there is awareness of Norse ancestry and pride in being part of the oldest Norse settlement in America, there is little contact with Old Americans and no subordination on an ethnic basis. What ethnic consciousness is present is, therefore, couched in terms of ancestral pride rather than the stigma of "foreignness."

The Norse in Jonesville not only had to make rapid adjustments to American society to maintain themselves in the town, but also were placed in direct relationships to Old Americans and found themselves subordinated and stigmatized as aliens. They were under social and economic pressure to hasten their assimilation, and they found that retention of ethnic traits was a barrier to social mobility. Furthermore, the Norse had entered Jonesville in hope of improving their economic status, yet they found themselves placed in the lowest occupations in the community. The Norse who entered the town were, therefore, subordinated in two respects: they were looked down upon as ethnics, and they were considered fit only for the undesirable, unskilled jobs. Both of these factors constituted a loss of status and security.

The feeling of subordination as a group was deepened for the upper-lower-class Norse by their relative loss of status when a portion of the ethnic group rose to the lower-middle class. The latter indicated their acceptance of the ethnic evaluation of the community by their efforts to rid themselves of the ethnic stigmata. In this way the lower-class Norse were subordinated not only by the community but by a portion of their own ethnic group which had achieved some degree of economic and social advance.

At the same time the entire Norwegian group felt the influence of an urban environment on the cohesiveness of its members. Intermarriage with other ethnic groups took place with greater frequency than was possible in the rural settlements, and divergent economic and social interests tended to disrupt their ethnic unity. This potential rapid disintegration of the Norse, plus the friction which arose in their contact with the Americans, served to heighten their consciousness of their ethnic heritage.

The Norse of Jonesville were then in a position which has many elements in common with the situation of preliterate groups which are placed in direct contact with modern civilization. They were placed in a new economic situation for which they had not been prepared. They found themselves not only unable to profit from the new economic basis but actually subjected to a loss of security and social position because of it. They were in contact with a dominant social group which subordinated them socially because of their different culture and dominated them economically as employers.

Among preliterate groups this situation often gives rise to a phenomenon which has been called the nativistic religious revival. Such religious movements have been interpreted as a reaction to the disruption of native social, economic, and religious life in the proc-ess of acculturation. The nativistic religious revival typically takes place after the period of initial contact with a dominant culture and serves to reintegrate the native social life in the face of the dis-integration which is threatening the group. The religious elements of such revivalism usually incorporate elements which were not originally present in native religion and stress the distinctness and power of the native society.

Revivalism is one form of response to the whole process of acculturation. "Revivalism is that portion of the response which expresses in ritual symbolism the basic feelings of acceptance or rejection of white culture, feelings of loss or damage, aggressive retaliation in response to deprivation suffered, and self-punishing assertions and practices in proportion to aggressive retaliation."[1]

The attempt to reintegrate the Norse through religious revivalism is best seen in the development of the Inner Mission Society. This semisecret organization stresses the use of the Norse language and emphasizes personal conversion and mystic religious experience. It began in a village east of Jonesville where there are only a few Norse present, but it now has its greatest strength in Jonesville. This group with its sympathizers is responsible for the retention of Norse services in the church long after the churches in the North Prairie area had become entirely English-speaking.

The distinctive ideology of the Norse involves the elements of rejection of the values of the dominant social groups of the community, and the taboos which restrict the activity of the sectarian seem to represent a degree of self-punishment through denial of the attractive aspects of the "world." The attempts to impose sectarian values on the rest of the community are not only efforts to safeguard the sect but expressions of aggression against the rest of the community and the values which the sect has rejected.

Faris has suggested that the sect results from an effort of a group to re-establish order when an earlier fixed order of society is breaking down.[2] Such social disintegration may be caused by a number of types of change. In the case of the Norse and the preliterate groups, it results from a rapid process of acculturation through direct contact with some dominant group of another culture and another economic system. The growth of the sect in Jonesville has certainly functioned to stabilize the Norse as a separate and distinct group in the community.

The fact that the Norse have been able to fix their position in

1 Phileo Nash, "Revivalism on Klamath Reservation," *Social Anthropology of North American Tribes,* Edited by Fred Eggan (Chicago: University of Chicago Press, 1937).

2 Ellsworth Faris, "The Sect and the Sectarian," *The Nature of Human Nature* (New York: McGraw-Hill Book Co., 1937), p. 48.

the community emphasizes the fact that the sect seems to be most strong among the Norse whose social mobility has been the least. The lower-class Norse and the middle-class Norse to a lesser extent have, by their acceptance of sectarian values and behavior, effectively prevented themselves from rising to the higher class levels. It has been pointed out that the restrictions imposed on members of the sect effectively bar them from participation in many activities which are necessary for complete integration into the community, especially in the higher classes. The total result of this restriction has been to reduce the mobility of the Norse as a group and prevent or reduce differentiation within the sect. This has preserved the homogeneity of the group and retarded the processes of assimilation which would otherwise have caused the Norse as such to disappear in the community. The achievement of this degree of social stability within the sect has functioned to keep the majority of the Norse in Jonesville in two class levels and has enabled them to maintain a degree of ethnic behavior which has not been maintained in the heart of the Norwegian settlement in North Prairie.

Chapter 12

STATUS IN THE HIGH SCHOOL

The school is the only community-wide, tax-supported institution in Jonesville devoted exclusively to the training of the young. All of the approximately 1,800 children, except some forty-odd enrolled in a local parochial school, attend the public schools.*

The state requires the school district to provide a common-school education at public expense; the courts of North Prairie have ruled that a common-school education includes four years of high school. State laws provide for the operation and maintenance of schools by residents of a local area with a minimum of supervision from state agencies. The operation of a school is essentially a community enterprise, particularly with respect to policies. State educational officials have little control beyond their power to withdraw state aid funds, in extreme cases, for local violations of law or administrative rulings. Other state functions include the licensing of teachers and school administrators, and the requirements that the schools be kept open a stipulated number of days each year and that certain subjects be taught.

The Jonesville area is organized into 33 school districts of which 32 are rural districts that support one-room schools where grades one through eight are taught. Each of these rural schools is administered by three adult trustees elected by the citizens of the district. These schools are supported largely by real estate taxes levied by the board on its district, and these funds are supplemented by some state aid. The rural schools have no integral connections with the schools in Jonesville.

* By A. B. Hollingshead. See List of Authors.

School districts are not required to maintain a high school; none of the rural districts within the communal area has established one. In accordance with the statutes, all land in Abraham County, not in a high school district, is organized into a non-high-school district and a tax is levied to pay for the tuition of pupils who attend high schools elsewhere. Since Jonesville has the only high school in the community the pupils from the non-high-school district come to Jonesville High School. Thus, the families in rural territory are in two districts—the common school district and the non-high district —and pay two taxes. The Jonesville school system is organized into one district under the jurisdiction of a Board of Education.

THE BOARD OF EDUCATION

Responsibility for the operation of the school system rests in a seven man Board of Education. The president of the Board is elected annually in April along with two members elected for three year terms. Theoretically, any adult citizen who is a resident of the district may be a candidate for the school board. In practice, the members of the Board of Education come from the two upper classes and have to qualify under three strictly administered ground rules: first, only men are eligible; second, Catholics, Jews, Irish, and Democrats are informally disqualified; and third, the Board is "non-political." To become a member of the Board a man has to be a Protestant, a Republican, a property owner, and a Rotarian or, at the very least, approved by the Rotarians. Rotarians are proud of the way they have controlled the selection of the Board for "more than twenty-five years."

The selection of a candidate to fill a vacancy is left to the president of the Board. He discusses possible candidates with his friends on the Board and in Rotary. Generally he invites a fellow Rotarian with whom he believes he can work to become a candidate. The president then files this man's name with the election clerk; nothing is said publicly about the impending vacancy or the forthcoming election until after the last date for filing has passed. Then the *Jonesville Eagle* runs a news item which notes that the date for filing for the school election has passed, and that such-and-such men have filed as candidates for the Board of Education, and Mr. X has filed again for president of the Board. Little additional publicity is given to the election until the *Eagle* carries the necessary legal notices of the polling places and names of candidates. When election day comes only a handful of voters go to the polls to elect the hand-picked candidates. In 1940, 132 votes were cast; 114 in 1941; and 84 in 1942.

This carefully controlled system for the selection of Board members has resulted in the election of middle-aged business and professional men from the top two classes who possess a highly developed sense of responsibility to these classes especially with respect to the preservation of economic interests, power, and prestige. The policies they have followed in the administration of the school system have reflected the community interests of their own social classes and, to a less extent, those of the little business and professional people in the lower-middle class. The relationship between their official positions as Board members and the education of approximately four-fifths of the children is not comprehended by either the Board members themselves or the rank and file of adults in the classes they represented.

Members of the Board have intimate and coordinate relations almost exclusively with people in their own classes who tend to think more or less alike on educational questions, particularly those that might raise the tax rate. They are out of touch with the opinions, beliefs, prejudices, and aspirations of some 75 percent of the people in the community. Contacts outside their class groups are largely superficial; their social positions make it difficult, even if they so desired, to bridge the gap between themselves and persons in the lower classes. People in the upper classes do not believe it wise or necessary to know what the common people are thinking. If they pick up information through gossip and chance remarks indicative of hostility or unrest, they tend to ignore it and consider the person voicing it as irresponsible, "radical," or "a local red." Persons in the Level Above the Common Man are satisfied with the Board since it represents the "finest people," "the good element," "the refined interests"; but, as one moves lower in the social structure, criticism of the Board of Education and its members is encountered with increasing frequency until the lower-lower class where the question of the school is ignored or avoided by most adults.

The Board of Education has been concerned primarily with two things: the operation of the schools as economically as possible, and conformity by teachers to conservative economic, political, religious, and moral doctrines, both in the classroom and in their private lives. The school is viewed as an indispensable but expensive institution by the members of the Board. They believe it should reflect in its administration and teaching all that is traditionally good and wholesome in Middle Western American small-town life —if it does not cost too much. The question of cost comes first whenever an innovation is suggested. Throughout its thinking on educational questions the Board compares the cost with the alleged value of the item or the program under consideration. Cost versus value is acute whenever an item that touches the high school enters the picture.

High school education is far more expensive than elementary; moreover, members of the Board are of the opinion that not everyone of high school age should have a high school education. No Board member was found who believed it was the responsibility of the community to provide educational facilities for *all* high school adolescents. They believed there are many boys and girls in high school who would be better off "on the farm" or "down at The Mill." They are interested, however, in seeing that "everyone who can profit by a high school education is provided with the necessary facilities," but they are not clear in the conception of who "can profit by a high school education." In general, they mean the sons and daughters of the three higher classes, and those in Class IV, if they "behave themselves." Adolescents in Class V are not considered to have enough ability "to profit from a high school education."

FINANCING THE SCHOOLS

The school system has been hampered for more than a generation by inadequate financial support. In 1931, the Taxpayers' League forced a 25 percent reduction in the evaluation of farm and town property. Since the tax rate was not increased, the amount raised by taxes to support the schools was reduced automatically. Teachers' salaries were cut from one-fourth to one-half and all other expenditures reduced to the absolute minimum. The Board of Education might have raised more money for schools by the reorganization of the system, but this would have meant an increase in taxes, and the interests of the Board were more concerned with low taxes than with an adequate school system.

After the cut in assessed values, real estate in the community was evaluated at $8,000,000 of which some $3,000,000 was in the town and $5,000,000 in the rural area. On the other hand, 62 percent of the population lived in town and 38 percent in the country. This created a situation where many people believed the owners of farm lands were not paying their share of the cost of maintaining the school system. This issue was centered in the high school because it cost the most to maintain, and the graduates from the 32 country school districts came to high school in Jonesville. In 1941-42, one-fourth of the high school students came from the rural area and three-fourths from the town. The non-high-school district paid the Jonesville Board of Education $10,142.04 tuition for these rural pupils. This represented one-fourth of the $42,468.19 high school budget. Some land-owners argued the rural pupils were paying their way. On the surface, this argument would appear to be sound, but the tuition paid by the non-high-school district was figured on current educational costs—instruction, plant operation, and fixed charges for insurance and depreciation. It did not attempt to include the original cost of the high school plant or a new one. Operation of the high school represented 55.2 percent of the $76,922 budget, but it included only 36 percent of the pupils serviced by the system.

Two radically different tax rates were levied on rural and town real estate to support the schools. In Jonesville, property owners were paying a $2.00 rate on $100 of assessed valuation. The non-high-school country district levied a rate of 44 cents on $100 of assessed valuation.

The state law allowed a school district to levy as much as $1.38 per $100 of assessed valuation without a special election. By special election, the people of a district could tax themselves more, as the people of Jonesville had done, but in the country no district came near approaching this maximum. The landowners feared that any change in the organization of the Jonesville school system would increase their taxes. The fear that the rate on the non-high-school land might be raised to the $1.38 limit, or higher, was the resistance point around which the landowners rallied to block attempts to reorganize the Jonesville school system on an adequate financial basis.

Although all the schools were involved in this argument in one way or another, it was centered in the high school because of the service the Jonesville High School performed for pupils from the rural area. Opposition to any change in the Jonesville school system from 1920 to 1941 came from families in the upper class who resided in Jonesville. These families were able to block all efforts to change the schools through the control of the Board of Education. It might appear paradoxical that a group of townspeople rather than the farmers opposed improvements in the schools. On the contrary, it is a logical product of the property and class systems. In 1940, 73.2 percent of all farm land was operated by tenants. This figure is for the county, but it is not believed the figure for the community is appreciably different since it covered one-half of Abraham County.

Six upper-class families owned more than 30,000 acres, an average of 5,000 acres each. Several others owned individually from one thousand to two thousand acres. One man, who was never spoken of as being a big landholder, casually remarked, "I have a real interest in this high school business because my wife and I own 10 farms in the county and I have a first mortgage on 18 more." Another large landholder said, "There is a lot of talk right now, but nothing will be done. The people in this town are interested in keeping taxes down and nothing else." A third powerful figure said, "Everyone's so excited about taxation that you would have a hell of a time putting any reorganization across."

The general consensus of the upper class was that the present school was adequate and nothing needed to be done. They were convinced also that the only way the schools could be changed would be through the united action of "the laboring class." As an astute upper-class political figure put it, "The laboring class are the people who always vote for that sort of thing anyway, but all the property owners in the group would be against it. I doubt whether the laboring people could swing it."

PROFESSIONAL PERSONNEL

Educational policies formulated by the Board are executed by the Superintendent of Schools, a professionally trained, licensed administrator hired by the Board from year to year and responsible directly to it. His contact with the community is professional and contractual, but his social relationships are far more important to his success or failure locally than his professional or contractual ones. The superintendent comes into a pre-existing socio-cultural complex with all its local values, beliefs, prejudices, and ground rules of what "to do" and "not to do." He must adjust to, and become a part of, a social system he did not help create. He is compelled by the pressures around him to organize his thoughts and activities in accordance with the demands made upon him by the people who wield the power in the community.

The superintendent's first responsibility is to the Board that hired him, and to which he must answer for his actions, as well as the actions of his teachers, and the pupils in the school system. He acts as liaison between the principals, teachers, and pupils, on the one hand, and, on the other, the Board and the schools' patrons. The superintendent is subject to many types of demands from the community as they relate to him as a person, the school system, and the Board, and from students and teachers. He knows that what teachers do in the classroom and community, especially what they are alleged to do, reflects on his standing with the Board. He is hired to keep the school system functioning smoothly, and his success depends upon the avoidance of criticism, rather than upon how well he educates the students.

The principals of the elementary schools and the high school are immediately subordinate to the superintendent. The elementary principal has jurisdiction over the four grammar schools and their 22 teachers. The high school principal is in charge of the high school and its 15 teachers.

The Board followed different employment policies in the two parts of the system. "Outsiders" were procured for all administrative positions and for positions in the high school; local girls were hired in the elementary schools whenever they were available. About three-fourths of the elementary teachers had been born, reared, and educated in the community. After high school they had gone away to teachers' colleges or universities for their professional training, then appointed back into the system. These women generally came from lower-middle-class families, with a few from upper-middle status; none was from the other classes. Local girls usually followed one of two paths: they either taught a few years, then married and raised a family, or stayed on year after year to become "maiden ladies." The local teachers lived with their parents, if they were living, or in the family home. Turnover in this group was in marked contrast to the outside teachers who left the system as soon as possible.

Salaries ranged from the superintendent's high of $3,500 to a low of $917 for beginning elementary teachers. (All salary figures are for 1941-42.) The principals' salaries were well above those for the teachers in the two divisions of the system. The high school principal received $2,415. The salaries of his teachers ranged from $1,300 to $2,050 with a mean of $1,525. The most frequent salary was $1,300. This figure was the "going" wage for "new" teachers. Some of these "new" teachers had had ten years' experience and held Master's degrees, but the majority were inexperienced college graduates who came to Jonesville for "seasoning" before they moved on to "better" positions. The agricultural teacher received $2,050 for twelve months' work plus his car. Actually he was paid less than the $1,300 teacher who was on a nine months' appointment, without the need of a car. The elementary principal's salary was $1,575. His teachers were paid from a low of $917 to a high of $1,391, with a mean of $1,000. The $1,391 teachers were local "girls"; all had been in the system for 15 or more years and two for 23 and 25 years, respectively.

"Outside" teachers from the superintendent to the least experienced girls, teaching on temporary limited licenses, expressed their desire to go elsewhere. One teacher stated,

"The low salaries they pay around here keep teachers moving in and out of the system. With the low salaries they pay, they cannot get anything but inexperienced teachers. Just as soon as they get a little experience, they are going to start looking for another job. The teachers here are always looking for better jobs. You can't blame them. The system is overcrowded, the facilities are poor, and we don't have the equipment we need. Besides, the community expects a lot from the teachers and does not give them anything in return."

This condition of frustration over low salaries and inadequate facilities, which grew out of the long-range policies followed by the Board, was summarized by the superintendent:

"There is insufficient money to build a new school, there is insufficient money to provide adequate facilities now and to pay livable salaries, and the result is a high rate of teacher turnover."

His words were punctuated by the hectic experiences he had in the two years he had been in the system. Eight of the high school teachers were new in the fall of 1941; five had been hired the week school started to replace teachers who had resigned at the last minute to accept positions elsewhere. Three teachers had been in the school a year or less; four from two to three years; one over four years. The principal had been there four years, but he was desperate to leave. (He did resign at the end of the year under pressure from the Board and the superintendent.) One-half of the teachers with experience in the community were married men with families. They desired to leave, but their family obligations made them hesitate even though they received salaries that were lower than the average semi-skilled mill worker.

"Trouble" in the School

Two superintendents administered the school system between 1925 and 1946. The first served for 14 years without seriously questioning policies or motives of the Board. In the spring of 1939, he was fired summarily after a year of quarreling among Board members, teachers, pupils, and parents. This fight developed out of the employment of a new high school principal in 1937. At that time, the man who had served as principal for six years resigned to go to law school. He left the profession because, as he said, "I saw no future in the Jonesville school system, or in school teaching for that matter."

The new principal performed his duties effectively, efficiently, and with a purpose the first year. He and his wife entered the Methodist Church (the superintendent went to the Federated), sang in the choir, and worked with the young people. He was invited into Rotary Club and his wife joined the Woman's Club. He assiduously cultivated the right people, did the right things, and said the correct word in the proper places. It was alleged he saw that the children of the Board members and other people who might do him some good received high grades. Shortly after his appointment was made for the second year, the next phase of his campaign to become superintendent was opened. He began, it was said, to hint to Board members how the school system was being "mismanaged." Petty things the superintendent did were related in a surreptitious manner. Failures in administrative detail were gloated over. Weaknesses in the school system were attributed to the policies of the superintendent.

When school opened in the fall, the high school principal carefully watched the superintendent, the principal of the grade schools, and certain teachers to see if they did anything he could use against them to further his ambitions. A few high school teachers worked with him in his scheme to have the superintendent fired so he could take over the job. One teacher was secretly promised the principalship when he became superintendent. This teacher's functions kept him in the Central School most of the day where he could observe the elementary school principal. By the middle of the year, the school system was in turmoil. The Board of Education was split between the principal and the superintendent. The teachers did not know where they stood, what to do, or whom to trust. The pupils knew of the fight and took sides. Wild stories of drinking, misuse of athletic funds, loose morals, and men teachers "laying hands on" girl students ran rife in the town. The basketball coach was alleged to have thrown a game with Diamond City to win a private bet. The Board threatened to fire the coach and the students went out on strike. The principal accused the superintendent, and was accused in turn of fomenting trouble. Clearly something had to be done—the Board acted with dispatch. It fired the superintendent, the elementary school principal, and nine teachers, but retained the high school principal.

The oldest teacher in point of service in the system characterized the Board's action as a "wild firing spree." The school fight, as this experienced teacher saw it, arose basically from the policies followed by the Board of Education over a long period. The Board had maintained a "weak character as superintendent who did exactly as the president of the Board desired. They paid him a poor salary and the teachers correspondingly lower. From year to year, things went from bad to worse with no one making an effort to correct the situation."

A new superintendent, elementary principal, and a new group of teachers were hired. But the Board did not change its policies. It proceeded on the assumption its actions were above reproach and that the trouble in the schools was traceable to the personalities involved rather than to a more basic set of conditions. The new superintendent moved slowly the first year. By quiet investigation he tried to trace gossip, rumor, and innuendo to their source. He made every effort to placate the teachers and place the system on a plane where it would be above reproach locally. He directed his energies toward building up *esprit de corps* among the teachers and generally raising morale. In spite of his efforts, one-third of the outside teachers resigned at the end of the year. The second year he reorganized the school records, put in a counseling service, and established student government in the high school. It was generally agreed he accomplished his objectives in a laudable manner, but the financial situation was no better than it was before.

A crisis was reached in the spring of 1941 when the North Central Association of Schools and Colleges removed Jonesville High School from its accredited list, and the State University threatened to do the same unless the Board of Education altered its policies and started some positive action toward the improvement of the high school plant, raised salaries, lowered teacher turnover, and made a number of other necessary changes. This action was the culmination of twenty years of criticism by the State Superintendent of Public Instruction, educational examiners from the State University, and the North Central Association. The Superintendent of Schools stated:

"This situation has been building up for a long time. In the summer of 1921, the University examiners told the Board of Education it had to raise more funds to operate the high school, and either the building had to be enlarged or a new one built, because the building was overcrowded to the point where it was dangerous. There were then 216 students and we have 426 enrolled now. Through the years the State University, the State Superintendent, and the North Central Association have written letter after letter to the president of the Board and to the different superintendents warning them the town had to do something about the high school or it would be cut off the certification list. As I have looked over these letters, I have seen they were getting tougher year by year. The situation has come to a head now and unless the Board of Education and the community do something, the University will drop us from the accredited list, too."

The action of the North Central Association hurt the community's pride, but it did not affect the state's financial assistance to the high school. If the State University disaccredited the high school, the school would be ineligible to claim state aid funds, which amounted to more than $8,000 a year, almost one-eighth of the high school budget. It was this possible loss that worried the Board of Education and served as a goad to action. Another practical consideration to some parents and many students was the fact that if the school were disaccredited by the State, its graduates would have to take entrance examinations before they could enter any college or university.

The North Central Association had adequate justification for the removal of the high school from its accredited list on the basis of the building's condition, without taking other factors into consideration. The building had been built in the late 1890's on one-fourth block in the marginal zone between the business and residential sections. The original brick building was two stories high, with a basement half below and half above ground. Furnace, toilet, cloak, recreation, and store rooms were in the basement; the superintendent's and principal's offices and two classrooms on the first floor; and the second floor was divided into three rooms. A wide central wooden stairway connected two halls about four feet wide, that led to the classrooms. Two flights of cement steps provided entrance and exit, one in front, and the other, on a side street. There was no direct entrance or exit at the sidewalk level to the basement.

This building had been adequate for the 75 to 80 students in the late 1890's and early 1900's; but by 1912 it was already inadequate. Four years of agitation for a new high school followed, but the power of the conservative forces kept the solution to a compromise.

The high school had become so overcrowded in the late 1930's that the Board of Education had adapted part of the Central School to high school uses. This building, located two-and-one-half blocks away on one-half block of land, was the only modern structure in the school system. It had been built in the early 1920's after a terrific struggle between the "better families" and the "laboring class" over the elementary school, a struggle which was resolved by building an adequate structure for the elementary grades and ignoring the high school needs which were even then pressing for attention.

The physical conditions at the high school were known generally in the community, but no one was interested enough to attempt to do anything. Although parents were urged to visit the school by the superintendent and the principal, they ignored the invitation. The principal reported that in the four years he had been connected with the school, only one parent had come to the high school, looked the building over, visited classes, and saw what was going on. A few other parents came to the high school at the express invitation of the superintendent or principal for conferences when their children had been involved in some delinquency which the school authorities desired to bring to their attention directly, but they came only to the front office and usually after school.

WHO GOES TO HIGH SCHOOL

"Learning things from books and life" in a friendly atmosphere was the ideal stressed in Jonesville High. Perhaps this preoccupation with friendliness on the part of the superintendent, principal, and teachers was related to the lack of friendliness in the student body, the schisms between class and religious groups, the club members and the nonmembers, the "rich kids" and the "poor kids," the "Americans" and the "Poles." Perhaps the students were learning about the business of life from their teachers and fellow students a little too realistically.

During the school year, 1941-42, there were 735 adolescents of high school age in the community who might have been in high school if they had all conformed to legal requirements or the ideal that the society should provide its members with a high school education at public expense. In the course of the year, 437 were enrolled in the high school at one time or another. The peak enrollment was reached early in September when 423 pupils crowded into the little rooms and narrow halls. By early June, through drop-outs, withdrawals, and transfers, which overbalanced the children enrolled from new families, the number had dwindled to 390, or 53 percent of the potential high school population.

Who was in school and who was out of school? Was there any relationship between age or place of residence and enrollment? What are the conditions under which some students persist in school and others withdraw?

It is a common belief in Jonesville that country children quit school oftener than town youngsters, but the facts refute this belief. Almost 75 percent of the 735 adolescents of high school age live in town and 25 percent in the country. The 390 who finished high school in 1941-42 were in almost the same proportion as the total: 75.9 percent lived in Jonesville and 24.1 percent in the rural area.

A second local myth is built around compulsory attendance. It is believed the authorities "make the children go to school" until they are sixteen years of age. Seventy-four percent of the 345 adolescents out of school in the spring of 1942 had withdrawn from school before they were sixteen years of age.

The people of Jonesville, both within and outside the school system, are unaware of the number or the proportion of young people of high school age who are not in school. The superintendent knew there were "some"; the president of the Board stated, "Certainly, there are a few youngsters not in school, but you will find that in any town."

Analysis of the data showed a high correlation between class position and continuance in, or dropping out of, school. All the young people in the classes Above the Common Man Level were in school; over 9 out of 10 in the lower-middle class; 6 out of 10 in the upper-lower class; but only 1 out of 10 in the lower-lower class.

We must conclude that the class to which a child belongs is a significant factor in his relations to the high school.

Table 14

SOCIAL CLASS AND SCHOOL ATTENDANCE

| | In School | | Out of School | |
Social Class	No.	Percent	No.	Percent
U	4*	100.0	..	..
UM	31	100.0	..	..
LM	146	92.4	12	7.6
UL	183	58.7	129	41.3
LL	26	11.3	204	88.7
	390	53.1	345	46.9

* Hereafter, the 4 cases in the upper class are combined with the 31 in the upper-middle class.

We believe this is a two-way relationship. On the one hand, the class culture of the child provides him with certain beliefs and values about the high school and what it has to offer. On the other, the institutional values of the school, represented by the Board of Education, the professional administrators and teachers, as well as the students, develop differential attitudes toward persons in different positions in the social structure which act as attractive or repellant agents to keep the adolescent in, or to force him out of, school.

WHO TAKES WHAT

The high school curriculum is built around three courses: College Preparatory, General, and Commercial. The entire College Preparatory Course is designed to meet the requirements for entrance into the State University. The General Course requires six units—three years of English, one of United States history, one of mathematics, one of some kind of science—and 10 units of electives. The Commercial Course is divided into two sections, General-Commercial and Secretarial-Commercial. Students enrolled in the College Preparatory Courses are placed in different classes from those taking

General and Commercial subjects. College Preparatory English is different from the English given to other classes. The College Preparatory students are given traditional algebra and geometry, whereas the other students receive what is called "Practical Mathematics," composed largely of problems in arithmetic.

Teachers in the College Preparatory Course consider it to be of higher educational value than the General or Commercial Courses. Those who teach both College Preparatory students and General students believe there is more ability in the former. They prefer to teach College Preparatory students because they are "more interested" and "do better work." These contentions may be true, but a more probable reason is that teaching the College Preparatory group satisfies the urge to teach the children who reflect the same academic values as one's own. Most teachers regard students in the General Courses as persons who do not have anything better to do with their time, mediocre in ability, and lacking motivation and interest in their subjects. Students in the Commercial Courses are rated even lower in ability than those in the General Course.

The students reflect attitudes held by the teachers in their evaluation of the three courses. Those who take the College Preparatory Course believe themselves to be on a higher intellectual level than the General students; the Commercial students, as we would expect, are placed on the bottom rung of the value ladder. A 1941 graduate, and a leader in her class, summarized the views of the students:

"If you take a College Preparatory Course, you're better than those who take a General Course. Those who take a General Course are neither here nor there. If you take a Commercial Course, you just don't rate. It's a funny thing, those who take College Preparatory set themselves up as better than the other kids. Those that take the College Preparatory Course run the place. I remember when I was a freshman, mother wanted me to take Home Economics, but I didn't want to. I knew I couldn't rate. You could take typing and shorthand and still rate, but if you took a straight Commercial Course, you couldn't rate. You see, you're rated by the teachers according to the course you take. They rate you in the first six weeks. The teachers type you in a small school and you're made in classes before you get there. College Preparatory kids get good grades and the others take what's left. The teachers get together and talk and if you are not in College Preparatory, you haven't got a chance."

Enrollment in the three courses is associated significantly with class: The adolescents from Above the Common Man Level concentrate in the College Preparatory Course (64.3 percent) and ignore the Commercial Course. The lower-middles are divided unequally: 51.4 percent are in the General, 27.4 percent in the College Preparatory, and 21.2 percent in the Commercial. The upper-lower children enter the General (58.5 percent) and Commercial (32.8 percent) Courses and avoid the College Preparatory (only 8.7 percent). The pattern for the lower-lowers is similar to the upper-lowers, but the number is too small to allow generalization.

The class bias in the different courses is particularly clear among the girls. For instance, 71 percent of the girls from the top class are in the College Preparatory Course, none in the Secretarial Division of the Commercial Course, and only one in the General Commercial Course. Girls from the upper-lower are concentrated in the Commercial Course with the greatest number in the Secretarial Division. Sixty-two percent of the girls in the Secretarial Division are from the upper-lower class and 38 percent from lower-middle. Most girls trained in the Secretarial Division find jobs in local offices as secretaries and clerks. The high school provides these girls with a specialized terminal education.

GRADES AND GRADING

The semester grades each student received were averaged, and the arithmetic mean used as an index of school performance. Individual mean grades were then tabulated on a three division scale: 85–100, 70–84, and 50–69. Distribution of grades by class is shown in the following table:

Table 15

GRADE DISTRIBUTION IN PERCENTS

Social Class	85-100	70-84	50-69
U + UM	51.4	48.6	..
LM	33.5	65.2	1.3
UL	18.4	69.1	12.4
LL	8.3	66.7	25.0
Total	23.8	66.3	9.9

Two points are clear here: (1) the grade distribution varies significantly from one class to another, and (2) the better grades go to the higher classes and the poorer grades to the lower classes.

Behind these figures lies the intricate pattern of human relationships, motives, and desires as they function in the class system. The struggle of the family to maintain a favorable prestige position is connected with the grades a child receives since grades are accepted in the culture as a symbol of intellectual worth. High grades are tantamount to quality and low grades to inferiority. Only a few may achieve high grades in a grading system where the teacher is constrained by the requirements of the normal curve to limit high grades to seven percent of a class. There are few boys and girls from the top classes, just as there are few high grades; there are more students from the lower than upper-middle class, likewise, more grades in a lower category; and so on down to the bottom where most of the boys and girls have dropped out of school. There are few students from these "poorer families," but what is more natural, the society being what it is, than that these students should receive the poor grades.

In the local social system offices, prestige positions, committee memberships, and exercise of power are accepted as the rightful due of the two higher classes. Teachers soon learn who is who and what must be done to satisfy the requirements of proper public relations in their associations with these people and their children. In the same informal way, they hear about families whose reputations are symbolic of all that is considered evil in the communal value system. They are told the children of these people "have to be watched," or, "you cannot expect anything from that tribe." Teachers experienced in the system warn the newcomers about this and that boy or girl, "their parents are touchy," "John comes from one of the best families here," "her mother expects her to make all A's," "all of Veronica's sisters have turned out to be prostitutes," "Jeannie's father was electrocuted a few years ago for murdering a prominent farmer; she's mean like he was." Narratives, gossip, a hint here, and a warning there give the teacher a feel of the situation. Remarks in teachers' meetings such as "we can't do anything there," said in relation to an upper-class boy caught copying an algebra problem on an examination, or "don't send her to detention [an upper-middle-class girl]—if you do our whole discipline program will be discussed in Board meeting"—in these none too subtle ways teachers learn to act judiciously in their relations with the children of the powerful.

It was believed widely in the lower classes and, to a somewhat less extent, in the lower-middle that the grades a high school student received were determined by who his parents were rather than by his ability or effort. This had some foundation, as one would expect in a belief that has persisted over a number of years and is documented by one story after another. In the stories, each case was personalized around the relations between the teacher, principal, superintendent, and the adolescent or his family. If the stories could be believed in their entirety, the honors in the graduating classes, from both the elementary and high schools, were deliberately given to the prominent families' children. It was charged that grades were changed, teachers threatened with dismissal, and examinations rigged. Several families in the top classes were alleged to have brought pressure on the superintendent or principal, through the Board of Education, to have grades changed after graduation so the child could enter college. We doubt that the process was as deliberate as we have been led to believe by some parents, but it undoubtedly happened in a few cases.

There is little question that the stories were rooted in fact, for the teachers did cater to the prominent families. The one teacher who had been in the high school for more than four years was highly regarded by the parents from the higher classes but hated and distrusted by many in the Common Man Level who were convinced she graded "with one eye on the social register and the other on her own advantage." An old lady who was often referred to as "the most powerful person in Jonesville" once told us, with reference to this teacher, that the town "is very fortunate to be able to keep 'Miss X.' She is such a wonderful teacher. She teaches every child in a different way; she knows each one's background and treats it accordingly."

EXTRA-CURRICULAR ACTIVITIES

An elaborate extra-curricular program brings the school's activities before the public on a broader front than its teaching functions. This, the circus side of school, entertains both student and adults in their leisure time. These entertainment activities are emphasized by the Board, the superintendent, the principal, teachers, and students. They want their athletic teams to win games, musical organizations to perform publicly at all possible times in a creditable manner, and the dramatics group to produce plays no one will criticize, but all will enjoy.

Extra-curricular activities that do not have spectator appeal or broad public relations value receive little emphasis. Girls' athletics, student government, school clubs, and dances are tolerated, but not encouraged. These minor programs are approved, and the administration "goes along" with the teachers and students interested in them, but they receive little support from the Board or the community. Clubs are fostered by the teachers in their departments and developed under their interest and leadership rather than through student interest. Any teacher can organize a departmental club if she is interested enough to take the time or trouble. For instance, the French teacher has a French Club; the domestic science teacher, the Homemaking Club; one English teacher developed a Library Club; and the agriculture teacher started a chapter of the Future Farmers of America for the boys in his classes.

Twenty-three extra-curricular activities ranging from organized athletics to the school paper are actively supported by the student body. They tend to be severely sex-graded, but some, such as the Dramatics Club, are composed of both boys and girls. It is possible for a boy to belong to eleven different organizations and a girl to twelve. In spite of the large number of activities and the wide range of interests they represent, one student out of three does not participate. Participation or nonparticipation is associated very strongly with class position as the following table shows:

Table 16

SOCIAL CLASS AND PARTICIPATION IN SCHOOL

Social Class	Participation	Nonparticipation
U + UM	100.0	. . .
LM	75.3	24.7
UL	57.4	42.6
LL	27.0	73.0
Total	65.9	34.1

Adolescents from the higher classes are found in far more activities than those from the lower classes, and the girls are in more than the boys.

Table 17

Social Class	Boys	Girls
U + UM	1.8	3.9
LM	1.1	2.0
UL	.8	1.0
LL	.6	.1
Total	1.0	1.4

In the two middle classes, the girls are in twice as many activities as the boys, but the difference is negligible in upper-lower, and in the lowest class the boys are more strongly represented than the girls. Eighteen girls are in six activities and seven in seven activities. Nine are upper-middle, six lower-middle, and three upper-lower. Since there are only fourteen girls in the upper-middle class, it is easy to see these girls enter as many activities as possible and give the impression to the other girls "they are in everything" as they, indeed, tend to be. The few hyperactive lower-middle-class girls represent only 11 percent of the girls in this class; moreover, they tend to be scattered in more activities so their presence in an activity is not so conspicuous. The three upper-lower girls in either six or seven activities represent less than four percent of the girls in the class; therefore, the roles they play are really different from the average girl in the class below. Boys do not allow themselves to become involved in as many activities as the girls. No boy participates in more than four, and only two are in this many—one, upper-middle, the other, upper-lower. Nevertheless, the upper-middle boys are in almost twice as many activities on the average as the lower-middle-class boys.

Participation in all extra-curricular activities except boys' athletics is biased in favor of some classes and against others. Boys' athletics is the one area where no association between class position and participation appears. The boys from the several classes turn out for all athletic teams in the approximate proportion represented by each class in the student body.

The invisible lines between the classes channelize the activities of an increasing proportion of the boys and girls out of extra-curricular activities as one moves through successive strata toward the bottom class, where the adolescents who are still in school are left out of the things that would give them vital training in getting along with persons in the other classes. As it is, each social class goes its way without paying too much attention to what is happening, simply as a result of the general indifference that characterizes the society.

Chapter 13

PARTY POLITICS: UNEQUAL CONTEST

A LOPSIDED TWO-PARTY SYSTEM

In Jonesville, as in other towns in America, the excitement and drama of government center in elections. And elections, generally speaking, involve political parties—either in primaries, where party standard-bearers are chosen, or in general elections, where one party is pitted against another. The men who devised the basic constitutional framework for the nation were anxious to prevent the formation of parties. However, parties soon came to play an important role in government, and today the American party system is recognized as an integral part of the foundations of our democratic institutions.*

The importance of parties in this country is reflected in the increasing degree to which they have been subjected to formal-legal rules, the usual reliance for safeguarding decision-making in government. The adoption of ballot reforms and the direct primary greatly increased the scope of formal-legal regulations, but even today the activities of parties are only partly under legal control.

To understand the way a political party functions in a given locality, it is necessary to go beyond a study of its formal organization. For the national scene, this task has been well accomplished by several books published in recent years. For the larger cities, the task has also been competently done, especially in studies of the political machine—beginning with a few scholarly studies, leaping into national prominence with the investigations of the Muckrakers, and developing more recently into systematic studies of

---

* By Joseph Rosenstein. See List of Authors.

party leadership and organization.[1] For towns the size of Jonesville, especially in the Middle West, there are no well-known studies showing how the political parties actually operate.

Jonesville, and the county in which it is located, are strongholds of the Republican party. For more than fifty years, no Democratic candidate for the presidency of the United States has carried Abraham County, with the single exception of Franklin D. Roosevelt, who won by a narrow margin in 1932. In the twentieth century, no Democrat has held county-wide office; even in 1932, when the Democrats were most successful, the Republican candidates for county office were elected by a comfortable majority. Politicians in Jonesville who attempt an explanation of this striking predominance of the Republican party almost invariably begin with a discussion of certain events in the early 1890's. A prominent Republican, now growing old, made the following observation about the party strife which preceded the present period of Republican domination:

"The government made a grant for the Illinois-Michigan canal. It was built about the time of the Irish immigration in 1840. The result was towns sprang up along it, Jonesville, Seneca, Marseilles, Ottawa, Utica, LaSalle, and so forth, and great numbers of Irish laborers came in and worked with wheel barrows and shovels. These towns along the canal filled up with Irish. From the Civil War till '95, the Irish played a big part in the politics of Jonesville. Those were the days of the 'Three Toms'—Tom Cronin the mayor, Tom Hunds a hunchback with a keen brain, and Tom Owens the backroom boss who ran things in the city council. In '93 and '94 a fight started. The American Protective Association (known as the 'A. P. A.') was really anti-Catholic and really against the Irish leadership of the Democratic party."

It was in this period that a newspaper man named Bailey came to Jonesville, and for nearly thirty years he played a prominent (later dominant) part in the politics of the county. An old-time politician says that he came to town "literally with patches on his trousers," as a representative of the American Protective Association. He took over one of the local newspapers, reputedly with the

[1] Outstanding volumes in this connection are M. Ostrogorski, *Democracy and the Organization of Political Parties* (New York: The Macmillan Co., 1922); Lincoln Steffens, *The Autobiography of Lincoln Steffens* (New York: Harcourt, Brace & Co., 1931); H. F. Gosnell, *Machine Politics: Chicago Model* (Chicago: University of Chicago Press, 1937).

backing of some leading landholders and businessmen. By rough-and-tumble politics, capitalizing on the religious issue and on his "connections" at the state capital, Bailey brought himself and the Republican party to a dominant position in the county. Shortly after the turn of the century, he became the "boss" of a highly organized county machine. His machine, a local informant says, "was looked upon by state leaders in the Republican party as the most efficient and powerful in the state."

Bailey, of course, was not singly and personally responsible for consolidating the local position of the Republican party. In the state and the nation, the period which followed his initial successes was one of general triumph for the party. Moreover, a continuing influx of Norwegians, who became staunch Republicans, also added to the party's local strength. Nevertheless, Bailey deserves the spotlight. Not only was he able to capitalize successfully on religious and ethnic rivalries in establishing the Republican party as "top dog"; he was equally skillful in mollifying and even absorbing opposition once the Republican party was dominant.

One incident will be reported in detail, partly as illustration and partly because the individual concerned later played a very prominent part in the politics of the county. The time was 1912. The man concerned was a young, highly ambitious lawyer named Ralph Bowman. Irish and Catholic, he was nevertheless a Republican. At that time, some of the "big" families in the county who had originally backed Bailey were engaged in a bitter factional fight with him. With the quiet, valuable backing of these wealthy families, but using the slogans and ideology of Teddy Roosevelt and La Follette, Bowman waged an active campaign for nomination as Republican candidate for States Attorney. The prestige of having "won" a sensational murder case as a special prosecutor helped him in the campaign. Looking back, he described the outcome:

"I was 26 or 27 then, and despite my lack of years was out to break the Bailey machine. I tied up La Follette's reforms with my speeches and went all over making speeches and creating a lot of public attention. That election was the hottest one ever held in the county. I was surprised someone wasn't shot. It turned out I was nominated and later elected States Attorney."

After Bowman was elected, Bailey proceeded to make peace with him, and Bowman became one of the prominent figures in Abraham County Republican circles. More than any other single incident, Bailey's political friendship with Bowman signalized the end of his political warfare with the Catholic Church. From that time on, the Republican party has been "open" to ambitious Catholic politicians, and Catholic voters have come into the party in large numbers.

In Jonesville, it was—and is—considered much "safer," from the standpoint of social and economic considerations, to vote Republican. There are at least three families in town, of high social prominence, who came into the community as Democrats but who have since become Republican. A leading Democrat epitomized the situation:

"People around here are scared to admit they're Democrats. Tim Rainey who was president of the bank came here from Tennessee. For awhile he didn't vote in the primaries. Then he started asking for a Republican ballot. I guess he figured it was good for the bank. I hate to think of what his ancestors down in Tennessee would think if they knew he was voting Republican."

Social and economic pressure is not confined to people in the upper part of the social scale. The same Democrat was discussing the workers in The Mill:

"Well, there are at least 500 voters out at The Mill and a good percentage of them live in the third precinct. If the vote shifts very much, you can pretty much bet that it's those mill workers changing and the men at The Mill know that. But it's not all based on fear. Suppose a man out there has a sick wife and wants to send her to the hospital. Our hospitals around here have a rule that they won't take any patients unless they can be assured of financial responsibility. This man will go to Phelps (a minor executive) and Phelps will say 'Go on ahead—take her to the hospital. I'll fix it up.' . . . They do a lot of things like that out there. Then at the time of the election, the worker will get called into the office and Phelps will say, 'I have a friend of mine here on the ballot—very good friend of mine—and I'd like to have you vote for him.' You'll notice that the man on the ballot is always on the Republican and not on the Democratic ballot."

In plants with strong, independent unions, such a situation might not be typical, but unions in Jonesville are not particularly militant.

In order to analyze the social characteristics of the voters who at present make up the mass base of the Republican party in Jonesville, a careful study was made of voting behavior since 1942.[2] Since that year, there have been five major elections—two primaries and three general elections. For the primaries, it is possible to determine which party a given voter prefers, because he must ask for a party ballot; for the general elections, it is impossible, of course, to determine from the official records which party an individual favors. For purposes of analysis, it is assumed that individuals who voted Republican in both primaries and who were active enough to vote in all three general elections are faithful partisans of the Republican party: voting behavior of individuals in this category—they will be called "solid Republican voters" in the following discussion—is analyzed in Table 18. In this table, the percentages of "solid Republican voters" in each of the five classes are taken as an index of the relative "Republican-ness" of the classes. The percentages, generally speaking, decrease as one goes down in the class scale, with by far the sharpest drop occurring in the lower-lower class. With the exception of that class, the percentages are all surprisingly high, in view of the fact that some of the elections did not include contests of great public interest. The contrast with the participation in the Democratic party is striking. Table 19 analyzes the class position of individuals who voted Democratic in either or both of the primary elections, regardless of whether they voted in general elections. Even with this much more liberal criterion, the Democrats in all classes made a very poor showing as compared with the Republicans.

Data on voting in the same five elections have been analyzed to determine whether religious and ethnic differences in party affiliations exist. An interesting contrast is that between members of the Catholic and of the Lutheran churches. Using the same criterion

2 The year 1942 was selected because that was when the present system of voting registration went into effect. The material presented in the following paragraphs is based on a person-by-person analysis of the official voting records. For data on the class characteristics and religious affiliations of these same individuals, the analyst was dependent on materials previously gathered in the course of the Jonesville research. The results of the analysis which are presented here are based on early tabulations and represent only about 80 percent of the full potential electorate. Specifically, the individuals considered in the statistical analysis are individuals who were twenty-one years or older in 1942, who registered for sugar ration coupons in Jonesville in May 1942, and for whom information on class position is currently available. The "class" of an individual is based on his I.S.C., as discussed elsewhere in this volume. Certain individuals are given a "derived" I.S.C. based on the I.S.C. of a member of the same family living at the same address.

as in Table 18, Table 20 shows that in all of the five classes[3] the percentage of solid Republican voters is much greater among Lutherans than among Catholics. Table 21 shows the percentage of

Table 18

PERCENTAGES OF "SOLID REPUBLICAN VOTERS" IN THE FIVE CLASSES

Class	Number of Individuals	Number of "Solid Republican Voters"	Percentage of Individuals who are "Solid Republican Voters"
Upper	108	30	28
Upper-middle	409	98	24
Lower-middle	1035	261	25
Upper-lower	1343	225	17
Lower-lower	415	28	7
Total	3310	642	19

Table 19

PERCENTAGES OF DEMOCRATIC VOTERS IN THE FIVE CLASSES

Class	Number of Individuals	Number of Democratic Voters	Percentage of Individuals who are Democratic Voters
Upper	108	2	1.9
Upper-middle	409	9	2.2
Upper and upper-middle combined*	517	11	2.1
Lower-middle	1035	20	1.9
Upper-lower	1343	35	2.6
Lower-lower	415	9	2.2
Total	3310	75	2.3

* Combination made because of small number in upper class.

Catholics in each class who are Democrats; for purposes of comparison, percentages of the class as a whole are presented from Table 19, since the same criterion is employed. In the entire group of Lutherans, there were only two Democrats, a number too small for a class breakdown so percentages are not presented. From

3 Except in the upper, where there are no Lutherans, and in the lower-lower, where the number of Lutherans is too small to give the percentage significance.

Table 20

PERCENTAGES OF "SOLID REPUBLICAN VOTERS" AMONG CATHOLIC AND LUTHERAN CHURCH MEMBERS IN THE FIVE CLASSES

Class	No. Catholics	No. Lutherans*	No. Catholics Who are "Solid Republican Voters"	No. Lutherans Who are "Solid Republican Voters"	% Catholics Who are "Solid Republican Voters"	% Lutherans Who are "Solid Republican Voters"
Upper	9	None	1	None	11	None
Upper-middle	53	27	6	5	11	18
Upper and Upper-middle Combined†	62	27	7	5	11	18
Lower-middle	159	93	26	30	16	32
Upper-lower	279	138	32	38	11	28
Lower-lower	44	13	4	1	9	8
Upper-lower and Lower-lower Combined†	323	151	36	39	11	26
Total	544	271	69	74	13	27

* This category includes wives of Lutheran members when wives have no other church affiliation.
† Combination made because of small numbers in certain categories.

Table 21, it is evident that, despite social and economic pressures, Catholics of all classes continue to vote in Democratic primaries in greater percentages than their non-Catholic counterparts.

The statistics which have been presented fail, of necessity, to take account of what might be called the "secret" Democratic vote. The pressures to "vote Republican" are such that voters with Democratic sympathies are extremely reluctant to vote Democratic in

Table 21

PERCENTAGES OF DEMOCRATIC VOTERS AMONG CATHOLIC CHURCH MEMBERS
IN THE FIVE CLASSES

Class	Number Catholics	Number of Democrats among Catholic Voters	Percentage of Democrats among Catholic Voters	Percentage of Democrats in Class as whole
Upper	9	2	22	1.9
Upper-middle	53	9	17	2.2
Upper and Upper-middle combined*	62	11	18	1.9
Lower-middle	159	11	7	2.2
Upper-lower	279	20	7	2.2
Lower-lower	44	1	2.3	2.1
Upper-lower and Lower-lower combined*	323	21	7	2.5
Total	544	43	8	2.3

* Combination made because of small numbers.

primaries, where they must publicly declare their party allegiance. But in the secrecy of the polling booth at a general election, the number of Democratic ballots cast is invariably larger than at the primaries. Even in a general election, however, the Democratic party generally makes a poor showing. The cumulative effect of Republican victories is considerable not only for the voters but also for those who plan to make a career of politics. For example, a young lawyer, who came from a family of Democrats and was politically ambitious, became active in the Republican party. Eloquently and succinctly, his words help explain his choice of party: "In this town, the saying is that Jesus Christ himself couldn't get elected if he ran on the Democratic ticket."

The long-continued local dominance of one major party over the other should be assessed in terms of the two-party system which characterizes the nation as a whole. In recent years, some political scientists have stressed the debt which democracy in America owes to our brand of the two-party system, contrasting it favorably with the multi-party system of some European countries and the monolithic one-party system of others. Paradoxically the local, even the sectional, dominance of one party or another is quite consistent with the operation of the two-party system in the country as a whole. Indeed, such local dominance may make a positive contribution to the preservation of the two-party system. During the long years of Republican domination, the Solid South did much to preserve the Democratic party as a major party. Similarly, during the more recent years of Democratic success, it was communities like Jonesville which kept the opposition party in readiness to attempt a comeback. In such perspective, the unequal contest between parties in towns like Jonesville is not fundamentally hostile to the American two-party system.

The internal organization and the operation of the two parties are generally the same throughout the country, varying correspondingly with the size and type of the town, the general area, dominance of the party, and other factors. In order to see the operation of a political party in Jonesville, we have to study the Republican since the Democratic party has been out of power for so many years that its organization is undernourished and its function incomplete.

THE REPUBLICAN PARTY: THE WHEEL HORSES

Family traditions and habits of the voters are not sufficient alone to account for the consistent success of the Republican party at the polls in Jonesville and Abraham County. The part played by a successful "boss" in consolidating the position of the Republican party in the county has already been mentioned; his successors among the local "big shots" in the party will be discussed later. Between the voters and the influential men behind the scenes there are a considerable number of party workers—the wheel horses—who devote time and effort to ensuring continued victory to the Republican party. Briefly, the party workers consist of precinct committeemen, "pay-rollers," and miscellaneous hangers-on. These categories are, of course, far from being mutually exclusive: some of the most active precinct committeemen are state pay-rollers, and some party workers who at present would be classified as mere hangers-on are past or prospective pay-rollers or precinct committeemen who have fallen from grace. These people have in common a strong interest: "getting out the vote" and ensuring, or hoping to ensure, that the objects of their attention vote "right." They also rely on the same technique—face-to-face contact with the people who vote.

In Jonesville, there are six precinct committeemen. They are close to the voters in several respects. First, they are directly elected by the voters. Moreover, at the time of an election—the most important time for any party—they are the lieutenants (or corporals) who operate directly on the scene, working to ensure a Republican vote as large and reliable as possible. They are close to the voters in another respect—class position. Five of the six precinct committeemen come from the upper-lower class, the largest class in Jonesville; the sixth is in the upper-middle class—appropriately enough, since he comes from what local politicians call the "silk-stocking precinct."

The literature on politics in large metropolitan centers has long recognized the importance of precinct committeemen.[4] There, the number of voters for city or county offices is so huge—running, perhaps into the millions—that candidates cannot expect to know personally a sizable proportion of the voters. Even the number of precincts is so large (in Chicago, over three thousand) that candidates would find it difficult to set up their own organizations in each precinct. Under such conditions, the "regular" party organizations find suitable conditions for their operation and depend upon the precinct committeemen as highly important cogs. The precinct committeeman in these metropolitan centers often serves as a kind of go-between for "his" people in their dealings with the highly complex governmental system of the metropolitan area. In communities like Jonesville, the candidates for city and county office do not find the party functionaries so indispensable, nor do the voters find the local government so complex or inaccessible without the help of their precinct committeemen. Hence, in Jonesville these party functionaries have a less critical role than their counterparts in a metropolis like Chicago or Philadelphia.

4 See, for example, Gosnell's volume on machine politics, previously cited, and J. T. Salter, *Boss Rule* (New York: McGraw-Hill Book Co., 1935).

Yet they are still active and perform essential duties. When an election is not imminent, their functions are less time-consuming and spectacular than those of precinct committeemen in Chicago: they are never called on to "fix" a traffic ticket, or arrange a tax adjustment. There are only a few far-sighted and efficient individuals who take their job as precinct committeemen seriously month in and month out: For example, one man made it a practice to devote at least one hour a day to the job, starting for work in the morning with an hour's margin to spare and varying his route from day to day to allow him to visit casually with most of his "constituents" in the course of a week. For most precinct committeemen, however, a few weeks prior to an election is the only time that political activities reach a high pitch. Nearly all of the Republican precinct committeemen make it a practice to conduct a house-to-house canvass in their precinct before an election; if a man does this personally in the evenings and does it conscientiously, it will take him about two weeks in the larger precincts.

Primary elections for county offices are supposed to be "open" in this community; that is, there are no "slates" presented for local offices. Therefore, the precinct committeemen are supposed to be "neutral" in the primary, confining their efforts to making sure that there is a large Republican turnout, without regard to the interests of particular candidates. One of the six Republican precinct committeemen in Jonesville was frank in expressing his divergence from the way a precinct committeeman is supposed to act. "I canvass before a primary," he said, "because there is generally one certain group that we want to get in there." The other precinct committeemen generally adhere closer to the expected course of action, although on occasion they may quietly help out a friend. For races involving state office, the code is less strict. At the time of the study, the committeemen were prepared to support state-wide candidates endorsed by the governor; even certain candidates for the state legislature had a recognized right to "use" precinct committeemen, if the latter were willing.

The electorate of the county is sufficiently small to permit candidates for county offices to make a direct personal canvass of a sizable proportion of the electorate. Indeed, within the last two years the incumbents in the offices of county clerk and county treasurer took full time to make a house-to-house canvass throughout the county six or seven weeks prior to the primary. The importance of precinct committeemen to candidates for local office is obviously small.

On primary election day, however, almost every candidate who is seriously contending for office will have "workers" out, many of them driving cars. It is on election day that the individuals previously mentioned as "hangers-on" take a conspicuous part in the electoral process. These "hangers-on" are available to candidates at rates which are fairly well standardized—fifteen dollars for driving a car, five or ten if not driving. At the time of the study, when there was relatively full employment, most election workers on primary day and general election day were women or old men. Most of them put in long hours and work hard. However, if the race is hot and the office lucrative, workers may be hired in such large numbers that many perform only nominal service. At the other extreme, there are party workers who are not at present precinct committeemen or state pay-rollers, but who have held office or hope to in the future, and therefore extend their electioneering efforts beyond mere service on election day.

For a general election, the hiring of party workers is more centralized than at a primary. A certain sum—sixty or seventy-five dollars for a large precinct—is allotted to each committeeman to hire workers. Only occasionally will a candidate hire his own workers, outside the party machinery, for a general election. The committeeman himself sometimes drives a car; more frequently, he will direct the other party workers in the precinct; frequently, he will keep a check on who has voted and send workers out to contact those who are still "missing."

The rewards of a precinct committeeman are not great. The sums made available to him at election time are seldom enough to pay the required number of workers and still compensate him for his time. He receives certain intangible rewards, some of which are important to people in modest circumstances—he may, for example, attend an inaugural on invitation from the governor he has helped to elect. At least one precinct committeeman finds his job a good substitute for joining a lodge that he cannot afford. The most tangible reward that a precinct committeeman can hope for is a job on the "pay roll"; and when his party is in power an efficient precinct committeeman can expect this sort of reward if he wants it. Three of the six Republican committeemen elected in 1946 later held state jobs.

At election time, a precinct committeeman can expect the support of a number of pay-rollers. Unlike paid party workers, they serve without cost. The number of such unpaid workers available at election time cannot be precisely estimated. In 1946 Abraham County had nearly 150 individuals on the state pay roll, of whom more than half came from Jonesville. However, in times of general prosperity, the state jobs with lower pay do not furnish much incentive for political work or attract ambitious individuals; hence, of the total named, only about a score were active and energetic in their political activities. Of course, pay-rollers can generally be relied on for their vote and the votes of their families. Taken together, the active and the passive support of the state pay-rollers is a factor of considerable political importance: to this fact, there is ample testimony, both from the difficulties encountered by the Republicans when they lacked state patronage and from the disorganization which befell the Democrats when they lost the patronage.

Many state jobs are ostensibly under civil service; however, appointment to all jobs of any consequence is controlled by the party organization. The precinct committeemen as a group elect a "county chairman," who in turn appoints a three-man patronage committee. Routine appointments to state jobs are "arranged" by the patronage committee. A leading local politician explained how the system worked in the days soon after the Republicans recaptured the leading state offices: "The signatures of all three members are necessary for a recommendation. After the three of us have made our decision we send in our papers, as in this case, to the state patronage committee. This procedure covers all the appointed jobs. Of course, the man we select may have to meet the requirements. They may have to pass the civil service test or something of the kind, so we have to be careful whom we recommend."

That is the way the patronage system works "on paper." However, in its actual operation the wishes and contacts of certain influential men in the community play a more important part than the foregoing quotation would indicate. Analysis of the informal processes of control and leadership in the party will take us farther behind the scenes of the Republican party.

THE REPUBLICAN PARTY: "BIG SHOTS"

The party wheel horses—the precinct committeemen, the hangers-on, the politically active pay-rollers—together with the candidates for local offices, are the men out front, talking politics with the voters, taking them to the polls, helping generally to maintain the local supremacy of the Republican party. But what goes on in the party behind the scenes? Is there a boss—or a small group of "big shots"—pulling strings to make the puppets dance? Forty years ago, the situation in Jonesville would have provided easy answers to these questions. In those days, Jonesville and Abraham County had a boss—old Dick Bailey. A backward look, sketching in the factional struggles down to the present day, will provide some understanding of control behind the scenes in the Republican party of Abraham County today.

During the period when Bailey was boss, he controlled not only the Republican precinct committeemen in the county but the Republican office-holders as well. It is often said of him that no election—even of a township treasurer or a school trustee—was too small for his attention. And he moved with equal ease among the larger concerns of the state capital, where he held important appointive positions and knew governors well.

Bailey was careful to keep on good terms with the leading politicians of the town. To the other politicians went offices and favors appropriate to their standing in the organization. Even potential politicians were not overlooked. Bowman describes his first morning in Jonesville, in the early years of the century: "I got off the train one morning about 10:30. By 10:45 one of Bailey's men was over to see me and to invite me to the Lincoln Club that night."

A politician's place in the county party system is related to his access to higher levels of party organization. This is one of the ways in which local politicians, who in the rural areas are in close contact with voters, are tied in with the party organization of the higher levels of government. Bailey's political interests were not confined to Abraham County. He came to Jonesville from the state capital, and he maintained his political interests there.

Bailey did not, of course, work alone. Through the Lincoln Club, "his" organization was in contact with large numbers of people interested in politics; by distribution of favors and offices among local politicians he placed many of them under personal obligation to him. The county party system in Bailey's time should not be visualized as one man "bossing" a mass. Rather, it consisted of one man in a dominant position working with and through other politicians with varying statuses and generally succeeding in the job of coordinating the cliques and economic interests involved.

Mr. Bowman ultimately succeeded Mr. Bailey. He is the man mentioned previously who, as a young lawyer, beat the Bailey machine in one of the hottest primaries the county has ever seen and who, in later years, made his peace with Bailey and became one of his closest associates. Shortly after Bailey's death, he maneuvered himself into election to an important position on the bench. The nature of this position is such that control of the local precinct committeemen is essential to continued election; for this reason, Bowman has maintained an active interest in controlling the precinct committeemen. However, his judicial position is not very favorable for a man who wants to play a lone hand as boss. As an experienced local man put it, "It's best for the boss who handles the patronage to be out of office." Bowman himself realizes that his private position, together with his age, limits his political activities. He is still consulted, however, on many important political decisions. Even the relatively low degree of political "organization" in the county may testify to his influence. Since his private position and advanced age keep him from certain political activities, he may want to make sure that no one else assumes too much power. This opinion was reflected in the comment of an ambitious politician: "There isn't any kind of political organization in this county at all. Bowman sees to it that it stays that way, too."

Another important man is Richard Bailey, the son of the old "boss." Unlike his father, he is more interested in money than in political power. A local politician said: "This Bailey has made a lot more money out of that paper than his father ever did, but he's not much of a politician because he isn't really much interested. You see, his father didn't really care so much about money. What he wanted was power. His son doesn't seem to care so much about power, but he's got the money."

Two quotations reveal the contrast between father and son. Of the dead "boss" an old associate said: "He was greedy for power. His face showed power. I'd look at it and think, 'By God, there's power there.'" Of the son, on the other hand, an officeholder remarked: "He's interested in power if he can get some money out of it."

Richard Bailey, the son, shows some interest in local politics. "He makes sure he gets the county printing bill," and is said to adapt local news stories to favor certain politicians and hinder others. Recently, he has "taken an interest" in a young man from Jonesville who was running for a high office in the state.

As publisher of the biggest newspaper in the county, Bailey has considerable standing. A veteran observer remarked: "He's important because he owns the newspaper here. Downstate it's customary for candidates for Congress to work through the newspaper editors if possible. That's true of an office-seeker in any large district."

Partly because of his father's reputation, partly because of his newspaper, partly because of his own activities, Bailey is still generally mentioned among those in the "control group" of the Republican party. However, enough has been said to indicate why he does not occupy the dominant position that his father did.

The man who has risen most rapidly in the past twenty years is Bill Stockton, an ambitious attorney. Unlike Bowman and Bailey, whose families' wealth was recently acquired, Bill Stockton comes from one of the wealthiest "old families" in the county. As a country squire, his father dabbled in politics, going along with the elder Bailey on local matters but disagreeing with him on state politics. The very election in which the local machine lost the governship was the one in which the elder Stockton backed the opposing candidate, thus bringing his family into a promising political position locally. Not long afterward, his son, Bill, was elected to an important county office. For a while, victory seemed somewhat hollow, since with the depression years the Republicans were replaced at the state capital by the Democrats. With the state patronage gone, the Republicans in Abraham County found it hard going. As the depression faded, the Republicans made a comeback in the state. Bill Stockton was on excellent terms with some friends of the new Republican governor; having consolidated his position locally during the depression, he found himself highly influential in the county Republican picture. This influence has persisted up to the present.

In a sense, all of the men who have been discussed were, or are, members of a group which "controls" the local Republican party behind the scenes. The extent and techniques of control have varied from time to time. The elder Bailey had well-developed methods for controlling both the party functionaries and the officeholders; the others have been either less ambitious or less successful. It is important to realize that "controlling" the party machinery of a county, especially a relatively small county like Abraham, involves being able to maintain two sets of relationships: one "outward" and one "local." The "outward" set of relationships are with the upper reaches of the party structure, particularly with the state "organization" but also with more powerful county organizations that may be in the same judicial or legislative districts. Without such relationships, patronage, favors, party workers, and campaign funds are hard to obtain. Parenthetically, the official channel for such relationships is not always the most important; though the chairman elected by the precinct committeemen of the county is supposed to handle these matters, in Abraham County he may do the legwork but is seldom mentioned as a "big shot"—instead, contests for the county chairmanship are generally discussed in terms of "who's behind" this candidate or that. The strength and importance of these outward connections vary with the individuals: the elder Bailey held an important appointive state office and was regarded as a leader of state-wide importance; his son has rather routine relationships with certain state candidates and a congressman because his newspaper is useful to them; Bowman has cultivated certain friendships that are useful to him in his political work; Bill Stockton has some friends at the state capital but lacks the close, high-grade connections that the elder Bailey enjoyed. The ability of an individual or clique to control the Republican party in Abraham County, or any similar county, will vary with the strength and quality of these "outward" relationships, extending outside the county.

The local set of relationships is also important. The two sets, separable analytically, have much in common. The same personal qualities and social skills that made the elder Bailey useful at the state capital served him well in dealing with the other local politicians in his own county. Another important common factor is the class position of the individuals involved: the ability to circulate socially in "important" circles at the state capital, the educational requirements of certain positions, practice in management and the exercise of initiative demand a middle-class social position as a sort of minimum if the outward connections are to be established and maintained. Correspondingly, on the local scene, the social skills and "connections" are most likely to be found in men of the upper-middle class or higher. As a matter of fact, all of the individuals mentioned as members of the behind-the-scenes "control" group are members of the upper or upper-middle class.

These class connections are of importance, too, in providing the sinews of war—campaign funds. Especially during the depression, some of the wealthy people in Jonesville contributed generously to the Republican party. These contributions, to be sure, reflect a recognition of economic interests; but the process of solicitation was made easier by the fact that the "treasurer" was an upper-class individual. It is worth noting that, of the six precinct committee-men in Jonesville, five are upper-lower class; the sixth, ranking in the upper-middle class, is treasurer of the committee at present. The class connections and the social skills of the lower-class individuals who serve as wheel horses simply do not qualify them for establishing successful relations either outside the county or with financially important groups within the county.

Not all financial contributions come from "respectable sources." In Abraham County, it is rumored that illegal businesses are heavily interested in politics. Some years ago, interest centered on a house of prostitution run by a colorful local character named Bertha Jennings who, for protection against the law, relied heavily on extravagantly generous charitable activities. Rumor also has it that the last raid on her place, years ago, was stopped cold when the man who requested the raid discovered that his partner was one of the regular patrons. At present, political interest and speculation center on gambling rather than bootlegging or prostitution; local people believe that the gamblers have placed their relations with "the law" on a financial basis less colorful but more efficient than Bertha Jennings. So far, the contributions from this source have not served to disturb the class relationships in politics which were previously discussed. Indeed, even if their stake and investment in politics should grow larger, the gambling interests would be anxious not to displace upper and upper-middle individuals, for the farther behind the scenes the gamblers operate the happier they are.

"DEMOCRATS ARE MADE, NOT BORN"

The Board of Supervisors in Abraham County is made up of men selected by township. In the southern part of the county, there are a few townships which vote Democratic consistently. An old newspaper, dating back more than fifty years, shows that this pattern of voting in these southern townships was established decades ago, probably at the time they were settled by a group of Irish immigrants. This same newspaper also shows that fifty years ago, before the advent of "Boss" Bailey, the Democrats were strong in Jonesville, too. Bailey was successful in driving the Democratic party in Jonesville into the ground, but he failed to make much headway with the southern townships. The result is that, even today, the Democrats have representation on the Board of Supervisors. At least two of them are very shrewd men—among the shrewdest on the Board. Capitalizing on the factional divisions among the Republicans and profiting from the efforts of the local Farm Bureau to work quietly for reforms in taxing procedure and highways, these Democrats have worked themselves into key positions on the Board. As long as they maintain their position and resist the temptation to play ball with the Republican organization, the Board of Supervisors is removed as a potential gear in the Republican "machine."

In the rural townships mentioned, the people are Democratic because of community and family traditions. In Jonesville, however, the number of families that traditionally vote Democratic is small, and even that number has been attenuated through the years because people believe it is socially or economically advantageous to show their allegiance to the Republican party. It is this situation that led one of the leading Democrats to observe, "In Jonesville, the Democrats we have aren't born to it; they have to be made."

Since the turn of the century, the biggest opportunity for "making" Democrats came during the depression of the thirties. During most of this period, the Democrats controlled the state, gaining influence through the expenditure of large sums of money for public works. One of the most active wheel horses in the Democratic party in Jonesville today looks back on his depression experiences and finds that, even twelve years later, he can rely on some of the votes "made" then. On election day, he explains, there are certain people that he always goes to:

"Mostly they are people that I helped out when they was on relief. You see, I was on the relief board, and people on relief wasn't all treated alike. You know that. There were some who got more and some who got less. Something else that I did that gives me an in with certain people is that I had the hiring on the big bridge across the river. Then I had a highway job for a while and I hired a lot of people for that. Hell, I was a big shot for a while. Particularly when I was handling the relief. I could do a lot of things for a lot of people, and naturally I did it in such a way that they would remember and in later years vote like I told 'em to."

Unfortunately for the Democrats, they found that most of the "relief" voters went back to the Republican party as soon as they got regular jobs again.

Another weapon held by the Democrats during the thirties was patronage, but it was not administered well because the party was small and beset by personal rivalries and factional difficulties. Before the depression, almost the only active Democrats were the country people. Prominent among them were the Democratic members of the Board of Supervisors. Competent in their own jobs and highly skilled at the bipartisan maneuvering on the Board, they were nevertheless "peanut politicians" when it came to a big job like changing a traditionally Republican county over into a Democratic one. One of the politicians from the southern part of the county was selected to handle the patronage; feeling that the job was too big for him, this man in turn selected Melvin Gray, a "professional" politician from the Republican ranks, to do the job. This "professional," who for several months had handled the local relief set-up, proclaimed himself a Democrat and was given full power to hire and fire. Gray entered the Democratic ranks at a time of heated contest among state candidates in the Democratic primary; this fact, added to his dubious party allegiance, created hard feelings within the Democratic party in Abraham County—feelings that have persisted even to this day.

This professional politician, who for years served as Democratic "boss" in the county, took the philosophy that "Democrats are made, not born" seriously. He used patronage to entice men into the Democratic party rather than to reward men who had been faithful Democrats for long years. His tactics were successful in that for a while he was able to get out a large Democratic vote in the primaries and the general elections. However, when the Republicans swept back into the state capital, the Democratic vote in the county, particularly in the primaries, quickly dwindled. If Democrats are to be made, it evidently takes plums of more enduring sweetness.

Today, Gray is an old man; even if the Democrats were to win the state again, he is getting too old to be very active. The most promising of the younger Democratic "big shots" is Jim Thorpe. He is a lawyer who came to Jonesville after Gray had established himself. For a while, he was on the other side of the fence, but in recent years the two men have cooperated closely. Unlike Gray, Thorpe comes from a "Democratic family" (he was born in the southern part of the county), but he agrees with Gray's tactics: If the Democrats have patronage again, he would use it to attract Republicans, not merely to reward faithful Democrats. Physically, Thorpe looks very much like a younger Herbert Hoover, but his politics are quite different: he likes to consider himself a liberal, reads the *New Republic,* and is a hearty admirer of Henry Wallace. He has been careful to establish good "outward" relations with some of the leading Democratic politicians in the state; as for his "local" relations, he has an enthusiastic following among most of the few Democrats in town and among many of the Democratic wheel horses in the county, but he is handicapped by long-standing feuds and factionalism among Democratic leaders.

This factionalism is so conspicuous that it calls for some comment. It appears to be related to the extreme weakness of the Democratic party on the local scene and the resulting dependence on "help" from the outside. Locally, the Democratic party is poor in resources—poor in terms of friends of the party who have money to contribute and poor in terms of voters with Democratic traditions. In order to produce votes at all, local leaders are highly dependent on outside help. When the Democrats hold major state offices, this help takes the form of patronage or of "favors" which can be converted locally into votes or campaign contributions. When the Democrats conduct an active state-wide campaign, help takes the form of campaign money which can be used to hire party workers. For help in all these forms, the "contact" men, of course, are the "big shots" in the local Democratic party; in jockeying for advantage among themselves, they have developed deep-seated rivalries and antipathies. Factional divisions in the state-wide party have accentuated the local rivalries.

The basic difficulty of the Democratic party, of course, is the formidable local position of its rival. Even during the depression years, when the local Republican party had no state offices to provide patronage or leverage, its leaders still had local offices and still had access to local people with money. This financial strength "at the top" is complemented by the skill with which the Republican party has cultivated the voters of all classes and religious groups over a period of years. Although that party originally consolidated its position in the county on the basis of religious strife, in later years the leaders of the party skillfully healed the breach once the position of the party was secure. Today, even though the Catholics in Jonesville are not as faithful adherents of the Republican party as members of certain other churches, large numbers of Catholics participate in the party as voters, and ambitious Catholic politicians find that the party is open to them. Among the various classes, too, the Republican party has been successful in establishing itself. The top positions of leadership go to men of the upper and upper-middle classes—men who have the social skills and contacts to establish the proper "outward" relations in the party and to maintain the local relationships demanded of leaders in the party. But, as the statistical materials show, staunch friends of the Republican party are found in all classes. People farther down in the class system vote Republican, not only because of family tradition and social and economic pressures in the community, but also because their participation is actively solicited by the "wheel horses" of the party—men who generally come from the lower classes, in close social contact with the mass of the voters. The efficient activities of these wheel horses can be traced partly to their own zeal for the party, but that zeal is reinforced by more tangible rewards—jobs and campaign money which, in turn, it is the function of the local "big shots" to ensure.

After surviving the depression years with so few scars on the local scene, the Republican party seems likely to remain predominant in the town for some years to come.

Chapter 14

TOWN AND COUNTRY:
THE STRUCTURE OF RURAL LIFE

The main highways out of Jonesville lead the automobile traveler directly into open Middle Western country. The first impression is of great flat expanses of cornfields interspersed with fields of oats and soy beans. About every half-mile along the highway one passes a farm house flanked by a prosperous-looking barn, crib, chicken houses, and hog sheds. A car, and usually a truck, are parked in the yard. A few dairy cattle graze quietly in a nearby pasture. Power and telephone lines lead into the farmstead. The farm wife may be hanging out the family wash or working in a garden near the house, while her husband cultivates the corn with a tractor in one of the fields. The total impression as the traveler drives along at fifty miles per hour is one of great uniformity almost to the point of boredom.*

But if the traveler slows to thirty miles per hour, he will begin to notice differences in the size of the farms, in the size and condition of the houses and barns, and in the names on the mail boxes. At one point a farm will extend for a mile along the highway, the house will be a large three-story brick structure in excellent condition, and the name on the mail box will be "Scott." A little farther along, another farm will extend only a quarter of a mile, the house will be an unpainted frame structure, and the name will be "Rasmussen." The first casual impression of uniformity will give way to one of diversity in both types of farms and types of people. If the

* By Evon Z. Vogt, Jr. See List of Authors.

traveler should happen to be a social anthropologist or sociologist interested in the ways that human beings organize themselves for social living, he should stop his car and spend several months living with, and talking to, these farm families. If he did this, he would find that the rural Jonesville people are participating in a complex and highly organized social system which provides them with prescribed ways of operating their farms, living together with their neighbors, and adjusting themselves to the town and to the outside world.

The region which we describe as Rural Jonesville covers the eight townships immediately surrounding the town and supports an agricultural population of approximately 4,000. The farm families in this area travel by automobile to Jonesville for most of their shopping, marketing, and recreation. When a farmer living in one of these townships says that he is "going into town," he means Jonesville.

Rural Jonesville is an open country type of farming community.[1] Each farm family lives on the farm it operates. Many of the rural administrative facilities are separately located in the town of Jonesville, but each township is a political unit with its own "town house" where the people go to vote and to hold occasional town meetings. The Farm Bureau and the school system also function on a township basis. The result is that the farm families are conscious of belonging to a particular township unit as well as to the larger Jonesville area.

The average size of the farms in Rural Jonesville is 200 acres. Approximately 60 percent of the land is tenant-operated and 40 percent, owner-operated. The present land-use pattern can be described as 75 percent cash grain, with crops of corn, oats, and soy beans, and 25 percent dairying, with the land planted in legume hay crops.

The township upon which we focused our study of Rural Jonesville lies immediately to the north of Jonesville in the area of Norwegian settlement. This township, with its 36 sections of farming land, supports a population of 700. For purposes of intensive interviewing and analysis of rural social relationships we used a sample of 49 contiguous farms in the center of the township. This research area contains 10,000 acres of land and a population of 60

[1] Zimmerman calls this a "pure isolated farm" type of rural community. See Carle C. Zimmerman, *The Changing Community* (New York: Harper and Bros., 1938).

farm families (207 individuals)—30 Norwegian, 26 Yankee (Old American), 2 German, 1 Swedish, and 1 English. The average size of the farm is 203 acres; 55.5 percent of the land is operated by tenants and 44.5 percent by owners. This area is typical of Rural Jonesville in size of farms and percentage of tenancy. It is also typical in having more than one type of farming population, but the types vary with different townships: Norwegian to the north and west, Irish to the south and east, etc.

"A LAND OF MILK AND HONEY"

North Township is in the heart of the American Corn Belt—one of the richest agricultural areas of the world. As one of the local ministers in Jonesville aptly pointed out: "This is really the land of milk and honey." The land is currently producing an average of 55 bushels of corn to the acre and selling at $250 an acre. In 1944 a survey of the area showed that the average farm of 200 acres had annual net earnings of almost $3,000.

Since the beginnings of settlement in Abraham County there have been no basic changes in crops or marketing, but there have been tremendous changes in the techniques for working the land. Corn has always been the principal crop, and Chicago has always been the market place for the Jonesville area. Oats was added to the economy as an important crop between 1880 and 1900. The third principal crop at the present time, soy beans, was introduced recently by the Farm Bureau and the Agricultural Adjustment Administration in the interests of soil conservation.

The agricultural techniques have undergone revolutionary changes with the application of machinery to the working of the land. The first automobiles were introduced about 1910 and came into general use in the years following World War I. The first tractors came into the community about the same time and were in general use by the 1920's. Today only one farmer in North Township uses horses to work his farm. Corn pickers began to replace hand picking in the early 1920's and are now used on 90 percent of the farms. Combines came in during the 1930's and are already used on over 60 percent of the farms.

The result of this mechanization has been a great decrease in the amount of farm labor required. This was well expressed in an interview with an old Yankee landowner: "Forty years ago one man could take care of only forty acres of corn. That was his job. Now a sixteen-year-old boy with farm machinery can take care of three or four times that much." The increased mechanization is also reflected in the tendency for an increase in the size of the farms. There are no figures for that period before 1880. But subsequent to that time the average size of the farm in the county has increased from 140 to 200 acres. Our analysis of the historical trends in Abraham County clearly shows that, as the farm population per township has become smaller, the cities have grown larger and have absorbed the rural surplus.

The high degree of mechanization enables most farm operators to get along without hired men. Farms of average size and smaller are worked by the farm operators with only the part-time help of their sub-adult sons and of their neighbors during periods of heavy operations such as harvesting.

The system of tenancy (under which almost 60 percent of the farms are now operated) usually operates as follows: the owner provides the land, the house, and the farm buildings; the tenant provides his own farm machinery, buys the seed, pays six to ten dollars an acre cash-rent for the pasture and hayland, and runs his livestock on the farm. Owner and tenant then split fifty-fifty on the cash-grain crops at the end of each growing season. There are a few cases in Abraham County where the owners give the tenants written leases of from one to five years. The most common arrangement, however, is a simple verbal agreement between the owner and the tenant which is renewed each year until one of the two parties desires a change. The data from North Township indicate a high degree of stability in this area. The average time for tenants remaining on the same farms is 11.4 years.

"There Are Two Classes in This Community—Yankees and Norwegians"

When Homer Johannsen made this statement about North Township, he was verbalizing the fact that his community was settled by two distinct streams of population and that the difference in social behavior between the two types is strong enough to constitute a basic social cleavage in this rural area. Almost every family in the community considers itself a member of either the "Yankee" or the "Norwegian" group. Intensive interviewing disclosed that the definition of these terms has both an historical and a behavioral reference. The members of the community define "Norwegians" as people (1) who were born in Norway, or whose ancestors were born in Norway; (2) who have retained a substantial portion of their original Norwegian culture; and (3) who are participating members of the Norwegian Lutheran Church. The "Yankees" are defined as "Old Yankee families" who came to Abraham County from the East in the early or middle nineteenth century. Some of these families trace their ancestry ultimately back to England, Wales, or Scotland. Others stem from early Pennsylvania Dutch or German settlements. Families who came directly from England or Wales within the last three generations are considered as "sort-of Yankees" by the rest of the community; in both behavior and attitudes they identify themselves with the Yankee group and are considered Yankees in this study.

The major cultural differences which tend to set the groups apart at the present time are language and a set of values associated with church participation. The linguistic difference manifests itself in terms of the first- and second-generation Norwegians who still prefer to speak Norse and in terms of the third and fourth generations who use certain expressions such as, "Would you like to go with?" instead of "Would you like to go with me?" or "I know you back" instead of "I recognize you," which are heard every day on the farms in North Township. Associated with the language difference are the names of the families. It is possible to take a roster of all the farmers in the township and predict with a high degree of accuracy, on the basis of names alone, whether a given family is Norwegian or Yankee. The Norwegians are "Rasmussens," "Peersons," "Rygs," "Knutsons," etc.; the Yankees are "Lynns," "Cates," "Scotts," "Joneses," etc. The members of the community are highly aware of these names as a means of determining the ethnic group of a particular family.

The interview material shows not only that the community is socially segmented along Yankee-Norwegian lines but also that the Old Yankees consider themselves superior to the Norwegians. This subordination of the Norwegians derives basically from the fact that the Yankees arrived first and were well established as farmowners with a well-organized rural social organization before the Norwegian immigration began. The oldest Yankee families first settled in the area in the early 1830's, and all Old Yankees arrived before 1870. Most of these early Yankee settlers were from families of some economic resources, and they all reached Abraham County with enough cash to buy land from the government at $1.25 an acre. The result was that the land was all taken up before the Norwegians began their settlement of this area. The Norwegian settlement of Abraham County was in the nature of an "invasion" of Yankee territory from the historic colony of Stavanger about 25 miles northwest of Jonesville. This "invasion" began about 1850, reached significant proportions in the 1870's, and continued to increase until 1920 when approximately 65 percent of the people in North Township were Norse. Since that time the number of Norwegians has remained about the same with the excess population leaving the farms for industrial jobs in nearby cities.

The Norwegians who came into the Yankee settlements of Abraham County possessed a "foreign" culture and few, if any, economic resources. They were, therefore, forced to start at the bottom of the agricultural and social ladder. The evidence indicates that the Yankee subordination of the Norwegians was very great when the Norse first came. As the Norwegians modified their way of life to be more in accord with the Yankees, as they climbed the agricultural ladder, and as the Yankee group was added to by later arrivals, the pattern changed. At the present time the "Old Yankees" still consider themselves separate from, but not categorically superior to, the Norwegian families.

"THE YANKEES OWN MOST OF THE LAND, BUT THE NORWEGIANS DO MOST OF THE WORK"

One of the most important determinants of the social position of an individual or family in a rural community is relationship to the land. In North Township a man is an owner, a tenant, or a hired hand; the place he occupies in the agricultural ladder is one of the factors in determining the amount of prestige that he enjoys in the community. An analysis of the pattern of land ownership and land operation in North Township clearly establishes the Yankees as the dominant landowning group and the Norwegians as the largest farm-working (tenants and hired hands) group. Of the 10,000 acres in the research area, the Yankees own 7,100 acres but operate only 4,000 acres, whereas the Norwegians own only 2,400 acres of land but operate 5,800 acres.

This pattern of dominant Yankee land ownership is a powerful factor in their subordination of the Norwegian group. For not only are the Yankees in possession of greater economic resources, but they are also in a landlord position over the Norwegian tenants and hired hands on the agricultural ladder.

In order to see what the dynamics of land ownership have been in North Township in the one hundred years since the land was first settled, we made a complete study of the land transfers which have been recorded in the county courthouse since the 1830's. The land was all held by the Yankees until the 1860's when the Norwegians began to buy land. The land ownership changes since 1860 tell a dramatic story. From the time the Norwegians began to acquire land in 1860 there was an increase in Norwegian ownership until 1920, with a marked increase in the 1870's. Norwegian ownership remained about the same during the decade of 1920 to 1930, but in the depression years of the early 1930's the Norwegians lost almost half their land.

In the 1860's almost all of the land was owned by rural Yankees. Between 1860 and 1900 the rural Yankee ownership was reduced by the amount that the Norwegians acquired. By 1910 a new group of owners had entered the picture—the urban Yankees, industrial managerial families in Jonesville who began to buy land as an investment for their surplus earnings and as a status symbol. Interview material from Jonesville clearly indicates that many of these rising industrial families were at first strongly subordinated by the old landed families in the community. By buying farms and acquiring the symbols of a "country gentleman" the industrial families succeeded in reaching the top of the class system in Jonesville. This pattern of the "country gentleman" with a "country estate" was carried over to America from England in the early days of the settlement of the Atlantic Seaboard. From there the pattern spread through the South and—in a somewhat attenuated form—to the American Middle West and to the Southwest where "Easterners" are buying ranches for country homes.

The great increase in urban Yankee ownership between 1910 and 1920 was due to two factors: (1) the urban industrial families acquired more farms, and (2) several of the rural Yankee families prospered on the high agricultural prices during World War I, moved into town on a retired status, and rented their land to tenants. This trend continued until 1930. During the depression of the 1930's the land lost by the Norwegians passed into the hands of upper- and upper-middle-class urban Yankee families.

The significant and sudden shift in land ownership during the

1930's had important effects on the rural community. The control of most of the land in North Township has shifted from independent farmers living on the land to absentee landlords who live in town and have only a "paper" relationship to the land. Whereas the first generation of rural Yankees who retired to the town retained a personal interest in the land and the problems of the tenants, the succeeding generations of the original farmers and the industrial families who acquire farms are less interested in the operation of the land except as a source of income and as a status symbol.

The changing pattern of land ownership also reflects the historical picture of the Norwegian "invasion" of this area. The Norse were successfully replacing Yankees in the ownership of the land until the great depression when the Norwegians lost out to absentee Yankees. The result has been a recent increase in the subordination of the Norwegian to the Yankee landlords of Jonesville.

THE YANKEE CLASS SYSTEM

From the problems of the relationship of the Yankee and Norwegian groups to each other and of both groups to the land, we shifted our attention to an analysis of the social structure within each group and found a number of significant differences. The Yankee group recognizes, and appears to organize most of its behavior around, a set of social-status distinctions which form an emerging social-class system in rural Jonesville. In the Norwegian group, on the other hand, the Lutheran Church is the structure around which the people organize most of their social behavior. Since this difference constitutes one of the keys to the understanding of human relationships in the rural area, we shall deal with it in some detail.

An analysis of the interview material from North Township reveals that most of the informants did not verbalize directly and openly about social-status differences. Only fifteen of the informants made direct references to social classes,[2] but twenty-nine made oblique or indirect references to people in inferior or superior social

2 The direct references to social class were predominantly from farm women who seem to be either much more aware of, or more likely to verbalize, social distinctions than the farm men. This difference may be due to the fact that farm men are brought into face-to-face relations with neighbors more frequently by the agricultural system (exchange work, farm meetings, etc.) than are farm women. The women gather more in meetings of various clubs in which it is possible to include "desirable" women and to exclude "undesirable" women.

positions. This distinction between direct and indirect references to social-class positions can be illustrated by the following excerpts from interviews.

George Washington Oliver has been a tenant on one of the Radcliffe ("Old Yankee") farms for the past twenty-seven years. His father was a Welsh coal miner who raised a large family in a nearby mining town. George started his working career as a miner, then turned to farm labor, and finally saved enough money to buy farm machinery and become a tenant.

The Olivers would like to own their own farm, but in twenty-seven years have not been able to accumulate the necessary capital to do so. When Mrs. Oliver was interviewed in her farm home, we obtained the following comments:

INTERVIEWER: "Who do you usually neighbor with, Mrs. Oliver—the McFaddens [an "Old Yankee" family related to the Radcliffes] who live across the road?"

MRS. OLIVER: "Oh, no. *Not* the McFaddens—they are old landowners. Of course, they are friendly, but they come from an old landowning family, and they are *above* us renters. We talk to them and all that, but we don't get too friendly with them, or press ourselves on them at all. We visit more with the Fishers [a tenant family who lives down the road]."

In this interview Mrs. Oliver was making a direct reference to the fact that renters rank below landowners in the social-class system.

Mrs. Ellis Reid is a member of one of the oldest Yankee families in the county. Her husband owns one of the finest farms in the area. The Reids have recently begun to sever their rural connections and have become interested in high-status "card clubs" and "Country Club" activities in Jonesville. In an interview with the Johannsens—a middle-class acculturated Norwegian family—the following comments were made about Mrs. Reid:

INTERVIEWER: "Is Mrs. Reid a member of the Rural Home Club?"

MRS. JOHANNSEN: "She used to belong, but she doesn't anymore."

MR. JOHANNSEN: "What's the matter, doesn't she *like* the people?" Here Mr. Johannsen was indirectly referring to the fact that the Reids have become "ritzy" and no longer choose to associate with their rural neighbors.

The reluctance to verbalize directly about social classes is a common phenomenon in our culture, especially in the rural areas where supposedly "people are all the same." James West, in his report on Plainville, makes the following statement:

The class system of Plainville might well be called a "super-organization," because it provides for every person living there a master pattern for arranging according to relative rank every other individual, and every family, clique, lodge, club, church, and other organization and association in Plainville society. . . . Yet, many, if not most, Plainvillers completely deny the existence of class in the community. . . . About Plainville and most of Woodland County they often say with some pride, "This is *one* place where ever'body is equal. You don't find no classes here."[3]

On the basis of the references to status distinctions occurring in the interviews and a detailed analysis of social participation over a period of five months, four social levels became discernible in the Yankee group in North Township. The top-ranking families in the area are called "squire farmers" or "gentlemen farmers." A middle group of families are labeled "old landowners" or "old settlers." Low-status families are thought of as "dirt farmers," "tenant farmers," or "renters." At the bottom of the hierarchy is a group of "lower-lower" people who are too few in number to have been given a name by the members of the community. They are the "shiftless" and nonrespectable members of the society—in a word, the Tobacco Road of North Township.

"SQUIRE FARMERS"

The "squire farmers" are landowning members of the "Old Yankee" families who have reputations as outstanding farmers and who have acquired a great deal of high-status urban culture patterns as compared to the other families in the township. These families live in large, modern farm homes which are comparable to the finest homes in Jonesville. The yards are landscaped with lawns, hedges, flower beds, and trees and are meticulously kept. There is never a stray piece of farm machinery or pile of old lumber in evidence.

The "squires" have outstanding reputations as expert farmers. Most of them are engaged in the development and production of hybrid seed corn which they sell to other farm operators. This hybrid seed corn business gives them a key role in the agricultural system as well as county-wide recognition, which is formally expressed by the

---

3 James West, *Plainville, U. S. A.* (New York; Columbia University Press, 1945), p. 115.

business group of Jonesville who have invited these farmers to become members of the Rotary Club (a predominantly upper-middle-class association). The actual labor involved in the agricultural operations is generally not done by the "squires" themselves. They either employ hired hands to do the work, or turn their farms over to tenants and act as supervisors.

The social participation of these families is almost entirely urban. The "squire farmer" families in North Township are all core members of upper- and upper-middle-class cliques in Jonesville. This participation brings them into frequent contact with the high-status families—both the retired landowning group and the industrial managerial families. At the present time, there is a great deal of social interaction between the town and the country at this class level. The "squire farmers" who still live in the country meet the upper classes of Jonesville at the Country Club, Rotary Club, Federated Church, Woman's Club, Hospital Aid, Daughters of the American Revolution, and in bridge playing cliques. On the other hand, the upper classes of Jonesville own—or have recently acquired —farms in the county as one means of achieving their high-status position. Evidence clearly indicates that the original upper class in Abraham County (including Jonesville) were the "Old Yankee" landowning families whose roots go back to the pioneering days of the 1830's and 1840's. With the rise of industrialism in Jonesville the managerial families rapidly acquired more wealth than the old landowners. But inasmuch as these rising industrial families were living in what was originally and essentially an agricultural community, they were subordinated socially by the old landowning group. In this context the motivation to buy farms on the part of the industrial families can be understood. Only after they had acquired the proper status symbols by buying land were they accepted by the original "aristocracy." At the present time the industrial families are becoming superordinate to the old landowning group and are "setting the pace" for the upper class in Jonesville.

The emerging structure in Abraham County is one in which the retired Yankee landowners and the high-status industrial families in Jonesville, on the one hand, and the still rural "squire farmers," on the other, are all becoming members of a county-wide upper-status group. The rural "squire farmers" are adapting themselves to the emerging social scene by acquiring the urban status symbols which enable them to participate in the Jonesville "society crowd." The other rural families consider them to be "ritzy."

With the exception of two Norwegian families who have sent their children to the state university, the "squire farmers" are the only families in North Township who send their children to college. In the 1946 graduation class of the Jonesville High School only one senior—the daughter of a squire farmer—from the township was planning to go to college.

The class position of these families is also expressed in certain aspects of their everyday behavior. Even while working, the "squires" never wear the traditional bib overalls, but wear khaki or corduroy pants and khaki shirts. They were never observed going to town in work clothes but "dressed up" in business suits. The families make frequent trips to Chicago, and they are interested in art and music.

The characteristics of this rural "upper class" were neatly summarized in an interview with the minister of the Federated Church: "You can call them gentlemen farmers. Where else would you find a farmer with the time to take art lessons like Michael Landers? Ellis Reid, he likes music and is artistic. They are also Rotarians. They are quite proud of their urban contacts and the friends they have in town. But in their thinking, I believe next would come their neighbors in the country of the same old landed group. They are proud of their friends in town, but they are also proud of their place in the country."

"Old Landowners"

The "old landowner" families are members of the same Old Yankee group as the "squire farmers." The basic difference between the two classes is to be found in the comparative lack of high-status urban culture patterns on the part of the "old landowner" group, whose social participation is still largely rural. They are active members of rural associations such as the Rural Home Club and the Home Bureau, and they have extensive visiting and clique relationships with their neighbors in the country. Their contacts in Jonesville are principally in the Daughters of the American Revolution and the Methodist Church (predominantly lower-middle).

The members of this class live is somewhat smaller houses than those occupied by the "squire farmers." The basic difference in house type, however, between the two classes is in interior decoration. The houses of the "old landowners" lack the "sophisticated" interior decoration of the "squire" homes. For example, instead of pastel colored walls, long sweeping drapes, and thick, plain-colored carpets, these homes are decorated with elaborate flower-designed wallpaper, short lace-trimmed curtains, and "old-fashioned" carpets. The front yards are usually landscaped, but less attention is paid to the upkeep of the yards and farm buildings.

In everyday dress and behavior this class shows some interesting variations from the "squire" group. The men do not generally wear bib overalls for working clothes, but like the "squires" they wear khakis or sometimes coveralls. They often appear in town during the week in their work clothes, but on Saturday nights they "dress up" in suits and spend two to three hours standing on the corners of the business district of Jonesville visiting with other farm families. Neither the men nor the women in this group participate in social drinking, nor do the women smoke.

There is a marked difference in the use of the English language between the "squire farmer" and "old landowner" class. In the latter group the "incorrect" use of the verb forms is common. For example, they say "he don't" instead of "he doesn't," "I come," instead of "I came," and "they run" instead of "they ran."

The symbols used by this group to subordinate the "dirt farmers" are centered around their status claims as "landowners" and as "Old Yankee families." (The label "old landowners" explicitly states this theme of "land" and "old family.") They have been landowners for at least three, often four, generations in North Township. Intermarriage among the Old Yankee families has been very extensive in the past and is continuing at the present time. The result is that these families are tied together by a complex of kinship relationships. To quote again from one of the Jonesville ministers (who always seem to know as much, or more, about the social life of a community as anyone else):

"You know, I have never been in a community where there were so many marriages within the community and so many relatives. I went to see three or four different people yesterday and found much to my amazement that they are all related. . . . There are the old families like the Radcliffes, the Blakes, and the McFaddens. They are all farm people. All intermarried. I guess it's because it's so easy to make a living here, and they have all stayed on through the years. Out of this has grown a feeling of aristocracy . . . the women especially of the old families are all associated with each other. They don't include anyone else. They're self-sufficient within their own area."

"DIRT FARMERS"

The "dirt farmers" are members of the more recently arrived group of Yankees—the "sort-of Yankees." They are all tenant farmers and hired hands with the exception of a few families who own very small farms, recently acquired.

The types of houses occupied by this class vary considerably in size and condition. The majority are small frame houses without indoor plumbing. The condition depends, to a great extent, upon whether or not the landlord furnishes material for repairs and adds modern improvements. Many of the yards have been landscaped, but little care is taken in keeping them up.

The formal participation of this group in either rural or urban associations is slight. Except for membership in Jonesville churches, only one man in this class is a member of a Jonesville association (the Independent Order of Odd Fellows—predominantly upper-lower). A few of the women belong to the Rural Home Club and the Home Bureau, but most of the families are members of no associations except the Farm Bureau.

At this social level in Rural Jonesville the traditional bib overalls are used as the standard work clothes and are usually worn to town. It is only on Saturday night and on Sunday for church that this class "dresses up" for a trip into Jonesville. Like the "old land-owner" class there is no social drinking or smoking on the part of the women. The language used by this group shows one interesting variation from the "old landowner" speech. In addition to the in-correct verb forms, this class also generally uses the word "ain't" to express negation.

"LOWER-LOWER"

At the bottom of the social-class hierarchy in rural Jonesville is a small group of people who constitute a rural "lower-lower" class. Most of them are not stable members of the community, but drift from farm to farm and in and out of the area. They are considered by the other members of the community to be "shiftless," "dirty," "immoral." Some of them are employed as hired hands by the farm operators, others cut wood for a living, some eke out an existence by part-time jobs in the country or in Jonesville and by government relief.

The members of this class come from southern "hillbilly" groups, who have drifted north from the mountains of Kentucky and Tennessee, or from old Abraham County families who have become disorganized and almost déclassé. We discovered that these rural people are connected by blood, in some cases, and by social participation, in nearly all cases, to the lower-lower residents of Towpath in the town of Jonesville. When one of these families moves into Jonesville, it always enters the urban class system at the lowest level.

Inasmuch as these people are economically and socially peripheral members of the rural community, they are always forced to occupy old ramshackle houses which the higher-class families have long since left vacant. "The farmhouse was old, badly in need of paint, several windows were stuffed with rags, and the screen door to the porch was full of holes."

The members of this class have "immoral" social reputations, do not believe in sending their children to school, and are frequently "in trouble with the law." A middle-class rural school teacher described the "lower-lowers" as follows:

"They are people who go into the woods to cut timber and don't believe in school. They keep their kids out of school. Like the Jim Porter family. He comes from an old pioneer family in this county, but he married a hillbilly woman. She's young and immoral. She's a drunkard, always goes to taverns in town, and doesn't take care of her family. I've had to help the family all this last year. I've gone to the social agency to get help for them and even taken them milk and clothes myself."

In North Township, Bob Sibley is another example of this rural "lower-lower." Sibley now works a farm belonging to a retired Norwegian landowner and lives alone in a four-room shack which had been deserted for many years before he moved in. He was arrested in Jonesville last spring for "window-peeping," and neighboring families continually gossip about his "entertaining women" in his house.

SOCIAL MOBILITY

Upward and downward mobility in the Yankee class system of North Township takes different forms at different class levels. Upward mobility from the "old landowner" to the "squire farmer"

class requires that a family withdraw from extensive rural participation and establish social connection with high-status people in
Jonesville. With this shift in participation an individual or family
must also acquire certain urban behavior patterns to enable them
to "behave properly" and "feel at home" in high-class social functions in town. They must learn how to participate in social drinking, to play a good game of bridge, to wear "fashionable" clothes,
to entertain large groups of people in their homes, to speak "correct" English, to talk about "art and music," to be interested in
sending their children to college and getting them into the "proper"
fraternities and sororities. This movement into the "squire farmer"
class also requires that a farmer become outstanding in his agricultural activity. This is necessary not only to give the family a
secure economic base so that it will have the leisure time to participate in urban social life,[4] but also to give the family county-wide
recognition.

The movement from the "dirt farmer" to the "old landowner"
class is a more difficult hurdle in the status hierarchy. Inasmuch as
the two classes are differentiated from each other chiefly on the
basis of land ownership and "Old Yankee" lineage, an individual
or family who succeeds in making the transition must buy a farm
and must establish kinship connections with the "Old Yankees."
Both of these goals are difficult to achieve. As pointed out above,
most of the land in the area is now in the hands of urban absentee
owners who are holding on to their farms. It is significant that
the interviews which show the most hostility toward the social-class
hierarchy are those with the wives of "dirt farmers" who are finding
it impossible to acquire land and thereby fulfill their ambitions of
upward mobility. The following interview is typical:

"This farm belongs to James Radcliffe. He owns a whole section
here. You know, we are really just hired men, and I think they
want to keep us that way. We want to buy a little piece of land
like the Stewart Fishers did over there. They got that farm from
an insurance company during the depression, but you just try
to buy a piece now. I think they just want us to be tenants. None
of them farm now themselves. They all li\ in town, and we are
just hired men. It's really a feudal system, and it's getting worse
all the time."

To acquire the family lineage necessary to being considered "old

---

[4] A farmer who customarily gets up at five o'clock in the morning to start his
work has neither the time nor the energy to participate in these social activities.

landowners" is an even more difficult process. There is one case in North Township of a man, originally a member of the more recently arrived Yankee group, who succeeded in climbing into the "old landowner" class by buying a farm and marrying one of the daughters of an "Old Yankee" family. The more frequent pattern of upward mobility at this level is to buy a farm and attempt to compensate for the lack of lineage by intense associational activity. Families who follow this pattern succeed in participating with the "old landowners" in formal associations such as the Rural Home Club and the Home Bureau, but the data indicate that they are still subordinated by the "Old Yankees." They are never fully accepted in the sense of being invited in for meals or other intimate social activities which symbolize relationships of equality.

There are no cases in the township of downward mobility from the "squire farmer" to the "old landowner" class. The evidence suggests that the "squire farmer" class emerged as a separate group within the past fifteen to twenty years. This fact appears in the interview material which contains statements to the effect that the fathers and mothers of the "squire farmers" were "good country people." It also appears in the data on club membership. A few years ago the "squire farmers" were active members of rural clubs such as the Rural Home Club and the Home Bureau. Now they have severed their connections with these rural organizations and "don't mix with country people" any longer. If this is the case, a pattern of downward mobility has probably not had time to develop at this level.

There are, however, cases of downward mobility from the "old landowner" to the "dirt farmer" level. The basic factors involved in this process appear to be: (1) "unfortunate" marriages, i.e., members of the families did not marry into other respected "Old Yankee" families and thereby tended to sever their contacts with their own class; and (2) bad farming practices which have resulted in heavy mortgages threatening the loss of their landowning position.

"A Man's Value Is Governed by His Activity in the Church"

As we turn our attention from the Yankees to the Norwegians in North Township, we shift from a group which is dominated by a system of social classes to a group where the church is the very core of the social life. The structure and ideology of the Lutheran Church have already been treated in full. In this chapter we are concerned with the place of the church in the lives of the rural Norwegian families.

The basic function of the Norwegian Lutheran Church is in its role as symbol and repository of both the sacred religious values and the ethnic cultural values of the group. The church with its auxiliaries (the Brotherhood for men, Ladies Aid for women, Lutheran Daughters of the Reformation for young women, etc.) provides a closed system of relations within which individual Norwegians can find satisfaction for almost all of their religious and social needs. This means that all members of the group, whether they are landowners, tenants, or hired hands, are brought together on an equal basis within the framework of the church. They not only appear in church on Sunday but also several times during the week. Periods of religious worship in the meetings in the church basement are always followed by long periods of visiting with neighbors. The women exchange recipes and ideas on child training and gossip about the members who are not present. The men talk about crops and the weather.

This all-embracing role of the church results in an entirely different set of prestige values for the Norse families. The respected members of the group are not necessarily the "old landowners" but rather the devout participants in the church. Nord Hansen, one of the deacons of the church and one of the most respected Norwegians in the township, has been a tenant farmer all of his life. The pastor says of Nord:

"He puts the Kingdom of God first. Regardless of what happens Christ comes first in his life, and he doesn't let anything interfere. Even during the war when it was hard to get help, he refused to work on Sunday and always came to church."

The combination of the two factors, subordination of the Norse by the Yankees and the strong attachment which the Lutheran Church has for the Norwegian families (by providing them with the social satisfactions they cannot obtain in the larger Yankee community), has effectively prevented the differentiation of the Norse group into the type of social-class system that is characteristic of the Yankees.

"HOMER JOHANNSEN DOESN'T SEEM TO HAVE NEED FOR THE THINGS OF CHRIST"

Although all of the Norse families in the township are members of the Lutheran Church and think of themselves as belonging to the Norwegian group, we found many significant variations in behavior from family to family. These variations can best be described in terms of acculturation of the Norwegian to the Yankee pattern of culture.[5] Some of the Norwegian families have retained a great deal of their ancestral way of life and are very devout members of the Lutheran Church; others have modified their social behavior to the extent that they talk and act just like the Yankees and are no longer very much interested in going to church. When the pastor of the North Township church said that "Homer Johannsen doesn't seem to have need for the things of Christ," he meant that this Norwegian farmer has drifted so far away from the ancestral pattern of Norse behavior that he is now only a peripheral member of the group.

The pattern of behavior of the least acculturated families was found to have the following characteristics: (1) A strongly patriarchal family in which the male head of the house makes most of the important decisions.[6]

(2) A firm belief in the sacred ideology of the Norwegian Lutheran Church and concommitantly a pattern of social participation which takes place almost entirely within the church and its auxiliaries. "We don't belong to any clubs. We just belong to the Grace Lutheran Church."

(3) A strict adherence to the taboos against movies, social dancing, and drinking. "These taverns and roadhouses are terrible. Boys and girls go there to drink and dance, and then they always go wrong."

(4) A deep-seated distrust of "city people."[7] This attitude was carried over from Norway where the *Boender* considered the urban people around Oslo as an "alien group."

(5) A strong emphasis on being "thrifty," an evaluation of money as something to be produced rather than consumed: "Oscar Swenson has a reputation for being very tight. I remember one time

---

[5] Acculturation is defined as the changes which result in the culture of a group when it comes into continuous first-hand contact with another group with a different culture. Cf. Robert Redfield, Ralph Linton, and Melville J. Herskovits, "Memorandum for the Study of Acculturation," *American Anthropologist*, 38: 149-152 (1936).

[6] One interesting manifestation of this patriarchal family structure is the fact that unacculturated Norwegian women never go into town without their husbands.

[7] This distrust of "city people" included distrust of the investigators. There were two unacculturated Norwegian households where we didn't get any farther than the kitchen door in an attempt to interview the families.

he came downtown to my office to get me to inoculate some hogs. He was chewing snuff so hard that I could hardly understand what he was saying. He said to me: 'Jim, I've got some hogs that need to be innoculated. Can you do it?' 'Yes, I can do it,' I said. 'Make it cheap, Bob, make it cheap,' he said."

(6) A preference for the Norwegian language in everyday conversation and in church services. "We just have a Norwegian service now once a year on New Year's Day. . . . You see, the young people do not understand Norwegian, and most of the old people now know English. Of course, I like the Norwegian service, myself."

(7) Certain personal habits such as snuff-chewing among the men and the lack of the use of cosmetics among the women.

(8) The eating of Norwegian dishes such as *lutefisk* and *lepsa*.

The pattern of behavior of the most acculturated families in the township showed a great number of significant changes: (1) The patriarchal family structure has been modified to the extent that the women play an important role in making family decisions. For example, the acculturated woman *usually* drives into town and does the family shopping by herself.

(2) There is less attachment to the sacred ideology of the Lutheran Church and less participation in the church activities. Both men and women belong to a great variety of clubs and associations outside of the Norwegian group.

(3) The families do not strongly adhere to the taboos on movies, dancing, and drinking. "We're weak Lutherans, I guess. We always go to movies. I like movies, and when I was young I always went to all the dances. Maybe we don't take our religion as seriously as we should, but I think you've got to get out and around. You can't hold down the young people too much."

(4) With the increased participation outside of the Norwegian Lutheran Church the suspicion of "city people" *per se* and the feelings of hostility toward them have almost disappeared.

(5) Money is evaluated as something to be consumed and not just produced. "I believe in getting some fun out of life. Spend your money while you can."

(6) Norwegian is no longer spoken or even understood by most of the acculturated families. "Chris don't speak Norwegian at all. I can understand a little simple conversation, but I don't get anything out of a sermon in Norwegian."

(7) Cigarette-smoking replaces snuff-chewing among the men, and the women usually wear cosmetics.

(8) The food served in the home is typically American.

These changes in behavior appear to be largely a function of the number of generations intervening between a Norwegian family and its immigrant forebears. The first generation finds itself in a strange culture with a different language and different pattern of behavior. The families arrive without economic resources and are subordinated in both the economic and social hierarchies. Their attachment to the ethnic language and culture is a natural result of these factors. As succeeding generations grow up in America, the social interaction with the larger community increases and the attachment to the ethnic group decreases.

One of the most important factors in acculturation in this rural area was the establishment of a community high school in Jonesville. As long as generations of Norwegians grew up out in the country and attended only the rural grade schools, first-hand contacts with the Yankees were at a minimum. Many of the one-room schools, serving only an area of four square miles, have only Norwegian children in attendance. But when the Norwegian children started to go to high school in Jonesville, they immediately came into continuous and intimate face-to-face relations with the Yankee group. The present situation in North Township is as follows: the grandparent generation have not been to high school, the parent generation attended high school, and the children are now all going to high school in Jonesville. This means that the current generation of children are the first to be reared by parents who have had extensive contacts with the Yankee community.

Another obvious and important factor in acculturation is the increased physical mobility in rural society as a result of the automobile and improved roads. When the parent generation were growing up, a Saturday trip to town was the rule. Now families in the township average a trip to Jonesville every other day. The radio and daily newspaper also figure importantly in this acculturation process by providing continuous and immediate news of the outside world.

The most acculturated Norwegian families in North Township are beginning to participate in the Yankee class system. They have modified their way of life to such an extent that they are accepted in the cliques and associations of the Yankee society. A few of these families who have large farms, college educations, and social contacts in Jonesville are entering the class system at the "squire farmer" level. Most of them, however, are participating with the "old landowner" or "dirt farmer" classes.

RURAL ASSOCIATIONS

The currently functioning formal associations in North Township are of two types: (1) those which have been organized by the state university agricultural extension service operating through the Farm Bureau, and (2) those which have been organized by the people in the township. Those associations organized around the Farm Bureau are the Farm Bureau itself, the Home Bureau, and the boys' and girls' 4-H Clubs. These associations are "open" or "inclusive" organizations in the sense that every family, regardless of status or ethnicity, is strongly encouraged to join. A large part of their activities are devoted to membership drives. The Farm Bureau attempts to improve the management of the farms by encouraging the adoption of scientific farming methods, good soil building practices, etc. The Home Bureau encourages farm women to adopt improved methods of running the home. The 4-H Clubs orient the young to the approved farm and home management methods of the adult organizations.

The Farm Bureau has been more successful in its membership drives than the Home Bureau or the 4-H Clubs. Only thirteen farm operators in the research area have not joined. Of these thirteen, eight are unacculturated Norwegians who still have a strong distrust for any associations outside of the Norwegian Lutheran Church; three are Yankee "dirt farmers" who are operating farms of less than 150 acres and who say that they cannot afford the fifteen dollars annual membership dues; and two (one Norwegian and one Yankee "dirt farmer") are against the policies of the Farm Bureau.[8]

The North Township Home Bureau has only twelve members—five acculturated Norwegian women, five lower class "dirt farmer" Yankee women, and two middle-class "old landowner" Yankee women.[9]

[8] These farmers were both active members of the Farmers' Union some years ago.

[9] The reason for the small number of members in the Home Bureau is the competition offered by the Rural Home Club described below.

The members of the 4-H Clubs represent twelve families in the research area—six acculturated Norwegian families, four lower-class Yankee families, and two middle-class Yankee families.

The Farm Bureau director from North Township is an acculturated Norwegian; the president of the Home Bureau is a lower-class Yankee woman; and the adult leaders of the 4-H Clubs are a lower-class Yankee man and an acculturated Norwegian woman.

It is clear that the core membership of these Farm Bureau associations, in both leadership and participation, comes from the acculturated Norwegian and the "old landowner" and "dirt farmer" Yankee families. The "squire farmers" do not actively participate in these associations, because they have severed their connections with rural clubs and are now interested in high-status urban activities.[10] The bulk of the Norwegian population continue to find satisfaction for their social needs within the interactive system of the Lutheran Church and are very reluctant to join these associations.

The Rural Home Club is a basically different type of association. Rather than an organization which is "artificially" stimulated from the outside, this club has its roots in the rural area. It is a "closed" or "exclusive" association in the sense that a woman must be invited to join and her name must be voted upon and passed by the members of the club before she is admitted. The club is affiliated with the county, state, and district federation of womens' clubs, and its annual program closely follows the federation plan. The meetings are organized around such topics as "International Relations," "Literature," "Music," "Education." The club meets once a month in the farm home of one of the members, and the program includes a talk by an outside speaker, musical entertainment, and refreshments.

The present members of the club come from the following types of families: forty-six are "old landowner" Yankees, nine are highly acculturated Norwegian women, and two are upward mobile "dirt farmer" Yankees. Fourteen of the forty-six "old landowner" members come from the Blake family—the oldest Yankee family in rural Jonesville. Ten of the members are wives of retired "old landowner"

---

10 While it is true that the "squire farmers" are formal members of the Farm Bureau and that they make their influence felt in the organization, they seldom attend meetings. Furthermore, their wives have dropped their memberships in the Home Bureau, and their children are not active in the 4-H Clubs.

Yankees who now live in Jonesville and are classified as lower-middle-class in the urban area.

When we asked "old landowner" Yankee members of the club about the number of Norwegian women who belonged, the usual response was: "Oh, we have a lot of Norwegian women in the Rural Home Club." But the membership analysis indicates that the Norwegian membership represents only 15 percent of the total in a rural area where the population is more than 50 percent Norwegian. The absence of any "squire farmer" class women and the fact that only two tenant farmers' wives are members indicate that the Rural Home Club is predominantly an organization for the "old landowner" Yankee women. The club never has membership drives; members are generally added to the organization by mothers' bringing in their daughters and daughters-in-law. The Norwegian women who are members are all third and fourth generation and are descended from the oldest landowning families of the Norwegian group. They have reached the point in the acculturation process where they have become "acceptable" to the Old Yankee group. The two Yankee tenant farmers' wives have the reputation in the community of being the type who "try to get into all the clubs and go to all the meetings." It is highly significant that the wives of the "squire farmers" dropped their memberships in the club the same year that these "dirt farmers'" wives were taken into the club, and also that one of these upper-class women commented at that time that the club was "taking in trash."

These data on the Rural Home Club suggest that the association functions in an important way to exclude and to subordinate the Norwegian and lower-class Yankee families in North Township. It also provides an opportunity for upward mobility for the lower-class Yankee and acculturated Norwegian women who are taken into the club.

INFORMAL GROUPINGS

An important part of the social structure in any rural community are the informal groupings which bring people into face-to-face relations. In rural Jonesville we found that "sales," "neighboring," "change work," and "Saturday night in town" are the most important types of informal groupings which enter into the structuring of human relationships.

Whenever a farmer decides to retire, he hires an auctioneer to sell off his livestock and machinery. The event is always advertised in the *Jonesville Eagle,* and farm families attend the sale in great numbers. Within a radius of twenty miles from Jonesville at least one farm sale occurs almost every day. Only a small proportion of the people actually do any buying when the auctioneer gets up with his cane (the symbol of his position) and starts to auction off hayrakes, tractors, chicken brooders, cows, and milking machines. Most of the families go to "see their neighbors and visit." An analysis of the people attending several of these sales indicated that nearly all of the Norwegian families and the "old landowner" and "dirt farmer" Yankees participate, but never the "squire farmers."

Informal visiting at another home is called "neighboring." [11] Although almost all of the families agreed that this form of social interaction does not occur so frequently as it did in the past, it still forms a significant part of the social life. While all of the families in the area knew almost all of the other families and would stop to visit with them if they happened to meet on the road or on the streets in Jonesville, we found that each farm family visited regularly with from one to three other families. This type of visiting took the form of driving to the home of the other family to spend the evening or to have dinner on Sunday.

The visiting relationships were classified according to the following scheme: (1) Visiting with immediate neighbors; (2) visiting with relatives in the township; (3) visiting within the same status level— i.e., visiting relationships which were neither with neighbors nor with kin, but which appeared to be motivated by a feeling of social equivalence. "We don't neighbor with the McFaddens [immediate neighbors]. We neighbor more with the Fishers [who live two miles away]."

In the Yankee group we found a total of seventeen specific visiting relationships. Four of these were visiting relationships with immediate neighbors; six were visiting relationships with relatives; and seven were visiting relationships with families of the same social class who were neither neighbors nor relatives. Many of the visiting relationships with neighbors and relatives also were within the same social classes. Of the total of seventeen relationships, thirteen were

11 Extensive "neighboring" is also done over the telephone. This is frequently more than a two-way conversation. "Rubbering in" (listening in on somebody's else conversation on a party line) is an important form of social control in rural Jonesville.

found to be within the same status levels and only four cut across status lines. The four which took place across status lines were cases of visiting with relatives.

In the Norwegian group there were a total of thirteen specific visiting relationships. Six of these were with immediate neighbors, four with relatives, and three with relatives who were also immediate neighbors.

These data on informal visiting suggest that the social stratification among the Yankees is of considerable importance in a family's selection of people they visit. In the Norwegian group, on the other hand, most of the visiting appears to be with neighbors, relatives, or both. These facts add significant corroborating data to the hypotheses that the Yankee social structure is dominated by a class system, and the Norwegian social structure by the closed interactive system of the Lutheran Church.

"Change work" is another form of social interaction which is still of considerable significance. Like "neighboring" it does not occur so much as in the past, but nearly every farm operator in the township does some exchange work. This exchange of labor occurs chiefly in connection with harvesting hay and grain, shelling corn, and butchering livestock. It is important to the social structure in that it brings two or more farm men into face-to-face relations. Every gathering of farmers to put up hay or to shell corn is accompanied by rather extensive visiting.

Exchange work is still largely carried on in the traditional way: neighbor exchanging with neighbor regardless of ethnicity and status. The interview material contains references to thirty-seven specific exchange-work relationships. These relationships were classified according to the same scheme used on the visiting relationships, i.e., exchange with immediate neighbors, exchange with relatives, or exchange with farmers in the same social class. In this case the relationships appear to be based almost entirely upon exchange with immediate neighbors. Of the thirty-seven cases, thirty-two were exchange work relationships with immediate neighbors, three with relatives who were not neighbors, and two with farmers of the same social class who were not neighbors and not relatives.

We advance the hypothesis that this system of cooperation in farm labor is one factor which has in the past tended to integrate the rural community across class and ethnic lines. As the amount of this exchange labor has decreased with the increased mechanization of farm operations, the integrative influence of the system has become less important and the differentiating factors of social class and ethnicity have come more into play, as evidenced by the data on informal visiting relationships. The data also suggest the hypothesis that the system of exchange labor is one of the factors accounting for less awareness of social class on the part of the farm men. Exchange work brings the men together but does not give their wives the same kind of contact with other wives.

We found from our research experience that almost all of the families in North Township could be found on the main street in Jonesville each Saturday night. The stores stay open until 9:30. The farmers begin to pour into town about 7:30 or 8:00, and for the next two hours every corner is packed with small groups of rural people exchanging the latest news and gossip. For most farm families this is an exciting experience; it is the one night of the week when they "always go to town." They not only see and visit with their rural neighbors on the streets but also come into contact with the townspeople and the "bright lights" of Jonesville.

TOWN AND COUNTRY

In order to determine how the social-class system of rural Jonesville correlates with the class system of Jonesville, we made a systematic study of the social interaction between the town and the country. Three types of data were used in this analysis: (1) The urban social-class position of immediate members of rural families who live in Jonesville; (2) the class level of the social participation which the rural families have in Jonesville and which urban families have in rural Jonesville; and (3) the urban class position of farm families who have moved into town from the country during the past few years.

The rural "dirt farmer" families in our research area have fifteen immediate members who live in Jonesville. Twelve of the fifteen are upper-lower class, and three are lower-middle class in town. The rural "old landowner" families have ten immediate members living in Jonesville. Eight of the ten are lower-middle class, and two are upper-lower class. The rural "squire farmers" have no immediate family members living in Jonesville. These data strongly suggest that the rural "dirt farmer" class is equivalent to upper-lower class in town, and that the rural "old landowner" class is equivalent to lower-middle in Jonesville.

The data on participation of the rural families in Jonesville associations and cliques corroborate the findings on the urban class position of immediate members of the rural families living in town and add evidence that the rural "squire farmer" class is the equivalent of urban upper-middle. The rural "squire" families are core members of a Jonesville upper-middle-class clique, of the Rotary Club (predominantly upper-middle), of the Woman's Club (predominantly upper-middle), and the Federated Church (predominantly upper-middle).

Most of the urban participation of the rural "old landowner" class takes place in the Lions Club (predominantly lower-middle), the Methodist Church (predominantly lower-middle), and the Daughters of the American Revolution (upper to lower-middle). Furthermore, ten of the members of the Rural Home Club—which was found to be predominantly rural "old landowner" class—are urban lower-middle-class women.

The urban participation of the rural "dirt farmer" class is very slight in comparison to that of the other classes, but the participation which does occur appears at the associational level of the Independent Order of Odd Fellows (predominantly urban upper-lower).

Four Yankee families have moved from North Township into Jonesville during the past ten years. Two of these were "dirt farmers" and they are now classified as upper-lower in Jonesville. Two were "old landowners" and are now classified as lower-middle in town. While the number of cases is small, such evidence as there is in this movement to town checks with the data presented above.

On the basis of these data we advance the hypothesis that the two class systems are correlated in the following way:

Rural	Urban
"Squire Farmers"	Upper-Middle
"Old Landowners"	Lower-Middle
"Dirt Farmers"	Upper-Lower
"Lower-Lower"	Lower-Lower

The interview material on town-country relations in Abraham County indicates that the attitudes depend upon a family's position in the social system. The higher-status Yankees and the acculturated Norwegians in the township believe that there is now no feeling of antagonism between city and country people nor a feeling of "city folks looking down on country folks," but the interview evidence from Jonesville indicates that the high-status people in town tend to "look down upon" country people (not landowners who live in town, but the people who live in the country and work the farms). The lower-status people, on the other hand, tend to "envy" farmers.

On the basis of our evidence from North Township we offer two tentative hypotheses in the form of predictions about the future course of events in rural Jonesville:

(1) As the acculturation process continues through time, the Norwegian group in North Township will gradually shift the center of its social participation away from the Lutheran Church and toward the cliques and associations of the Yankee community. This shift in participation will be accompanied by changes in behavior from the ancestral Norwegian pattern to the Yankee pattern. The result will be the emergence of a system of social-class stratification in the township which will cut across both groups, Yankee and Norwegian. Specifically, it is predicted that if all the Norwegian families in the research area are interviewed a generation from now (twenty-five years hence), a large number of the Norse families will respond affirmatively to questions about social-status differences between owners and tenants, "old families" and "new families."

The most crucial factors operating in this process appear to be found in the cessation of Norwegian immigration, the attendance of Norwegian children at the Jonesville Community High School, and the dynamics of land ownership. Immigration from Norway has ceased (the last migrant to North Township from Norway arrived in 1900), and there are no new immigrant generations entering this rural community to carry on the traditions of the ancestral culture. The social participation of the young in the activities of the high school brings them into continuous first-hand contacts with the Yankees and effectively increases their external relations with the wider community. The evidence from the township indicates that the younger Norwegians are becoming increasingly interested in attending movies and social dances and less interested in participation in the Lutheran Church activities. The recent trend of events in the changing pattern of land ownership makes it increasingly unlikely that the sons of Norwegian tenants will acquire land. These descendants of Norwegian tenants will either continue as tenant families or will leave the township for industrial jobs in Jonesville or other nearby towns. In either case, as the cohesive influence of the Norwegian Lutheran Church comes to have less importance in the lives of these younger generations, the differentiating factor of a class system based, among other things, upon ownership of the land will tend to place the sons of Norwegian owners in a superordinate position to the sons of tenants.

(2) The rural Yankee class system will increasingly become a part of the urban class system of Jonesville. The evidence clearly indicates that social interaction between the town and the rural township has increased markedly over the last forty to fifty years. The top of the rural class system (i.e., the "squire farmers") is already an almost integral part of the Jonesville social structure. Over half the land in North Township is owned by urban families who have thereby become the landlords for a great many rural tenant families. The data on the life careers of "surplus" children in the township indicate that they are moving to industrial jobs in Jonesville and other nearby towns. The young now attend high school in Jonesville, and there is a movement underway to establish a consolidated grade school in town. If this movement is successful, the children from all the rural families in the area will begin to participate in the urban social structure during grade school. The families in the township now average a trip to town every other day as compared to one trip a week a generation ago. These factors suggest that rural families will increasingly participate in the Jonesville social structure and that the four social classes in the rural area will become integral parts of the upper-middle, lower-middle, upper-lower, and lower-lower classes in the urban community.

Chapter 15

JONESVILLE GOES TO WAR

Before Pearl Harbor, Jonesville, in the heart of the Middle West, was isolationist country. The average man in the town was a Republican: he read the *Chicago Tribune,* and believed that the war was not our war. The draft, lend-lease, the arguments for the United States getting into the war were "New Deal propaganda" and directly attributable to "that man in the White House." Shortly before Pearl Harbor, a well-informed man, prominent in the political and social life of the city, summarized the attitudes of the town about international affairs when he said: "We all think like the *Chicago Tribune* here, and it's not only because we read it. If the goddamned *Tribune* didn't exist we'd still think like it, that's just the way we are. It's not the *Tribune,* it's us."*

Three days after Pearl Harbor, he told us, "Well, I guess for the most part you'd call it isolationism, but I think to most people all that meant was that we didn't want to get into a war unless we had to. Now that war has been thrust upon us, it's entirely different."

STRANGERS IN TOWN

Months before Pearl Harbor, equipping the nation's new army brought changes to the life of the common man in Jonesville. Fifteen miles southeast of town, two large areas of rolling corn land were suddenly engulfed by buildings, men, and machines; one became a powder plant, the other a large shell loading plant. In a little village fifteen miles down the river a barge plant, employing less than a hundred men, was leased by a Chicago steel company with the an-

* By Wilfrid C. Bailey and Walter Eaton. See List of Authors.

nouncement that it had a contract to build fifty million dollars' worth of landing ships and would employ 10,000 men. In less than a year the village's population skyrocketed to 6,000 and its workers spread over a 35-mile radius.

For the common men of Jonesville and America all this meant new jobs at undreamed-of pay. Men began to shift from old jobs to the new ones, strangers drifted into Jonesville looking for a place to live, vacant houses were converted into two-family dwellings, there was "doubling up" and a pleasant boom in business.

The rise in population was not great—from 6,145 in 1940 to 6,771 in 1943; meanwhile, 500 young men had gone into the armed forces. But new faces, in a town where everyone knows everyone else, stand out like sore thumbs. One group of newcomers were the workers who, the townspeople said, were mostly "poor whites" from the South. They were equated with, and treated as, lower-class Southern whites who had been moving into the area and settling along the river and north of the tracks.

For an accurate check on the validity of this opinion, let us turn to the employment records of the nearby shipyard. They show that 70 percent of the workers were from Illinois; of the remaining 30 percent, two-thirds were from the Southern states and the remainder from all over the United States.

The landlords dismissed lists of waiting "defense workers" to rent to the "more desirable" technical staff. The children of the workers were treated like other lower-class children at school. Mary Lou Calhoun, for example, moved to Jonesville with her family from Tennessee and enrolled in school. She found that in Jonesville children enter first grade at the age of six not at the age of seven as at home. The Jonesville schools, struggling to maintain their accredited status, believed Southern schools to be inferior and automatically put her back a grade. This put her two whole grades behind her age mates and made her feel inferior. Jonesville said, "You know those poor white trash can't compare with our children. Just look how they have all failed and are a grade or two behind our children."

The other group of newcomers were technical and managerial staff, sent in to run the plants. Because of their social and educational background they entered the community at a good solid middle-class level. They were the ones who became active in the churches and organizations in town. The ministers made strong efforts to bring these "desirable additions to the community" into their churches.

Not all of the people who went to work in the new industries, or defense plants as they were called, were newcomers. Many Jonesville men left their old jobs, sometimes abandoning long seniority, to take advantage of the new high wages and of the possibility of advancing from unskilled and semi-skilled jobs into the skilled crafts. Some held back because these new jobs offered no security in the future, but others had dreams that their new high salaries would continue indefinitely.

The industries helped stimulate the shift in occupations. Accompanying their labor drive they established training schools for welding and other crafts. Some jobs such as welding were opened to women at the same wage as men. The prevailing wage in Jonesville for women rose from forty-five cents per hour to a maximum of $1.20. Women left their jobs as maids, laundresses, and store clerks to work in the shipyards and powder plants. Other women who normally did not work, including some who had thought it beneath their position, went to work. It was patriotic and at the same time profitable. Wives of the service men wanted to save money for a new start after the war; they wanted to feel that they were helping their husbands win the war. Upward economic mobility increased tremendously in amount and speed; women advanced to jobs never before available to them, ethnic and racial groups raised the ceiling on their job expectations, unskilled workers learned new skills.

Before the end of the fighting war, the war plants began to slow down. Within a month after V-E Day, the powder plant and shell loading plants had closed. The last landing barge was launched in the summer of 1945. Thus, before the final surrender of Japan, the nearby boom towns were settling back to normal and the men of Jonesville began to drift back to their old peacetime jobs.

The small city of Jonesville, thousands of miles from the fighting and of little importance to the war effort, had been organized to act as if it were immediately behind the battlefronts. More than one pair of eyes had looked into the heavens expecting to see a fleet of German bombers, eyes that a few months before had read with approval the editorials of the *Chicago Tribune,* which said the whole of the United States was far beyond the limits of possible attack. Jonesville was divided into 120 blocks, each with its block captain and his deputy as air raid wardens. Disaster crews were organized among members of the fire department, police department, medical men and nurses, assisted by trucks and equipment of large businesses such as The Mill. The newspaper cooperated by giving many columns of publicity to Office of Civilian Defense activities and instructions on what to do in case of air raids. The postmaster announced with great ceremony that the Post Office had prepared itself by arranging for an emergency building, renting of trucks from local trucking companies, and placing their supply of stamps and bonds in two different spots for safekeeping. The intensity of this movement was climaxed by the great trial blackout of August 1942. After weeks of training and planning it took place. Instead of going to places of safety the citizens of Jonesville dashed out into the streets to see what the town looked like all blacked-out. A few laughed at the whole procedure, but it served its purpose by causing everyone in the mid-continent homes of Jonesville to think of the enemy as a threat to their own security.

Throughout the war the concept of doing one's part for the war effort was stressed. People had a genuine interest in actually making a contribution; others wanted simply to make their fellows believe they were contributing.

This feeling of contributing to the war effort even invaded the courts. The people along the railroad brought formal complaint against the company because of the shrill train whistles and other noise. The representative of the railroad said in defense that, "The clanging of an engine bell, the shrill sharp sound of the locomotive whistle, the rhythmic roar of a speeding train, these things today are the symphony of victory. These sounds, in ever-increasing crescendo, should gladden the hearts of every American." The citizens dropped the complaint.

"Our Heroes"

Despite the elaborate organization to help win the war, the one influence in Jonesville that brought the people face to face with the realities of war and stirred within them a genuine feeling of concern was their connection with relatives and friends in the armed forces. Almost every individual had many relatives and close friends in the service. This applied to all from the upper-class manufacturer living in Top Circle to the lower-lower charwoman living in a shack along The Canal, each of whom had a flag in the window displaying three blue stars. It was around this one factor that there was the greatest feeling of being at war and of everyone's being part of it. It was a theme of perpetual interest and concern to the entire community. This feeling probably reached its climax on June 6, 1944, D-Day in Normandy, when the President led the nation in prayer and thousands flocked to the churches for special services.

The community would first learn of the fate of a new group of civilian draftees when the newspaper carried an announcement that the draft board had received a quota to send so many men. This would be followed by a list of names. For the next few days the paper would be full of little news items such as, "Mrs. Kenneth Lee entertained a number of friends at a special dinner. The guest of honor was Kenneth Lee, Jr., who will leave soon for the army. He was presented with a watch and a writing kit." Or "The Marco Club of the Methodist Church had a picnic last night in honor of Larry Evans who is leaving soon for the navy. Reverend Withington expressed the appreciation of the group for the fine work Larry had done in the church and presented him with a devotional guide and a writing kit."

On the eve of the departure the *Jonesville Eagle* would publish a front-page picture of the young men standing on the Post Office steps with the caption, "Men from Abraham County reported today at the office of the Selective Service Board at the Federal Building for instructions for their induction soon into the armed services." This was a signal to all that they were leaving on the morning train.

At 6:30 next morning a crowd of people gathered outside a local cafe where the selectees were having their breakfast and receiving final instructions. Outside, the high school band would fall into position and next a color guard from the American Legion. As the boys came out of the door of the cafe, they lined up and the head of the draft board called "Forward march." They marched down Liberty Street to the railroad station where a large crowd had gathered. Here they fell out and waited for the train. Everywhere little groups of people surrounded individuals about to leave. As the train would come around the curve from the west the conversation would pick up tensely and the band begin to play. Hurried kisses, embraces, and handshakes from relatives and friends. One by one the boys shook hands with the draft board and climbed onto the train. The train pulled out and the buzz of excitement in the crowd was drowned out by the band playing the Marine Hymn. Within a minute or two the station became deserted except for the two men loading mail and baggage onto a truck. Jonesville had made another contribution to the war.

There were many lines of communication between the community and its sons in the armed forces; the most general of these was the newspaper. A daily column called "Our Men and Women in Service" was of great interest to everyone. It consisted of one- or two-sentence communications such as "S1/c John Harvey has just returned to Great Lakes after a short leave in Jonesville," or "New address for Pvt. Charles Lind is as follows: 16205550, Hq. 2913 O/H Det. W.R.C., Apo. 227, care Postmaster, New York, N. Y." Any friend or relative could use this medium to inform the community at large concerning his "Service Man's" latest move by calling the *Jonesville Eagle* office. Although personals and society news tend to be limited to the middle and upper class, this column included items running from the very top to the very bottom of the social scale. The armed forces included men from all parts of the community, and it was popularly assumed that the past made no difference as they were all fighting for the common cause.

Almost every church and many other organizations and institutions had newsletters distributed to both their representatives in the service and the people at home. The newsletter acted as a distributor of information of a common concern and also served the purpose of keeping the service man in touch with the symbol system and the sacred ideology of the particular group he went out from. The American Legion and other organizations, together with their auxiliaries, on various occasions would send small gifts to long lists of local boys. When a boy was home on furlough there were the usual rounds of parties and dinners with friends and relatives. Churches and clubs would entertain him and have him as guest speaker. In December 1942, the Rotary Club announced that the next meeting would be guest night. Each member was to bring some-one in uniform and two gifts to send to those unable to be home at Christmas time. Community unity of wartime spirit as expressed through pride over its men in the armed forces reached a peak in October 1944 with the dedication of the Jonesville Honor Roll.

Every war produces its heroes who become the symbol of their nation's sacrifice and gallantry in battle. Within a few months after Pearl Harbor the nation had its heroes to be praised in spoken word and song. In April 1943, the navy notified the community that a destroyer escort was to be named after Pvt. John Taylor. John

Taylor, lineal descendant of old Will, was a marine private in a gun crew aboard a plane carrier. He was killed when the ship was sunk in a naval battle. The gun crew received a citation which read, "As result of the gun crew actions, they effectively assisted in the defense of their ship by fast, accurate fire under extremely difficult circumstances, and thereby set an example of courage and devotion to duty of the highest order." The letter accompanying this citation was so worded that it seemed as if there was much more to the story that could not be told for reasons of security. Upon receipt of the news, the community rallied to send the Taylor family to the launching. There they heard their son lauded as a hero and the crew of the ship ordered "to go out and complete the task that Private Taylor had started to do." Their entire trip was fully reported by the local newspaper, and mementos of the event were displayed in a downtown store window.

The name of John Taylor was permanently preserved as that of the community hero for World War II when the newly formed Veterans of All Wars adopted the name of John Taylor Post 9701, Veterans of All Wars. His name was selected by unanimous vote when research revealed that he was the first boy from Abraham County to lose his life. His family gave their permission in a letter that told of the contribution that the U.S.S. Taylor had made to victory.

Off to War

Greetings; having submitted yourself to a local board composed of your neighbors for the purpose of determining your availability for training and service in the land or naval forces of the United States, you are hereby notified that you have now been selected for training and service therein.

These words launched millions of young men into a new phase of their life. To most it was a side track to the normal path that they were traveling, the induction of young men into an adult position in the community. For this reason the effect of going into the armed forces varied according to the individual. Some were just completing high school and had not had a chance to obtain their first jobs. Others were either well established in their economic sphere or were undergoing advanced training to enter this sphere. Some were still in the high school date patterns, some were about to be or just married, and others were married and had children. In age, they ranged from 17 or 18 at the time of their induction into the army or navy to almost middle age. In the service some merely advanced in age and experience while others progressed in their adjustment to adult life by gaining experience and training. Some married and became fathers without being able to enter into family life.

The Jonesville Honor Roll displays 889 names of which 750 identify boys who were living in or around the town. Twenty-four young women served as nurses or in the women's branches of the army, navy, marines, and coast guard. The remainder are largely accounted for as boys who had left the community but still had friends and relatives there.

Table 22

STATUS DISTRIBUTION OF YOUNG MEN

Class	Total Group		Military Service					No Military Service	
			Army		Navy		Total			
	No.	%	No.	%	No.	%	No.	%	No.	%
U	12	1.34	5	1.21	5	2.62	10	1.66	2	0.68
UM	47	5.25	21	5.08	10	5.24	31	5.13	16	5.48
LM	278	31.03	125	30.27	67	35.08	192	31.78	86	29.45
UL	410	45.76	193	46.73	84	43.98	277	45.86	133	45.55
LL	149	16.62	69	16.71	25	13.09	94	15.56	55	18.84
Total	896	100	413	68.38	191	31.62	604	57.54	292	42.46

We made a study of who went to war and who didn't and why. Accurate data are available on the young men born between 1914 and 1926. Of the total of 896 boys in this group, 604 or 57.54 percent saw military service and 42.46 percent or 292 remained civilians. The younger age groups furnished a high proportion of men to the armed forces: half of the total were born in 1921 and later.

The distribution of the 1914-1926 age group by status is shown in Table 22. There is no great difference between the status profiles of those who remained civilians and those who went into the service or between branches of service. Ten out of twelve upper-class boys entered the service and the navy attracted a greater number of them than expected from its size relative to the army. Conversely a larger number of lower-lower boys remained civilians and they also contributed more heavily to the army than the navy. These figures would seem to contradict the popular opinion in Jonesville that the draft board showed favoritism for upper-class boys.

A leading citizen, who was in one of the classes above the Common Man Level, and who was well informed on the activities of the draft board, claimed that not a single man needed on a farm was drafted. This was an important issue to the community as it is located in the center of a rich agricultural area. Breaking down our figures on military service into rural and urban shows that 26.42 percent of the group are rural boys but they contributed only 18 percent of those in military service; 61.41 percent of the rural boys were deferred against 42.46 percent of the total group and 35.66 percent of urban boys. The deferment of rural boys was for agricultural labor to help on their fathers' farms. Comparison of tables would seem to indicate a weighting in favor of the middle and upper classes. The situation is proportionately reversed for the lower classes. The deferment of the three upper-middle-class and upper-class boys was well known to the community. These well-known cases were the cause of the complaints against the draft board.

It is difficult to determine the true cause of deferment in most cases because it was complicated by frequent changes in regulations and the practice of allowing occupational classification in cases where the individual was not physically qualified for military duty. Because of the many nearby industries engaged in war work and the scarcity of farm labor there was a great temptation to obtain draft-exempt jobs. This was counteracted by social pressure. The young man not in uniform was constantly the recipient of blunt questions regarding his draft status. A frequent complaint was, "Why don't they have everyone wear a pin of some kind giving their draft status? Then we would know."

There were only two cases of overt action against young men not in the service. The fronts of their brothers' shops were daubed with yellow paint and both boys enlisted. Most of the action was covert as in the case of Norman Steadman. Norman lived on a farm all of his life and was employed as a farm hand. He sang in the choir of the Federated Church. One Sunday he came home and told his father that he was not going to sing any more. He said that all through the church service Mrs. Lundin sat down there and just glared at the choir. He knew that she was looking at him, and he knew she was mad because her boys had been drafted and he was still deferred. He refused to sing again and within a month volunteered. His brother, employed in a foundry, soon followed him.

What happened to the people of Jonesville during the war, with few variations, happened to all the American people. The cities, towns, and villages went through the conflict by directing all their efforts at home to production of equipment to win the war; they sent their young men away from civilian life into the fighting forces to win the war but they expected all their men to leave military life and return to civilian existence immediately after hostilities ceased. When the "veterans" returned home a new chapter was added to the stream of events that make Jonesville and America what they are.

Probably no one has described the nature of veteran readjustment more clearly than the Jonesville veteran who said, "Well, I'll tell you what it is. From one life to the other, isn't it? You left here as a civilian. You get in and you have to take a lot of bull. You come back out and you don't have to take no more bull. That's readjustment—that's the veteran's idea of it. In other words, you go right back to where you started out from."

To learn how Jonesville's veterans got back where they started—and to find whether most of them actually got there at all—a research was begun in September 1945. About 500 Jonesville veterans contributed to the study. All were living in Jonesville at the time of their induction, and most of them have returned since their separation from service. Because Jonesville, as we have seen, is a typical American community, what these veterans have said and done is probably the story—in substance, if not in exact detail—of thirteen million other ex-GI's.

THE VETERANS RETURN TO JONESVILLE

A majority of the Jonesville veterans came home after at least two years of service, about eighteen months of which were spent overseas. When they got home there were two things they wanted. First they wanted to see their families and friends, and next they wanted to get out of uniform and into a white shirt, a civilian suit, and a colored tie—preferably "a big red tie with green dragons," as one veteran described it. Seeing their families and friends was easily accomplished; obtaining civilian clothing presented a more difficult problem. Colored ties—particularly the hand-painted ones at ten dollars apiece—were available in abundance. But civilian suits and that most civilian symbol of all, the white shirt, were almost impossible to purchase by the time most of the veterans came home. These shortages were disturbing. The more serious shortages of homes, cars, and jobs continued to harass the veterans long after civilian clothing was obtainable.

During his first weeks in Jonesville, the ex-GI dressed like a civilian and tried hard to feel like one, but he acted much more like a serviceman home on leave. "It's a sort of a prolonged leave," an ex-army flier said. "That's the prevailing atmosphere, I think. When I came back I found that to see my old cronies I had to go to Mac's Tavern or out to the Three Little Fishes. And that's the same bunch of guys that three years ago or five years ago you'd never have seen at either place. If I want to see anybody, that's where I've got to go now. And I get a certain big bang out of it, too. I don't know—the town may settle down to where it was before, but in general you've got a big shift in night life to that sort of place."

One young veteran saw it another way: "While I was overseas, I used to think about the things I'd done as a kid and look forward to doing them again—you know, just playing around and relaxing. But after I got on the ship and headed for home those things sort of lost some of their glory. I began to come right down to reality, you might say. Of course, I was looking forward to getting rid of the uniform and more or less being John Q. Citizen again, but I suppose I'd never thought much about it really. It's a little bit like when I came home on furlough. I had the idea of getting away from it all, more or less. I figured I was really going to kick over the traces—go out and raise hell—take off. But then I got home here and I found that the town sort of restricts you. There's a lot of public opinion you're up against. Even the beer is scarce, and that sort of restricts you a little bit. You can't take off the way you thought you could. Even if you go up to Chicago—no matter where you go— you'll find it's just as dead but on a big scale, so that makes a guy kind of restless."

This restlessness is the outstanding trait of returning servicemen. He is above all a displaced person, a migrant and an immigrant. He returns to his old community as a traveler from far places who has accustomed himself to a radically different way of life. He has been trained to unquestioning obedience to the commands of others, and as a veteran he finds himself once more responsible for issuing his own commands. He has become accustomed to the extravagant freedom of week-end passes, secure in the knowledge that the service will feed and clothe him during the coming week, whatever happens; and as a veteran he quickly discovers that such excursions and their consequences must be at his own expense. He has traveled at staccato speeds through countries which were often excitingly different from his own, and as a veteran he finds himself stopped suddenly in the midst of alarmingly familiar scenes. In part, his restlessness is the result of sheer momentum. "I still get that itchy feeling," an ex-GI said. "One reason I took to truck driving was when you get that itchy feeling you can hit the road." This feeling may go on for six days, six months, or for the veteran's lifetime. While it persists, the veteran is still on his last furlough, the furlough which begins with the wearing of civilian clothes and continues until he is so thoroughly accustomed to civilian life that he is unaware, except perhaps on Armistice Day, that he is a veteran at all.

Marriage and Family Adjustment

The marriage adjustment of Jonesville's ex-servicemen was characterized by certain typical difficulties. One of the foremost of these was the housing shortage, which had its greatest effect upon veterans who had married while in service or soon after their discharge. During their first months at home, nearly all of these veterans found it necessary to live with relatives. Their ultimate aim, of course, was to establish a new home, but in trying to accomplish this they were faced not only with the shortage of housing but with inflated prices in real estate, home furnishings, lumber, and anything else a permanent household requires. The migratory existence these families led was reported by one newly-married veteran: "Frankly, I don't know what married life *is* like. First, we were living with my folks. Then it just happened that this friend of mine decided he was going down to Florida and we could take his place, so we got to live there for two months. Then, as luck would have it, we managed to squeeze in here a couple of weeks before they really had the place ready— they want too much for it, but what can you do? I'll tell you the truth, I haven't had time to know what I do think about things."

Furthermore, it was almost inevitable that the veteran's restlessness should be expressed in his marital behavior. As one wife said,

"When my husband got home, I never saw anything like it. We'd go
to bed early, and then he'd be up at five o'clock in the morning. He'd
be going all over the house. He'd pull out the dresser drawers and
go through all of them. Then he'd go through every closet in the
house. He'd go up to town and come back again—just fidget around
—it seemed like that was all he'd ever do. It got on his nerves, and
it got on my nerves, too. But my goodness, it was just that in the
army he had been used to being kept busy and having some place to
go all the time. Then he came home and here he didn't have anything to do." If there were children in the family, the problem was
likely to be still more complex. The wife of an ex-sergeant complained: "I think getting along with the children is the hardest for
him. Naturally, the baby changes the home schedule a lot, and I
don't think he realizes that you kind of have to change to that, too.
He wants everything to go on just as it was, you know. He doesn't
realize that a child has to have naps and follow its eating schedule.
Then he objects that the baby is spoiled. Well, it *is* spoiled. You
see, both of the grandparents have been here, and of course they
thought, 'Oh, the poor child—here all alone with no father.' And
they just gave it everything it wanted, and more than it needed,
really. But mostly," this wife added, "he just doesn't seem used to
the responsibility of children. When he wants to go, that's all there
is to it—he can't be bothered with the child. I suppose this is mostly
because his home responsibility is so much different from army
responsibility. In the army, the men just worked for a while and
then they forgot about it; they'd be off duty, and they could go anywhere they pleased. But here at home it's twenty-four-hour responsibility."

Perhaps the chief source of the average veteran's marital difficulties is in working out a satisfactory division of labor between husband and wife. Usually, during the husband's absence, the wife
became accustomed to performing many of the tasks which had
formerly been the husband's responsibility. She had learned to
handle the family's money, pay the bills, buy gas and oil for the
car, and arrange for its maintenance, do all of the family shopping,
and—if there were children—perform to the best of her ability the
roles of both mother and father. Frequently she was compelled to
supplement the family's wartime income by obtaining employment
outside the home, in which case her new self-sufficiency was intensi-
fied by the feeling of independence that wage-earning permits.

Under these circumstances, the husband's return very often pre-
cipitated confusion if not outright conflict. The wife, however willing she may have been, found it hard to give up the rights and duties
she had learned to consider her own; and the husband, for all his
eagerness to become a "family man," was alternately jealous of his
privileges in one sphere and forgetful of his responsibilities in
another. As one wife said, "We're always getting mixed up about
who's going to do this and who's going to do that. He's been away
for a long time, and little things just don't come into his head. I
don't want you to think we argue about it, because we don't, but it's
just been hard for both of us to know what each should take care of."

Not until this division of labor has been decided upon and become
habitual, can the veteran's marital adjustment be complete. Once
this has been accomplished, the veteran is probably a civilian again
—at home. Whether he will feel and act like a civilian in the other
areas of his behavior depends, it seems, on factors of a somewhat
different order.

THE JOB

What is it that ordinarily makes the veteran feel like a civilian
in his behavior as a whole? Almost instinctively the veterans appear
to know the answer. As one particularly restless ex-serviceman described it, "I really need to get to work. I think it would be a good
thing for me. I've done an awful lot of sitting around these taverns
since I got back, and I'm getting tired of it. If I get a job I may do
a little drinking at night, but I know you can't hold a job and
drink in the daytime. But when you're not working, what else can
you do? The trouble is I keep meeting people who want to buy
me drinks, and a guy just can't say no even if he's already got a
pretty good skinfull. So I keep on. It's not so good. Well, I'll lay
around for a while and then get back on the ball again." The ritual
of "laying around" is something the veteran promised himself during long months of overseas duty, but it often becomes a tenaciously
established way of life.

Approximately 45 percent of the Jonesville veterans obtained jobs
soon after their discharge from service. A fortunate few—perhaps
five percent—coasted into civilian life and came to a gentle stop in
the offices of their fathers, the merchants, professional men, and
plant superintendents of Jonesville. For these veterans, readjustment presents few problems, and those which do arise can be met

with the confidence of men whose social and economic status is secure. Furthermore, the very fact that these—the veterans with silver spoons—have a position in the community to maintain tends to discipline their readjustment. As one such veteran said, "I can't afford to do some of the things that other fellows can—I suppose in the long run that makes it easier for me. Whenever I have to blow off some steam I've always tried to keep it in the family."

The great majority of veterans who immediately obtained employment did so, however, under less benevolent circumstances. This group consisted of the older, married veterans, many with families to support, for whom employment was not a matter of kind, parental invitation but of urgent necessity. Much as they usually disliked their pre-war jobs at The Mill, they grudgingly returned to them. "There's really not much choice around here," one of these veterans pointed out. "In order to do anything, you have to get out of town, and to do that you have to make fairly good money. I might get something that would pay a little more, but as it stands now I have to take almost anything I can get. You know, a few years back if I'd thought I was going to have four kids I'd probably have passed out." Yet the surprising fact remains that veterans whose economic circumstances thus compelled them to accept employment soon after their discharge show the best general adjustment of any ex-service group in Jonesville, on the basis of tests designed to measure this factor.

Perhaps the most significant finding of the veteran study has been that successful adjustment involves a narrowing of the range of alternatives, a restriction—whether by personal choice or environmental circumstances—of the various things which the individual may want to do. In the case of the veterans with silver spoons, this restriction is provided by the obvious desirability of carrying on a well-established familial enterprise. In the case of the married veterans with families to support, a similar if less attractive restriction is provided by the immediate need of a regular income. In both cases it is apparent that successful adjustment is often in part compulsory.

The second largest group of Jonesville's ex-servicemen, comprising nearly 40 percent of the total number, can perhaps best be described as the adolescent veterans. Whatever maturity these veterans may have gained in military situations, they have returned to civilian life as adolescents armed with little more than discharge papers and high school diplomas. The civilian job experience they may have had was usually limited to vacations or the few months between high school graduation and entrance into the armed forces, and the skills they perhaps acquired while in service are difficult to convert to civilian use. In general, these are the veterans who have neither an adult way of life to readjust *to,* nor sufficient occupational training to readjust *with.* As a result, the adolescent veteran drifts from one marginal job to another, believing always that his next employment will be more satisfactory than his last. He is perpetually discontented and perpetually hopeful. An easy prey of vocational guidance "experts," he moves from job to trade school to university and back again, periodically tempted to give up the quest entirely and return to the peacetime quiet and accustomed certainties of military life. Of the 500 veterans who were studied, approximately 85 have moved from Jonesville since their separation from service; of these, by far the greater number were classified as adolescent veterans. Thirty-five of the younger veterans have entered trade schools or universities, thirty-nine have obtained employment in other cities, and eleven re-enlisted in the armed forces within a period of three months following their discharge.

Every Tuesday morning in Jonesville, members of the local "52-20" veterans' club line up at the employment service trailer parked in front of the City Hall and enter their claims for adjustment compensation. Since most of the "52-20" veterans are unmarried and living with their families, the twenty dollars of weekly compensation—Jonesville calls it "rocking chair money"—is enough to keep them in cigarettes, beer, and other last furlough necessities.

Service experience, however, often raised the occupational level of men who had previously done only unskilled work. The various branches of the service spent millions of dollars on special training programs, and, as a consequence of this, hundreds of thousands of discharged servicemen returned home with a new estimate of their vocational aptitudes and a determination to use these aptitudes in future employment. The difficulty, in Jonesville as in most American towns, was in making these aspirations effective. An ex-sergeant described the problem: "Before I got in the army, I worked eleven years at The Mill. Now that I'm home, I'm not crazy about going back there. Maybe I will when I get in harness, but I sure can't see myself going back there for eleven more years. You see, I had a desk job in ordnance. It was a job you had to be trained for or else have a lot of experience. Up in the Aleutians I even did the work of a technical sergeant for a while. Whereas at The Mill it's practically unskilled labor. They call it semi-skilled, but that's just because you have to know what the different types of boxes are and where they're located—that sort of thing. In the army, I got used to doing another kind of work." The Mill, unfortunately, can offer Jonesville's veterans only their old jobs of remembering where the boxes are.

Another aspect of service experience that has prevented veterans from cheerfully returning to their pre-war employment is the relentless discipline which service life entails. "I've taken orders long enough," one ex-navy radioman said. "I don't want to go back to the goddamned factory. When you've been in the navy, you don't want to go back under those bosses—you feel that way. You want to be more or less on your own, without some foreman giving you orders, telling you what to do all the time. I'd kind of like to get into some electrical work, or radio, or something along that line. I was a radio operator for about two and a half, maybe three, years. Did a little repair work on them, monkeyed around with them. I'd like to take a course in that and then open a radio shop of my own, but I don't know whether I'd make a go of it or not. I don't want to start something like that and go broke—then I'd be out altogether."

As the veteran study proceeded, it became increasingly apparent that one of the urgent tasks of our economy is to offer veterans the jobs they *want*—jobs that will give them some measure of the abundance, independence, and vocational advancement they have every right to expect. For such jobs the rocking-chair way of life is a poor substitute.

What Did the War Win?

One of the conclusions of the Jonesville research has been that overseas veterans often came home with a feeling of ill-will for their former Allies. In fact, as far as the average ex-GI was concerned they were hardly Allies at all. Except for the Russians, their military assistance was regarded with tolerant contempt; and their friendship, for the most part, was either distrusted or rejected altogether. One 28-year-old veteran summarized his European impressions as follows: "England? My God! You never saw so many perverts in your life. It's full of them. And France, I'd say, is a country without morals. They aren't perverted or anything else—they just don't give a damn. I never saw anything like it. The country is full of disease. And the French are the most two-faced people you ever saw. They'll be nice to you to your face, and as soon as you turn around they'll be swearing at you in French. I don't have any use for them, frankly."

Another Jonesville veteran, asked if he had ever thought of going back in the army, said: "Definitely not—unless they were having a war with England and France, and then I would join right up. I'd just love to clean hell out of the frogs and the English. Those English and French are a bunch of phonies. They will try to screw you every chance they get. The French are the worst, though. They charged us ten prices for everything, and you couldn't do anything about it or you'd be court-martialed. As for the Italians, they didn't have brains enough to get mad at."

Why World War II was fought is a question the majority of Jonesville's veterans have never heard answered satisfactorily. Apparently the orientation courses to which they were subjected while in service failed either to hold their interest or compel belief. "I got a little of it—not very much," an ex-corporal recalled. "It didn't interest me because, in a manner of speaking, their version of it was probably right, but if you'd asked the average fellow in the front lines why he was fighting the war, chances are you'd run into a brick wall. He'd say he was just there fighting because he had to be there, that's all." Most of the veterans admitted, of course, that this country was justified in defending itself against Hitler and probably also against the Japanese. As one ETO veteran explained, "I think you'll find most of the GI's who've been up where the action was, well, even though they regretted some of the stuff they were going through, they realized it was pretty well necessary. They realized that the Jerries would have caused trouble wherever we'd been. You saw some of the countries the Germans had gone through, and you knew it was pretty important that we were over there. We had to get them out of the way sooner or later." To this extent, Jonesville's servicemen knew what the war was against. But few, even as veterans, had any idea of its purpose.

The typical opinion of the Jonesville veterans, however, was expressed by a former tech sergeant, recently discharged from the

Marine Corps: "I really couldn't say why we fought the war. It just seemed like we worked into it. If a man got into a fight himself, he'd know who started it and what he was fighting for. But just fighting for someone else, you don't know." The average serviceman was never quite able to believe that the war was his war, that its objectives were his objectives, that its successful conclusion meant anything more personal to him than the privilege of going home. He saw the war as a vague conspiracy conceived by men of whom he knew nothing and motivated by forces of which he had no comprehension. As a veteran, his attitude remain unchanged. "I just think there's a lot of money tied up there, that's all," said one veteran. "It started so suddenly and ended so suddenly that it sort of looked like it might have been a few of the big politicians—a few of the big businessmen. At the present time, just ordinary people don't have much to say about it. It's just the political people that have got the say. We go to war because it's their way of looking at things." "They"—"the government"—"the political people"—these, according to the average Jonesville veteran, must assume responsibility for planning both the war and the postwar future.

The general attitude of Jonesville's veterans was summed up by the ex-corporal who said: "I never follow politics any more. It don't make much difference to me who gets in. After all, I figure if a man runs himself and minds his own business, he'll get along all right."

VETERANS' ORGANIZATIONS

In view of this political passivity on the part of the average veteran, it is perhaps surprising that two veterans' organizations—the American Legion and the Veterans of Foreign Wars—are among the most politically active of America's pressure groups. Seemingly the explanation lies in the fact that political expressions of these two organizations are almost entirely divorced from the usual post activities of their memberships. In Jonesville, during a recent six months' period, neither the American Legion nor the VFW posts found occasion to discuss a single issue of general political importance. Such questions were not discouraged—they simply were not raised. Wherever the policies of the Legion and VFW are formulated, it can safely be assumed that it is not in the broad memberships of these organizations. The Jonesville veteran—like the average veteran elsewhere—joins one of his local veteran groups for social, not political, reasons.

During the years prior to World War II, Jonesville's only veteran organization had been the American Legion. At that time the Legion's active membership was extremely small and was recruited mainly from the lower-middle and upper-lower classes. Early in 1943, however, the Jonesville post, revitalized by the prospect of vastly increased membership, conducted an extensive money-raising campaign which made possible the purchase of a Jonesville building suitable to accommodate the expected World War II members. And, as Jonesville's ex-servicemen returned, a large number—approximately 500—did join the Legion. Many, however, were soon dissatisfied.

Through no fault of the World War I members, an annual election of officers had taken place in June 1945, the month just preceding a vast influx of ex-GI's which continued until spring of the following year. As a result, Jonesville's World War II veterans found themselves silent partners in a Legion post whose officers, with one exception, were the veterans of another war. This fact, together with the ex-serviceman's typical restlessness in any organizational situation, led a number of veterans to establish a Jonesville post of the VFW. After a flurry of enthusiasm, during which some 200 veterans joined the new organization, it quickly became apparent that differences between the VFW and the Legion were little more than insignia-deep. Both protested feelingly but ineffectively at the discrimination of Jonesville auto dealers against veterans and in favor of more prosperous clients; both concerned themselves briefly with the housing problem, and found its solution hopeless; both appointed sports committees and began the hurried recruitment of basketball and softball teams, in season; both contributed generously to the high school band and other equally deserving causes, planning stag nights and carnivals to defray these expenses and accrue some modest profit besides. Both, in short, behaved like social organizations and, as far as Jonesville's veterans are concerned, that is what they are.

The experiences of the citizens of Jonesville who stayed home or who were members of the military and returned had a profound effect on the community. No one felt himself to be quite the same, for life during wartime was different. That the effect of World Wars I and II was more than what happened to each individual who experienced them is displayed in the organizations of veterans, but this permanent effect on the group is even more deeply felt in the secular and sacred ideologies of the community. The first part of the concluding chapter will be concerned with how the feelings and beliefs of those who experienced war are organized into an ideology which reflects our basic ideals.

Chapter 16

WE HOLD THESE THINGS TO
BE TRUE: SOCIAL LOGICS
OF JONESVILLE

MINE EYES HAVE SEEN THE GLORY

Despite the pessimistic events of the first years of World Wars I and II, the people of Jonesville and America derived deep satisfaction from them; for it is in time of war that human beings get some of their deepest satisfactions as members of the community.* It is a mistake to believe that the American people hate war to the extent that they derive no satisfaction from it. Verbally and superficially they disapprove of war, but this is only partly revealed in their deeper feelings. In simple terms, most of them had more fun in the second World War, just as they did in the first, than they have had at any other period of their lives. The various men's and women's organizations, instead of inventing things to do to keep busy, had to choose among activities which they knew to be vital and significant to them and to others.[1]

* By W. Lloyd Warner. See List of Authors.

[1] Part of the materials used in this chapter have been previously published in *American Society in Wartime,* Edited by W. F. Ogburn (Chicago: University of Chicago Press, 1943) in a chapter by W. Lloyd Warner entitled "The American Town." The thesis expressed in the first section of this chapter was first developed in the Yankee City research. The research in Jonesville further confirmed what had been found out in Yankee City. The whole thesis will be published in detail in the fifth volume of the "Yankee City Series" on symbolic behavior. See W. Lloyd Warner, "Yankee City Series," Volume V.

The strong belief that everyone must sacrifice to win the war greatly strengthens people's sense of their significance. Everyone is believed to be giving up something for the common good—money, food, tires, scrap, automobiles, or blood for blood banks. All of it is contributed under the basic ideology of common sacrifice for the good of the country. These simple acts of giving by all individuals in the town, by all families, associations, schools, churches, and fac- tories, are given strong additional emotional support by the com- mon knowledge that local young men are representing the town in the military forces. It is known that some of them may be killed while serving their country. It is believed that they are sacrificing their lives in order that their country and democracy may live. In this belief, all acts of giving to help win the war, no matter how small, are made socially significant and, as sacrifices, add to the strength of the social structure. The collective effect of these small renunciations (it is believed) is to lessen the number of those who must die for their country.

Another important integrative factor in strengthening the social structure of the small town and city is that in wartime internal antagonisms are drained out of the group onto the common enemy. The local antagonisms which customarily divide and separate people are often suppressed. The feelings and psychic energies involved, normally expended in local feuds, are vented on the hated symbols of the enemy. The local ethnic groups, too frequently excluded from participation in community affairs, are given an honored place in the war effort, and the symbols of unity, rather than the separating differences, are stressed. The religious groups and the churches tend to emphasize the one-ness of the common war effort rather than their differing theologies and competitive financing. The strongest pressure to compose their differences is placed against the several classes. The small number of strikes is eloquent proof of the effectiveness of the pressure on management and labor. A common hate of a common enemy, when organized in community activities to express this basic emotion, provides the most powerful mechanism to energize the lives of our towns and to strengthen our feelings of unity. Those who believe that the war's hatreds can bring only evil to our psychic life might well ponder the therapeutic and satisfying effects on the minds of people who are turning their once private hatreds into social ones and joining their townsmen and countrymen in this basic emotion.

Each year various groups of people in Jonesville, Deep South, Yankee City, and hundreds of other places, engage in thousands of significant patriotic rites, always symbolic, which give visible and audible form to the feelings and beliefs of the participants. These symbolic events may be very elaborate religious ceremonies or extremely simple secular ones.

The religious ceremonies are one of the several forms of collective representations which Durkheim so brilliantly defines and interprets in his book, *The Elementary Forms of the Religious Life*.[2] He said, "Religious representations are collective representations which express collective realities." Religious collective representations are symbol systems which are composed of beliefs and rites that relate men to sacred beings. Beliefs are "states of opinion and consist in representations"; rites "are determined modes of action" which are expressions of, and refer to, religious belief. They are visible signs (symbols) of the invisible belief.

The religious ceremonies, periodically held, function to impress on men their social nature and make them aware of something beyond themselves which they feel and believe to be sacred. This intense feeling of belonging to something larger and more powerful than themselves and of having part of this within them is found in the belief in sacred beings, which is given a visual symbol by use of symbolic designs, the emblems of the sacred entities.

That which is beyond, yet part of, one is no more than the awareness of individuals and the collectivity of individuals of their participation in a social group. The religious symbols as well as the secular ones must express the nature of the social structure of the group of which they are a part and which they represent. The beliefs in the gods and the symbolic rites which celebrate their divinity are no more than men collectively worshiping their own images—their own since they were made by themselves and fashioned from their experiences among themselves.

The integration and smooth functioning of the social life of a modern community like Jonesville are very difficult because of the heterogeneity of the parts. We should expect conflicting parts to have conflicting symbols; therefore we know it is necessary for the community to provide itself with symbol systems which function to integrate the people into total community activities and permit

2 Emile Durkheim, *The Elementary Forms of the Religious Life* (translated by J. W. Swain, Glencoe, Illinois: The Free Press, 1915).

the interrelation of these segmenting symbols. A considerable degree of unity is necessary if the community is to maintain the ordinary functions of the group.

Our communities are filled with churches, each claiming great authority and each with a separate sacred symbol system. Many of them are in conflict, and all of them in opposition. Many of our associations, such as the Masons, Odd Fellows, and the like, have sacred symbol systems which partly separate them from the whole community. The ethnic traditions contribute to the heterogeneity of symbolic life. The evidence is clear on symbolic differentiation and the conflict among these systems. Do we have sacred symbol systems which permit integration and collective action through their use by everyone in the community?

Memorial or Decoration Day ceremonies and subsidiary rites such as those of Armistice Day are rituals which express a sacred symbol system functioning to integrate the whole community, with its conflicting symbols and its opposing, autonomous churches and associations. In the Memorial Day ceremonies the anxieties man has about death are confronted with a system of sacred beliefs about death which give the individuals involved and the collectivity a feeling of well-being. Further, the feeling of triumph over death by collective action in the Memorial Day parade is made possible by recreating the feeling of euphoria and the sense of group strength and individual strength in the group's power, which were felt so intensely during the wars when the veterans' associations were created and when the feeling so necessary for the Memorial Day's symbol system was originally experienced.

Ministers often express the theme of the sacrifice of the individual for national and democratic principles. One introduces Divine sanction for this sacrificial belief and thereby succeeds in emphasizing the theme that the loss of an individual's life rewards him with life eternal. Another uses one of our greatest and most sacred symbols of democracy and the only very powerful one that came out of World War I, the Unknown Soldier. The American Unknown Soldier is Everyman of the mystery plays. He is the perfect symbol of equalitarianism.

In all services, the same themes are used in the speeches, most of which are in ritualized, oratorical language, or expressed in the ceremonials themselves. Washington, the Father of his country, first in war and peace, devoted his life not to himself but to his country.

Lincoln gave his own life in sacrifice on the altar of his country. Most of the speeches imply or explicitly state that Divine Guidance is involved and that these mundane affairs have supernatural implications. They state that the revered dead have given the last ounce of devotion in following the ideals of Washington and Lincoln and the Unknown Soldier and declare these same principles must guide us, the living.

The beliefs and values of which they speak refer to a world beyond the natural; their references are to the supernatural.

The Memorial Day rites of Jonesville, Yankee City, and hundreds of other American towns are a modern cult of the dead and conform to Durkheim's definition of sacred collective representations. They are a cult because they consist of a system of sacred beliefs and dramatic rituals held by a group of people who, when they congregate, represent the whole community. The members of the cult are not formally organized into an institutionalized church with a defined theology but depend on informal organization to order their sacred activities. By expressing their sacred ideals (about themselves and democracy), the people ritually relate the living to the sacred, in the Memorial Day ceremonies.

The cult system of sacred belief conceptualizes in organized form sentiments common to everyone in the community about life and death. These sentiments are composed of fears of death which conflict with the social reassurances our culture provides to allay our anxieties. These assurances, usually acquired in childhood and thereby carrying some of the authority of the adults who provided them, are a composite of theology and folk belief. The deep anxieties to which we refer include anticipation of our own deaths, of the deaths of loved ones and, less powerfully, of the deaths of those they know and of men in general.

Each man's church provides him and those of his faith with a set of beliefs and a mode of action to face these problems, but his church and those of other men do not equip him with a common set of social beliefs and rituals which permit him to unite with all his fellows to confront this common and most feared of all his enemies. The Memorial Day rite and other subsidiary rituals connected with it form a cult which partially satisfies this need for common action on a common problem. It dramatically expresses the sentiments of equality and unity of all the living among themselves, of all the living with all the dead, and of all the living and dead, as a group, with the gods. The gods, Catholic, Protestant, and Jewish, lose their sectarian and class definitions, limitations, and foreignness among themselves and become objects of worship for the whole group and the protectors of everyone.

The unifying and integrating symbols of this cult are the dead. The graves of the dead are the most powerful of the visible emblems which unify all the activities of the separate groups of the community. The cemetery and its graves become the objects of sacred rituals for the collective dead which permit opposing organizations, often in conflict, to subordinate their opposition and to cooperate in collectively expressing the larger unity of the total community. The rites show extraordinary respect for all the dead, but they pay particular honor to those who were killed in battle "fighting for their country." The death of a soldier in battle is believed to be a "voluntary sacrifice" by him on the altar of his country. To be understood, this belief in the sacrifice of a man's life for his country must be judged first by our general scientific knowledge on the nature of all forms of sacrifice. It must then be subjected to the principles which explain human sacrifice whenever and wherever found. More particularly, this belief must be examined with the realization that these sacrifices occur in a society whose Deity is a man who sacrificed his life for all men.

The principle of the gift is involved. In simple terms, when something valuable is given, an equally valuable thing must be returned. The speaker who, quoting scripture in his Memorial Day speech, said, "Whosoever shall save his life shall lose it and whosoever shall lose his life in My name shall save it," almost explicitly stated the feelings and principles involved. Finally, and most particularly, the analysis we make of the belief in "the sacrifice of American citizens killed in battle" is that the sacrifice is for their country and its people and their collective moral principles.

The Memorial Day ceremonies consist of a series of separate rituals performed by autonomous groups which culminate in a consecrated area set aside by the living for their dead. In such a place the dead are classed as individuals, for their graves are separate; as members of separate social institutions, for they are in family plots, and formal ritual respect is paid them by church and association; and as a collectivity, since they are thought of "as our dead" in most of the ceremonies. The fences surrounding the cemetery place all the dead together and separate all the living from them.

The Memorial Day rite is a cult of the dead, but not just of the dead, since by symbolically identifying sacrifice of human life for the country with the Christian Church's sacred sacrifice of its god, the deaths of men also become powerful sacred symbols which organize, direct, and constantly revive the collective equalitarian ideals of the community and the nation.

Just as the totemic symbol system of the Australians represents the idealized clan,[3] and the African ancestral worship symbolizes the family and state,[4] so the Memorial Day rites symbolize and express the sentiments the people have for the total community and the state. But the separate values and ideas of various parts of the community are also portrayed. The ideas and values of several religious and ethnic groups and social classes are symbolically expressed and their place within the social structure of the community clearly indicated.

THE IDEOLOGY OF DEMOCRACY IN A CLASS SYSTEM

Five generations have lived on the banks of The River since Will Taylor and his people founded the City of the Common Man and the other Jonesvilles of the midland prairie. All that has happened and is happening in Jonesville has happened to America. We said earlier that this community "reflects and symbolizes the significant principles on which the American social system rests. Borrowing from the Gospel of John," we went on to say, "Jonesville is in all Americans, and all Americans are in Jonesville, for he that dwelleth in America dwelleth in Jonesville and Jonesville in him." Easily the most important fact about this community is that its beliefs and values are founded on basic contradictions, and its social logics, the basic precepts on which action is founded, are a series of paradoxes.

Some of our basic social logics, many of them contradictory, are enumerated below:

(1) All men are equal.

(2) Some men are superior in status, others inferior.

---

3 W. Lloyd Warner, *Black Civilization* (New York, Harper and Brothers, 1937).

4 Audrey Richards, *Hunger and Work in A Savage Tribe* (London: Routledge, 1932).

The two propositions are restated in the social logics of

(3) "All men are equal, but some of us are more equal than others"; sometimes expressed in another form, more subtle and less easy to see at a glance, "all of us are equal because all of us have an equal opportunity to achieve," or, more pessimistically, "from shirtsleeves to shirtsleeves."

(4) All men are equal in the sight of God, but within His church and among His people power and position are too often present.

These four statements apply to every aspect of the society. There are many other basic propositions contained within them which are their corollaries and help buttress their power:

(5) All occupations are to be respected, for all are necessary for the common life, but they have varying degrees of prestige and power and are ranked accordingly.

(6) The values inherent within occupational ranking place the skilled jobs above those with less skill and reward them accordingly.

(7) These same occupational values rank jobs demanding more schooling above those requiring less.

(8) Clean jobs outrank dirty ones; white-collar men, those who labor.

(9) Jobs may be organized into interconnected hierarchies (factories, etc.) where the success or failure of a man may be measured by his movement up or down the hierarchy.

Our social logics about money, as revealed in behavior, reflect some of the fundamentals of our value system. Some of the more important ones are

(10) The greater amount of money a family or individual possesses, the higher the economic ranking; however,

(11) While the possession of larger and smaller amounts of money is a factor in social class, the mere possession of money is insufficient for achieving social status, for the successful use of money for class purposes demands its translation into socially approved behavior which expresses prestige in the values of the superior classes. Therefore,

(12) It is better to spend one's money on good works, philanthropy, higher education, and the works of God, or objects of conspicuous display, and achieve contact and perhaps identification with the great and highly placed than to hoard it and live in the lowly position of the miser or in the respected but subordinate position of the common man.

(13) Those who accumulate money but hoard or invest it and refuse to translate their money symbols into social and status symbols accumulate economic power which is recognized, but they never achieve top social status, no matter how large their accumulated wealth, for such status depends on their recognition by others and acceptance by those at the top.

(14) Any kind of money is important and necessary for maintaining social advantage, but the income from investments is better than other sources, for the coupon-clipper who has made his money is superior to him who still earns profits or fees.

(15) Unearned income is better than earned wealth, for income from investment, although highly evaluated, is not ranked as high as inherited symbols of money. In other words, to have a silver spoon in one's mouth at birth is better than being a self-made man. Successful social mobility in the American mind is a magnificent performance but is never as good as being born to the group of those who already belong.

(16) Profits and fees as forms of income are better than salaries, but salaries *as forms* of getting money are better than wages.

(17) Wages, while low, are earned money and as such are better than public or private aid; for the recipient of unilateral "gifts" is always subordinate and in an inferior position. Truly in America when one is poor it is better to give than to receive.

(18) Recipients of "public welfare aid," the lowest *form* of income, are ranked accordingly and penalized by social sanction.

No doubt the reader has noticed that the writer has emphasized a sharp distinction between the *form* of getting money and the amount. We all know the amount of money that a man has is of great importance, but everyone knows that the small salary that supports a clerk's family is superior to what might be the larger combined income of a family whose form of income is public relief. Each realm, the form and the amount, has its own hierarchy of values; each realm of value interpenetrates the other in practice, yet each too is at the same time separate. Occupation, and source and amount of income have their own rankings, and their values are reflected in social-class position. Other value systems are ranked and contribute their share to the status a man or his family enjoys or suffers in Jonesville. Certain other propositions about the social logics of status need to be added.

(19) A family's house, its furniture, and other such equipment

express and help symbolize its social-class position. Inferior families live in inferior houses, superior families in superior houses. For example, well-cared for, large houses which express the values of the elect are superior; the poorly cared for small houses are likely to be those of the inferior classes.

(20) The dwelling areas of Jonesville are socially graded. Those who live in inferior areas are likely to be inferior; those who live in superior areas are likely to be superior.

(21) Learning too is graded and ranked. Those who have been exposed to the higher grades of learning are superior; those stopping further down are inferior. But

(22) It is whom you know not what you know that is important.

(23) The way each of the above prestige-giving factors operates in the life of an individual in his community depends on how the other members of the community evaluate them and incorporate them into his social reputation and membership in the status-giving institutions of Jonesville.

(24) It is possible for individuals to move up or down in this social-class hierarchy.

(25) The principal methods of upward mobility are accumulation of money and its transformation into socially approved symbols, educational advancement, recognition of trained talent, marriage into a higher level, the use of beauty and sex, the acquisition of moral and ethical social codes of superior groups, the acquisition of secular rituals at superior levels, learning the social skills (speech, etc.) of those in the higher groups, and participation in cliques, associations, and churches that are frequented by the higher groups.

(26) Downward mobility is caused by loss of money, marriage at lower levels, loss of moral and ethical behavior, and participation in associations, cliques, churches, and other institutions below those you previously used.

Clearly these propositions just reviewed indicate that the equalitarian principle expressed in the precepts sacred to our democratic creed are in opposition to the hard facts that press upon the citizens of Jonesville when they experience the secular realities of social class. It is clear that the "truths" of either system, social hierarchy or democratic equality, are not true in themselves. Each is made known to us only by understanding what the other is and by ferreting out the way the two contradictory systems are interrelated. We cannot give our entire attention to one and not recognize the other, for the two constitute the realities of American democracy. The democracy of the American Dream is true only because of the social gradation on the ladder where successful men are permitted to realize their ambitions. The social-class system is true only because the precepts of the Dream provide the moral code which enforces the rules of social mobility by insisting that all able men who obey the rules of the game have "the right" to climb. To many it will seem paradoxical that the truth about American belief can only be found by relating two contradictory principles of human value and human action. Careful scrutiny of what is involved scientifically reduces this paradox to simple scientific propositions.

Complete equality does not exist in any society which is highly complex and differentiated into many occupations and positions. All the parts of a complex society are always evaluated and ranked. The operation of the family system throughout the generations helps to perpetuate this system of ranking and to select certain kinds of people for higher and lower social positions. No society with a large population can exist without a high division of labor to perform the tasks necessary for its survival; hence it is certain that no populous society can exist without one or more systems of rank.

If this last statement is true, the fundamental question for Americans to answer should be "Is the American insistence on equality nonsense and sentimental delusion and should honest men abandon such ideals and principles?" The answer is clearly no; for these equalitarian beliefs and values are of absolute importance to us. Without them our social-class system would become rigid and inflexible; there would be little or no movement between the classes. The worth of the individual under such circumstances would be decided by the principles of fixed status rather than by the flexible rules permitting social mobility. Although our system is not entirely democratic and equalitarian, belief in a democratic ideology provides an ideal toward which we strive. The strength of the democratic ideal provides the counterbalancing, opposing force against the power of our social hierarchy which, although naturally and inherently a part of our complex culture, if unopposed would reduce American life to a fixed rank order and destroy our present system of open classes where the individual is defined as someone who has choice about what he does. This is a system whose principles say that no man or family shall remain in the status to which he was born.

The extreme political right constantly attacks our principle of equality; the extreme political left constantly attacks the phenomenon of social class. If the goals of the first are what they seem to be—an effort to guarantee the position of those at the top and reduce competition from those at the bottom, their behavior is understandable and, from their point of view, perhaps defensible; if the goals of the extreme left are to substitute an entirely new system, a totalitarian and fixed social system, for the present one by destroying our beliefs in our present one, then their attacks on the phenomenon of social class are, from their point of view, sensible and correct. But should either the left or the right triumph, the worth of the individual, as we understand it, would vanish, for our system of open social classes would be destroyed. If Americans by disinterest, lack of understanding, or apathy, allow the channels of mobility to be blocked, social and political catastrophe will certainly result, for a society of fixed status will then govern our lives. It might be fascist, communist, or have some other authoritarian or totalitarian political name attached to it, but the underlying social reality will be the same. For our democratic system, in which people can compete for social reward, can survive only as long as the principles of rank are tempered by those of equality.

ACKNOWLEDGMENTS

The authors are indebted to a large number of people for their help in the field research, the analysis of the evidence, and the preparation of the material for this publication.

First of all, we owe a deep debt of gratitude to the many citizens of Jonesville who generously gave us their time and knowledge to help us understand their city. Because we have tried to keep the town anonymous and not reveal the sources of our information, we cannot publicly thank them as individuals. It is to be hoped that each person who helped us, when he reads this statement, will accept it as our expression of gratitude to him for the help and the many kindnesses shown us and for the valuable information given to our group.

We wish to thank the Committee on Human Development, under whose auspices the research was conducted, for their generous support. Particularly, we would like to express our gratitude to Robert Havighurst and Ralph Tyler, members of the Executive Committee on Human Development. Each was a source of strength to all of us. When occasional difficulties arose during the research their wise counsel and warm friendship always solved all problems.

The research files in the office of the Committee on Human Development are filled with interview and field documents collected by two score or more field workers. The authors of the chapters in this book have greatly benefited and each has used all or most of these valuable materials. We cannot list the names of all of the research people here but we do wish to thank all of them and to acknowledge our indebtedness.

Several scientific journals have published some of the results that have been used by the various authors of the present volume. We appreciate the editors' kindness in allowing us to use these materials.

Some of the authors received fellowships and scholarships from various scholarly institutions and foundations during the time that they did their research and wrote their chapters. Rather than list all of them here, it seemed wise to thank them generally, thus allowing each author, when he publishes his own articles and books, to acknowledge specifically his separate indebtedness.

All of the individuals described and analyzed in this volume, as well as their families, cliques, associations, or political, religious, and economic institutions, are composite representations and do not in any instance represent one particular individual or group. In some cases, several individuals, situations, or associations are compressed into one. In others, the individuals and situations are in part or entirely imaginary. Factual generalizations have also been employed. We have excluded all material which might identify specific persons. These various techniques have been used to prevent possible identification of individuals or organizations; they have been used in such a fashion that the story of Jonesville is told as economically as possible and with no distortion of the facts. All proposed changes in our material for the purpose of preventing identification were first critically considered by the staff to insure against changing the social reality of the points of the original interview or other data.

A NOTE ON THE AUTHORS

This book was written by several authors who were collaborators on the study of Jonesville and on the analysis of the material collected. All data gathered by them and other researchers in the Jonesville study were shared.

The authors are:

WILFRID C. BAILEY, a social anthropologist now teaching at the University of Texas, wrote the chapter on the churches (Chapter X) and was co-author of the chapter on the veterans (Chapter XV). He has spent several years doing research on Mormon communities in Arizona and Utah.

ARCH COOPER, one-time research assistant on the Jonesville research, is a social anthropologist. He is now completing the write-up of his field study of an isolated group of people living in the interior of the island of Jamaica. He collaborated on Chapter II, on social class.

WALTER EATON, a sociologist, presently teaching at Roosevelt College, collaborated on the chapter on veterans (Chapter XV).

A. B. HOLLINGSHEAD, a sociologist and professor at Yale University, has published extensively in sociology journals. He wrote the chapter on the schools (Chapter XII). He is now studying the social life of children.

CARSON McGUIRE, associate professor of Educational Psychology and Human Development, University of Texas, is author of the chapter on social mobility (Chapter IV). He is making an extensive study of this phenomenon of social class.

MARCHIA MEEKER, social anthropologist and research associate in the Committee on Human Development, University of Chicago, is co-author of the book, *Social Class in America*. She wrote the two chapters on associations (Chapters VIII and IX) and collaborated on the chapter on the factory (Chapter VII).

BERNICE NEUGARTEN, research associate in the Committee on Human Development, University of Chicago, is a psychologist. She wrote the chapter on children (Chapter V).

JOSEPH ROSENSTEIN is a sociologist. At the time of the study he held a Marshall Field fellowship in the Department of Sociology at the University of Chicago. He is just completing a study of the relation of political organization to community life.

EVON Z. VOGT, JR., social anthropologist now teaching in the Department of Social Relations, Harvard University, wrote the chapter on rural Jonesville (Chapter XIV). He is presently studying the Navajo Indians.

W. LLOYD WARNER, director of the community research in Jonesville and editor of this volume, teaches at the University of Chicago. He has done research in contemporary American and European communities and studied the Australian aborigines. He wrote the chapter on the history of the community (Chapter I), the chapter on ecology (III), "Room at the Top" (VI), the concluding chapter (XVI), and the introductory statement, "What this Book is About." He also collaborated on the chapters on The Mill (Chapter VII) and on social class (Chapter II).

DONALD WRAY, sociologist and professor at the University of Illinois, wrote the chapter on the Norse (Chapter XI). He is presently doing research in the social organization of American industry.

Index

Ability, academic and class, 87; and job mobility, 113; and popularity of children, 78; and social mobility, 66. *See* Talent

Acculturation, and associations, 258; and behavior differences, 253-254, 255; and church, 264; and ethnic education, 184-185; and revivalism, 191; and social class, 263. *See also* Assimilation

Achievement level, and upward mobility, 65, 69, 71, 72

Activity deviation, and social mobility, 62

Age grading, in associations, 118; among Norwegian-Lutherans, 174, 175, 181, 188

Aggression, and lower-class children, 85; and upward mobility, 69

Agricultural Adjustment Administration, 238

Agricultural background, 17, 19-20, 25. *See also* Rural Community

American Dream, 54, 58, 114, 297

American Legion, 125, 142; in World War II, 270; and World War II veterans, 284-285

American Protective Association, 165, 215

Appearance, personal, and class attitudes of children, 78; and social mobility, 75

Aristocracy, xiii; as social principle, xviii. *See also* Upper class

Armed forces, 266, 270, 271, 272; enrollment by class, 272-274

Armistice Day, as symbolic rite, 290

Army, enrollment by class, 272-274

Assimilation, of ethnic groups, 176, 184, 188-192. *See also* Acculturation

Associations, 115-129, 130-148, 151, 161; lower-lower-class, 143-144; lower-middle-class, 138-143; and Norwegian-Lutherans, 175, 255; rural, 244, 247, 249, 257-259; and sacred symbol systems, 290; and social mobility, 74, 144-148; upper-class, 117, 131-134; upper-lower-class, 138-143; upper-middle-class, 134-138; in wartime, 287-288; women's, xvii

Automobile, effect of, 21; and acculturation, 256

Auxiliaries, church, 165; lodge, 125, 143

Bailey, Wilfrid C., 149, 266, 301

Baptist Church, organizations, 127-128, 142; and social class, 53, 153-155, 159, 160, 161-162, 164, 166; and social mobility, 167

Beauty, and social mobility, xvi, 63, 75, 78, 296

Behavior, differences within Norwegian-Lutheran group, 253-254, 255; differences in rural community, 239; of ethnics in relation to dominant culture, 75; and social class, 34, 86; and social mobility, 28, 68-69, 75; and social status, 67, 247

Beliefs, social, xviii, 291; supernatural, 291

"Best Friend" technique, 78-83

Bill of Rights, xiii

Board of Education, 205; and churches, 150; and Catholic Church, 194; and class attitudes, 95, 97, 195-196; policies, 203 and social class, 194-196

Bridge, cliques, 246; parties, 29, 178. *See also* Cliques, Clubs

hARPER ✦ CORChBOOKS

HUMANITIES AND SOCIAL SCIENCES

American Studies: General

HENRY STEELE COMMAGER, Ed.: The Struggle for Racial Equality   TB/1300
EDWARD S. CORWIN: American Constitutional History. △ *Essays edited by Alpheus T. Mason and Gerald Garvey*   TB/1136
CARL N. DEGLER, Ed.: Pivotal Interpretations of American History   TB/1240, TB/1241
A. S. EISENSTADT, Ed.: The Craft of American History: *Recent Essays in American Historical Writing*
Vol. I   TB/1255;   Vol. II   TB/1256
CHARLOTTE P. GILMAN: Women and Economics ‡ TB/3073
OSCAR HANDLIN, Ed.: This Was America: *As Recorded by European Travelers in the Eighteenth, Nineteenth and Twentieth Centuries. Illus.*   TB/1119
MARCUS LEE HANSEN: The Atlantic Migration: 1607-1860. *Edited by Arthur M. Schlesinger*   TB/1052
MARCUS LEE HANSEN: The Immigrant in American History   TB/1120
JOHN HIGHAM, Ed.: The Reconstruction of American History △   TB/1068
ROBERT H. JACKSON: The Supreme Court in the American System of Government   TB/1106
JOHN F. KENNEDY: A Nation of Immigrants. △ *Illus.*
TB/1118
LEONARD W. LEVY, Ed.: American Constitutional Law
TB/1285
LEONARD W. LEVY, Ed.: Judicial Review and the Supreme Court   TB/1296
LEONARD W. LEVY: The Law of the Commonwealth and Chief Justice Shaw   TB/1309
RALPH BARTON PERRY: Puritanism and Democracy
TB/1138
ARNOLD ROSE: The Negro in America: *The Condensed Version of Gunnar Myrdal's An American Dilemma*
TB/3048
MAURICE R. STEIN: The Eclipse of Community: *An Interpretation of American Studies*   TB/1128
W. LLOYD WARNER: Social Class in America: *The Evaluation of Status*   TB/1013

American Studies: Colonial

BERNARD BAILYN, Ed.: The Apologia of Robert Keayne: *Self-Portrait of a Puritan Merchant*   TB/1201
BERNARD BAILYN: The New England Merchants in the Seventeenth Century   TB/1149
CHARLES GIBSON: Spain in America †   TB/3077
LAWRENCE HENRY GIPSON: The Coming of the Revolution: 1763-1775. † *Illus.*   TB/3007

PERRY MILLER: Errand Into the Wilderness   TB/1139
PERRY MILLER & T. H. JOHNSON, Eds.: The Puritans: *A Sourcebook*   Vol. I   TB/1093;   Vol. II   TB/1094
EDMUND S. MORGAN, Ed.: The Diary of Michael Wigglesworth, 1653-1657: *The Conscience of a Puritan*
TB/1228
EDMUND S. MORGAN: The Puritan Family: *Religion and Domestic Relations in Seventeenth-Century New England*   TB/1227
RICHARD B. MORRIS: Government and Labor in Early America   TB/1244
KENNETH B. MURDOCK: Literature and Theology in Colonial New England   TB/99
JOHN P. ROCHE: Origins of American Political Thought: *Selected Readings*   TB/1301
JOHN SMITH: Captain John Smith's America: *Selections from His Writings. Ed. with Intro. by John Lankford*
TB/3078
LOUIS B. WRIGHT: The Cultural Life of the American Colonies: 1607-1763. † *Illus.*   TB/3005

American Studies: From the Revolution to 1860

JOHN R. ALDEN: The American Revolution: 1775-1783. † *Illus.*   TB/3011
RAY A. BILLINGTON: The Far Western Frontier: 1830-1860. † *Illus.*   TB/3012
EDMUND BURKE: On the American Revolution. ‡ *Edited by Elliott Robert Barkan*   TB/3068
WHITNEY R. CROSS: The Burned-Over District: *The Social and Intellectual History of Enthusiastic Religion in Western New York, 1800-1850*   TB/1242
GEORGE DANGERFIELD: The Awakening of American Nationalism: 1815-1828. † *Illus.*   TB/3061
CLEMENT EATON: The Freedom-of-Thought Struggle in the Old South. *Revised and Enlarged. Illus.*   TB/1150
CLEMENT EATON: The Growth of Southern Civilization: 1790-1860. † *Illus.*   TB/3040
LOUIS FILLER: The Crusade Against Slavery: 1830-1860 † *Illus*   TB/3029
WILLIAM W. FREEHLING, Ed.: The Nullification Era: *A Documentary Record ‡*   TB/3079
FELIX GILBERT: The Beginnings of American Foreign Policy: *To the Farewell Address*   TB/1200
FRANCIS GRIERSON: The Valley of Shadows: *The Coming of the Civil War in Lincoln's Midwest: A Contemporary Account*   TB/1246
ALEXANDER HAMILTON: The Reports of Alexander Hamilton. ‡ *Edited by Jacob E. Cooke*   TB/3060
JAMES MADISON: The Forging of American Federalism: *Selected Writings of James Madison. Edited by Saul K. Padover*   TB/1126
BERNARD MAYO: Myths and Men: *Patrick Henry, George Washington, Thomas Jefferson*   TB/1108

---

† The New American Nation Series, edited by Henry Steele Commager and Richard B. Morris.
‡ American Perspectives series, edited by Bernard Wishy and William E. Leuchtenburg.
* The Rise of Modern Europe series, edited by William L. Langer.
** History of Europe series, edited by J. H. Plumb.
¶ Researches in the Social, Cultural and Behavioral Sciences, edited by Benjamin Nelson.
§ The Library of Religion and Culture, edited by Benjamin Nelson.
Σ Harper Modern Science Series, edited by James R. Newman.
° Not for sale in Canada.
△ Not for sale in the U. K.

1

JOHN C. MILLER: Alexander Hamilton and the Growth of the New Nation TB/3057
RICHARD B. MORRIS, Ed.: The Era of the American Revolution TB/1180
FRANCIS S. PHILBRICK: The Rise of the West, 1754-1830. † Illus. TB/3067
TIMOTHY L. SMITH: Revivalism and Social Reform: American Protestantism on the Eve of the Civil War TB/1229
ALBION W. TOURGÉE: A Fool's Errand ‡ TB/3074
GLYNDON G. VAN DEUSEN: The Jacksonian Era: 1828-1848. † Illus. TB/3028
LOUIS B. WRIGHT: Culture on the Moving Frontier TB/1053

American Studies: The Civil War to 1900

W. R. BROCK: An American Crisis: Congress and Reconstruction, 1865-67 ° △ TB/1283
THOMAS C. COCHRAN & WILLIAM MILLER: The Age of Enterprise: A Social History of Industrial America TB/1054
W. A. DUNNING: Reconstruction, Political and Economic: 1865-1877 TB/1073
HAROLD U. FAULKNER: Politics, Reform and Expansion: 1890-1900. † Illus. TB/3020
HELEN HUNT JACKSON: A Century of Dishonor: The Early Crusade for Indian Reform. ‡ Edited by Andrew F. Rolle TB/3063
ALBERT D. KIRWAN: Revolt of the Rednecks: Mississippi Politics, 1876-1925 TB/1199
ROBERT GREEN MC CLOSKEY: American Conservatism in the Age of Enterprise: 1865-1910 TB/1137
ARTHUR MANN: Yankee Reformers in the Urban Age: Social Reform in Boston, 1880-1900 TB/1247
WHITELAW REID: After the War: A Tour of the Southern States, 1865-1866. ‡ Edited by C. Vann Woodward TB/3066
CHARLES H. SHINN: Mining Camps: A Study in American Frontier Government. ‡ Edited by Rodman W. Paul TB/3062
VERNON LANE WHARTON: The Negro in Mississippi: 1865-1890 TB/1178

American Studies: 1900 to the Present

RAY STANNARD BAKER: Following the Color Line: American Negro Citizenship in Progressive Era. ‡ Illus. Edited by Dewey W. Grantham, Jr. TB/3053
RANDOLPH S. BOURNE: War and the Intellectuals: Collected Essays, 1915-1919. ‡ Ed. by Carl Resek TB/3043
A. RUSSELL BUCHANAN: The United States and World War II. † Illus. Vol. I TB/3044; Vol. II TB/3045
THOMAS C. COCHRAN: The American Business System: A Historical Perspective, 1900-1955 TB/1080
FOSTER RHEA DULLES: America's Rise to World Power: 1898-1954. † Illus. TB/3021
JOHN D. HICKS: Republican Ascendancy: 1921-1933. † Illus. TB/3041
SIDNEY HOOK: Reason, Social Myths, and Democracy TB/1237
ROBERT HUNTER: Poverty: Social Conscience in the Progressive Era. ‡ Edited by Peter d'A. Jones TB/3065
WILLIAM L. LANGER & S. EVERETT GLEASON: The Challenge to Isolation: The World Crisis of 1937-1940 and American Foreign Policy Vol. I TB/3054; Vol. II TB/3055
WILLIAM E. LEUCHTENBURG: Franklin D. Roosevelt and the New Deal: 1932-1940. † Illus. TB/3025
ARTHUR S. LINK: Woodrow Wilson and the Progressive Era: 1910-1917. † Illus. TB/3023
GEORGE E. MOWRY: The Era of Theodore Roosevelt and the Birth of Modern America: 1900-1912. † TB/3022
RUSSEL B. NYE: Midwestern Progressive Politics TB/1202
WILLIAM PRESTON, JR.: Aliens and Dissenters TB/1287
WALTER RAUSCHENBUSCH: Christianity and the Social Crisis. ‡ Edited by Robert D. Cross TB/3059

JACOB RIIS: The Making of an American. ‡ Edited by Roy Lubove TB/3070
PHILIP SELZNICK: TVA and the Grass Roots: A Study in the Sociology of Formal Organization TB/1230
IDA M. TARBELL: The History of the Standard Oil Company. Briefer Version. ‡ Edited by David M. Chalmers TB/3071
GEORGE B. TINDALL, Ed.: A Populist Reader ‡ TB/3069

Anthropology

JACQUES BARZUN: Race: A Study in Superstition. Revised Edition TB/1172
JOSEPH B. CASAGRANDE, Ed.: In the Company of Man: Portraits of Anthropological Informants TB/3047
W. E. LE GROS CLARK: The Antecedents of Man: Intro. to Evolution of the Primates. ° △ Illus. TB/559
CORA DU BOIS: The People of Alor. New Preface by the author. Illus. Vol. I TB/1042; Vol. II TB/1043
RAYMOND FIRTH, Ed.: Man and Culture: An Evaluation of the Work of Bronislaw Malinowski ¶ ° △ TB/1133
DAVID LANDY: Tropical Childhood: Cultural Transmission and Learning in a Puerto Rican Village ¶ TB/1235
L. S. B. LEAKEY: Adam's Ancestors: The Evolution of Man and His Culture. △ Illus. TB/1019
EDWARD BURNETT TYLOR: The Origin of Culture. Part I of "Primitive Culture." § Intro. by Paul Radin TB/33
EDWARD BURNETT TYLOR: Religion in Primitive Culture. Part II of "Primitive Culture." § Intro. by Paul Radin TB/34

Art and Art History

WALTER LOWRIE: Art in the Early Church. Revised Edition. 452 illus. TB/124
EMILE MÂLE: The Gothic Image: Religious Art in France of the Thirteenth Century. § △ 190 illus. TB/44
MILLARD MEISS: Painting in Florence and Siena after the Black Death: The Arts, Religion and Society in the Mid-Fourteenth Century. 169 illus. TB/1148
ERICH NEUMANN: The Archetypal World of Henry Moore. △ 107 illus. TB/2020
DORA & ERWIN PANOFSKY: Pandora's Box: The Changing Aspects of a Mythical Symbol. Illus. TB/2021
ALEXANDRE PIANKOFF: The Shrines of Tut-Ankh-Amon. Edited by N. Rambova. 117 illus. TB/2011
JEAN SEZNEC: The Survival of the Pagan Gods △ TB/2004
OTTO VON SIMSON: The Gothic Cathedral △ TB/2018
HEINRICH ZIMMER: Myths and Symbols in Indian Art and Civilization. 70 illustrations TB/2005

Business, Economics & Economic History

REINHARD BENDIX: Work and Authority in Industry TB/3035
THOMAS C. COCHRAN: The American Business System: A Historical Perspective, 1900-1955 TB/1080
THOMAS C. COCHRAN & WILLIAM MILLER: The Age of Enterprise: A Social History of Industrial America TB/1054
ROBERT DAHL & CHARLES E. LINDBLOM: Politics, Economics, and Welfare TB/3037
PETER F. DRUCKER: The New Society: The Anatomy of Industrial Order △ TB/1082
EDITORS OF FORTUNE: America in the Sixties: The Economy and the Society TB/1015
ROBERT L. HEILBRONER: The Great Ascent: The Struggle for Economic Development in Our Time TB/3030
ROBERT L. HEILBRONER: The Limits of American Capitalism TB/1305
FRANK H. KNIGHT: The Economic Organization TB/1214
FRANK H. KNIGHT: Risk, Uncertainty and Profit TB/1215
ABBA P. LERNER: Everybody's Business TB/3051
ROBERT GREEN MC CLOSKEY: American Conservatism in the Age of Enterprise, 1865-1910 TB/1137
PAUL MANTOUX: The Industrial Revolution in the Eighteenth Century ° △ TB/1079

Education

Historiography & Philosophy of History

History: General

History: Ancient

History: Medieval

History: Renaissance & Reformation

HAJO HOLBORN: Ulrich von Hutten and the German Reformation TB/1238

JOHAN HUIZINGA: Erasmus and the Age of Reformation.△ Illus. TB/19

JOEL HURSTFIELD, Ed.: The Reformation Crisis △ TB/1267

ULRICH VON HUTTEN et al.: On the Eve of the Reformation: "Letters of Obscure Men" TB/1124

PAUL O. KRISTELLER: Renaissance Thought: The Classic, Scholastic, and Humanist Strains TB/1048

PAUL O. KRISTELLER: Renaissance Thought II: Papers on Humanism and the Arts TB/1163

NICCOLÒ MACHIAVELLI: History of Florence and of the Affairs of Italy TB/1027

ALFRED VON MARTIN: Sociology of the Renaissance. Introduction by Wallace K. Ferguson △ TB/1099

GARRETT MATTINGLY et al.: Renaissance Profiles. △ Edited by J. H. Plumb TB/1162

MILLARD MEISS: Painting in Florence and Siena after the Black Death: The Arts, Religion and Society in the Mid-Fourteenth Century. △ 169 illus. TB/1148

J. E. NEALE: The Age of Catherine de Medici ○ △ TB/1085

ERWIN PANOFSKY: Studies in Iconology: Humanistic Themes in the Art of the Renaissance △ TB/1077

J. H. PARRY: The Establishment of the European Hegemony: 1415-1715 △ TB/1045

J. H. PLUMB: The Italian Renaissance: A Concise Survey of Its History and Culture △ TB/1161

A. F. POLLARD: Henry VIII. ○ △ Introduction by A. G. Dickens TB/1249

A. F. POLLARD: Wolsey. ○ △ Introduction by A. G. Dickens TB/1248

CECIL ROTH: The Jews in the Renaissance. Illus. TB/834

A. L. ROWSE: The Expansion of Elizabethan England. ○ △ Illus. TB/1220

GORDON RUPP: Luther's Progress to the Diet of Worms ○ △ TB/120

G. M. TREVELYAN: England in the Age of Wycliffe, 1368-1520 ○ △ TB/1112

VESPASIANO: Renaissance Princes, Popes, and Prelates: The Vespasiano Memoirs: Lives of Illustrious Men of the XVth Century TB/1111

History: Modern European

FREDERICK B. ARTZ: Reaction and Revolution, 1815-1852. * Illus. TB/3034

MAX BELOFF: The Age of Absolutism, 1660-1815 △ TB/1062

ROBERT C. BINKLEY: Realism and Nationalism, 1852-1871. * Illus. TB/3038

ASA BRIGGS: The Making of Modern England, 1784-1867: The Age of Improvement ○ △ TB/1203

CRANE BRINTON: A Decade of Revolution, 1789-1799. * Illus. TB/3018

D. W. BROGAN: The Development of Modern France. ○ △
Volume I: From the Fall of the Empire to the Dreyfus Affair
Volume II: The Shadow of War, World War I, Between the Two Wars. New Introduction by the Author TB/1184
TB/1185

J. BRONOWSKI & BRUCE MAZLISH: The Western Intellectual Tradition: From Leonardo to Hegel △ TB/3001

GEOFFREY BRUUN: Europe and the French Imperium, 1799-1814. * Illus. TB/3033

ALAN BULLOCK: Hitler, A Study in Tyranny ○ △ TB/1123

E. H. CARR: German-Soviet Relations between the Two World Wars, 1919-1939 TB/1278

E. H. CARR: International Relations between the Two World Wars, 1919-1939 ○ △ TB/1279

E. H. CARR: The Twenty Years' Crisis, 1919-1939 ○ △ TB/1122

GORDON A. CRAIG: From Bismarck to Adenauer: Aspects of German Statecraft. Revised Edition TB/1171

DENIS DIDEROT: The Encyclopedia: Selections. Ed and trans. by Stephen Gendzier TB/1299

WALTER L. DORN: Competition for Empire, 1740-1763. * Illus. TB/3032

FRANKLIN L. FORD: Robe and Sword: The Regrouping of the French Aristocracy after Louis XIV TB/1217

CARL J. FRIEDRICH: The Age of the Baroque, 1610-1660. * Illus. TB/3004

RENÉ FUELOEP-MILLER: The Mind and Face of Bolshevism TB/1188

M. DOROTHY GEORGE: London Life in the Eighteenth Century △ TB/1182

LEO GERSHOY: From Despotism to Revolution, 1763-1789. * Illus. TB/3017

C. C. GILLISPIE: Genesis and Geology: The Decades before Darwin § TB/51

ALBERT GOODWIN: The French Revolution △ TB/1064

ALBERT GUÉRARD: France in the Classical Age: The Life and Death of an Ideal △ TB/1183

CARLTON J. H. HAYES: A Generation of Materialism, 1871-1900. * Illus. TB/3039

STANLEY HOFFMANN et al.: In Search of France TB/1219

A. R. HUMPHREYS: The Augustan World: Society, Thought, and Letters in 18th Century England ○ △ TB/1105

DAN N. JACOBS, Ed.: The New Communist Manifesto & Related Documents. Third edition, Revised TB/1078

LIONEL KOCHAN: The Struggle for Germany: 1914-45 TB/1304

HANS KOHN: The Mind of Germany △ TB/1204

HANS KOHN, Ed.: The Mind of Modern Russia: Historical and Political Thought of Russia's Great Age TB/1065

WALTER LAQUEUR & GEORGE L. MOSSE, Eds.: International Fascism, 1920-1945 ○ △ TB/1276

WALTER LAQUEUR & GEORGE L. MOSSE, Eds.: The Left-Wing Intellectuals between the Wars, 1919-1939 ○ △ TB/1286

WALTER LAQUEUR & GEORGE L. MOSSE, Eds.: 1914: The Coming of the First World War ○ △ TB/1306

FRANK E. MANUEL: The Prophets of Paris: Turgot, Condorcet, Saint-Simon, Fourier, and Comte TB/1218

KINGSLEY MARTIN: French Liberal Thought in the Eighteenth Century TB/1114

L. B. NAMIER: Facing East △ TB/1280

L. B. NAMIER: Personalities and Powers: Selected Essays △ TB/1186

L. B. NAMIER: Vanished Supremacies: Essays on European History, 1812-1918 ○ △ TB/1088

JOHN U. NEF: Western Civilization Since the Renaissance: Peace, War, Industry, and the Arts TB/1113

FRANZ NEUMANN: Behemoth: The Structure and Practice of National Socialism, 1933-1944 TB/1289

FREDERICK L. NUSSBAUM: The Triumph of Science and Reason, 1660-1685. * Illus. TB/3009

DAVID OGG: Europe of the Ancien Régime, 1715-1783 ** △ TB/1271

JOHN PLAMENATZ: German Marxism and Russian Communism. ○ △ New Preface by the Author TB/1189

RAYMOND W. POSTGATE, Ed.: Revolution from 1789 to 1906: Selected Documents TB/1063

PENFIELD ROBERTS: The Quest for Security, 1715-1740. * Illus. TB/3016

PRISCILLA ROBERTSON: Revolutions of 1848: A Social History TB/1025

GEORGE RUDÉ: Revolutionary Europe, 1783-1815 ** ○ △ TB/1272

LOUIS, DUC DE SAINT-SIMON: Versailles, The Court, and Louis XIV. △ Introductory Note by Peter Gay TB/1250

ALBERT SOREL: Europe Under the Old Regime. Translated by Francis H. Herrick TB/1121

N. N. SUKHANOV: The Russian Revolution, 1917: Eyewitness Account. △ Edited by Joel Carmichael
Vol. I TB/1066; Vol. II TB/1067

A. J. P. TAYLOR: From Napoleon to Lenin: Historical Essays ○ △ TB/1268

A. J. P. TAYLOR: The Habsburg Monarchy, 1809-1918 ○ △ TB/1187

4

G. M. TREVELYAN: British History in the Nineteenth Century and After: 1782-1919. △ *Second Edition*
TB/1251
H. R. TREVOR-ROPER: Historical Essays º △ TB/1269
ELIZABETH WISKEMANN: Europe of the Dictators, 1919-1945 ** º △ TB/1275
JOHN B. WOLF: The Emergence of the Great Powers, 1685-1715. * *Illus.* TB/3010
JOHN B. WOLF: France: 1814-1919: *The Rise of a Liberal-Democratic Society* TB/3019

Intellectual History & History of Ideas

HERSCHEL BAKER: The Image of Man TB/1047
R. R. BOLGAR: The Classical Heritage and Its Beneficiaries △ TB/1125
RANDOLPH S. BOURNE: War and the Intellectuals: *Collected Essays, 1915-1919.* ‡ △ *Edited by Carl Resek*
TB/3043
J. BRONOWSKI & BRUCE MAZLISH: The Western Intellectual Tradition: *From Leonardo to Hegel* △ TB/3001
ERNST CASSIRER: The Individual and the Cosmos in Renaissance Philosophy. △ *Translated with an Introduction by Mario Domandi* TB/1097
NORMAN COHN: Pursuit of the Millennium △ TB/1037
C. C. GILLISPIE: Genesis and Geology: *The Decades before Darwin* § TB/51
G. RACHEL LEVY: Religious Conceptions of the Stone Age and Their Influence upon European Thought. △ *Illus.* Introduction by Henri Frankfort TB/106
ARTHUR O. LOVEJOY: The Great Chain of Being: *A Study of the History of an Idea* TB/1009
FRANK E. MANUEL: The Prophets of Paris: *Turgot, Condorcet, Saint-Simon, Fourier, and Comte* TB/1218
PERRY MILLER & T. H. JOHNSON, Editors: The Puritans: *A Sourcebook of Their Writings*
Vol. I TB/1093; Vol. II TB/1094
MILTON C. NAHM: Genius and Creativity: *An Essay in the History of Ideas* TB/1196
ROBERT PAYNE: Hubris: *A Study of Pride. Foreword by Sir Herbert Read* TB/1031
RALPH BARTON PERRY: The Thought and Character of William James: *Briefer Version* TB/1156
GEORG SIMMEL et al.: Essays on Sociology, Philosophy, and Aesthetics. ¶ *Edited by Kurt H. Wolff* TB/1234
BRUNO SNELL: The Discovery of the Mind: *The Greek Origins of European Thought* △ TB/1018
PAGET TOYNBEE: Dante Alighieri: *His Life and Works.* Edited with Intro. by Charles S. Singleton TB/1206
ERNEST LEE TUVESON: Millennium and Utopia: *A Study in the Background of the Idea of Progress.* ¶ *New Preface by the Author* TB/1134
PAUL VALÉRY: The Outlook for Intelligence △ TB/2016
W. WARREN WAGAR, Ed.: European Intellectual History since Darwin and Marx TB/1297
PHILIP P. WIENER: Evolution and the Founders of Pragmatism. △ *Foreword by John Dewey* TB/1212
BASIL WILLEY: Nineteenth Century Studies: *Coleridge to Matthew Arnold* º △ TB/1261
BASIL WILLEY: More Nineteenth Century Studies: *A Group of Honest Doubters* △ TB/1262

Literature, Poetry, The Novel & Criticism

JACQUES BARZUN: The House of Intellect △ TB/1051
W. J. BATE: From Classic to Romantic: *Premises of Taste in Eighteenth Century England* TB/1036
RACHEL BESPALOFF: On the Iliad TB/2006
R. P. BLACKMUR et al.: Lectures in Criticism. *Introduction by Huntington Cairns* TB/2003
JAMES BOSWELL: The Life of Dr. Johnson & The Journal of a Tour to the Hebrides with Samuel Johnson LL.D: *Selections.* º △ *Edited by F. V. Morley. Illus. by Ernest Shepard* TB/1254
ABRAHAM CAHAN: The Rise of David Levinsky: *a documentary novel of social mobility in early twentieth century America. Intro. by John Higham* TB/1028

ERNST R. CURTIUS: European Literature and the Latin Middle Ages △ TB/2015
ÉTIENNE GILSON: Dante and Philosophy TB/1089
ALFRED HARBAGE: As They Liked It: *A Study of Shakespeare's Moral Artistry* TB/1035
STANLEY R. HOPPER, Ed.: Spiritual Problems in Contemporary Literature § TB/21
A. R. HUMPHREYS: The Augustan World: *Society in 18th Century England* º △ TB/1105
ALDOUS HUXLEY: Antic Hay & The Giaconda Smile. º △ Introduction by Martin Green TB/3503
ARNOLD KETTLE: An Introduction to the English Novel △
Volume I: *Defoe to George Eliot* TB/1011
Volume II: *Henry James to the Present* TB/1012
RICHMOND LATTIMORE: The Poetry of Greek Tragedy △
TB/1257
J. B. LEISHMAN: The Monarch of Wit: *An Analytical and Comparative Study of the Poetry of John Donne* º △
TB/1258
J. B. LEISHMAN: Themes and Variations in Shakespeare's Sonnets º △ TB/1259
ROGER SHERMAN LOOMIS: The Development of Arthurian Romance △ TB/1167
JOHN STUART MILL: On Bentham and Coleridge. △ *Introduction by F. R. Leavis* TB/1070
KENNETH B. MURDOCK: Literature and Theology in Colonial New England TB/99
SAMUEL PEPYS: The Diary of Samuel Pepys. º *Edited by O. F. Morshead. Illus. by Ernest Shepard* TB/1007
ST.-JOHN PERSE: Seamarks TB/2002
V. DE S. PINTO: Crisis in English Poetry, 1880-1940 º △
TB/1260
ROBERT PREYER, Ed.: Victorian Literature TB/1302
GEORGE SANTAYANA: Interpretations of Poetry and Religion § TB/9
C. K. STEAD: The New Poetic: *Yeats to Eliot* º △ TB/1263
HEINRICH STRAUMANN: American Literature in the Twentieth Century. △ *Third Edition, Revised* TB/1168
PAGET TOYNBEE: Dante Alighieri: *His Life and Works.* Edited with Intro. by Charles S. Singleton TB/1206
DOROTHY VAN GHENT: The English Novel TB/1050
E. B. WHITE: One Man's Meat TB/3505
BASIL WILLEY: Nineteenth Century Studies: *Coleridge to Matthew Arnold* º △ TB/1261
BASIL WILLEY: More Nineteenth Century Studies: *A Group of Honest Doubters* º △ TB/1262
RAYMOND WILLIAMS: Culture and Society, 1780-1950 △
TB/1252
RAYMOND WILLIAMS: The Long Revolution. △ *Revised Edition* TB/1253
MORTON DAUWEN ZABEL, Editor: *Literary Opinion in America* Vol. I TB/3013; Vol. II TB/3014

Myth, Symbol & Folklore

JOSEPH CAMPBELL, Editor: Pagan and Christian Mysteries. *Illus.* TB/2013
MIRCEA ELIADE: Cosmos and History: *The Myth of the Eternal Return* § △ TB/2050
MIRCEA ELIADE: Rites and Symbols of Initiation: *The Mysteries of Birth and Rebirth* § △ TB/1236
THEODOR H. GASTER: Thespis º △ TB/1281
DORA & ERWIN PANOFSKY: Pandora's Box: *The Changing Aspects of a Mythical Symbol.* △ *Revised Edition. Illus.* TB/2021
HELLMUT WILHELM: Change: *Eight Lectures on the I Ching* △ TB/2019
HEINRICH ZIMMER: Myths and Symbols in Indian Art and Civilization. △ *70 illustrations* TB/2005

Philosophy

G. E. M. ANSCOMBE: An Introduction to Wittgenstein's Tractatus. º △ *Second Edition, Revised* TB/1210

C. G. JUNG & C. KERÉNYI: Essays on a Science of Mythology: *The Myths of the Divine Child and the Divine Maiden*　　　　　　TB/2014

JOHN T. MC NEILL: A History of the Cure of Souls TB/126

KARL MENNINGER: Theory of Psychoanalytic Technique　　　　　　TB/1144

ERICH NEUMANN: Amor and Psyche △　TB/2012

ERICH NEUMANN: The Archetypal World of Henry Moore. *107 illus.*　　　　TB/2020

ERICH NEUMANN: The Origins and History of Consciousness △　Vol. I *Illus.* TB/2007; Vol. II TB/2008

C. P. OBERNDORF: A History of Psychoanalysis in America　　　　　　TB/1147

RALPH BARTON PERRY: The Thought and Character of William James: *Briefer Version* TB/1156

JEAN PIAGET, BÄRBEL INHELDER, & ALINA SZEMINSKA: The Child's Conception of Geometry ○ △　TB/1146

JOHN H. SCHAAR: Escape from Authority: *The Perspectives of Erich Fromm*　TB/1155

MUZAFER SHERIF: The Psychology of Social Norms　　　　　　TB/3072

Sociology

JACQUES BARZUN: Race: *A Study in Superstition. Revised Edition*　　　　TB/1172

BERNARD BERELSON, Ed.: The Behavioral Sciences Today　　　　　　TB/1127

ABRAHAM CAHAN: The Rise of David Levinsky: *A documentary novel of social mobility in early twentieth century America. Intro. by John Higham* TB/1028

THOMAS C. COCHRAN: The Inner Revolution: *Essays on the Social Sciences in History*　TB/1140

LEWIS A. COSER, Ed.: Political Sociology TB/1293

ALLISON DAVIS & JOHN DOLLARD: Children of Bondage: *The Personality Development of Negro Youth in the Urban South* ¶　　　　TB/3049

ST. CLAIR DRAKE & HORACE R. CAYTON: Black Metropolis: *A Study of Negro Life in a Northern City. Revised and Enlarged. Intro. by Everett C. Hughes*
　　　　Vol. I TB/1086; Vol. II TB/1087

EMILE DURKHEIM et al.: Essays on Sociology and Philosophy. *With Analysis of Durkheim's Life and Work.* ¶ *Edited by Kurt H. Wolff*　TB/1151

LEON FESTINGER, HENRY W. RIECKEN & STANLEY SCHACHTER: When Prophecy Fails: *A Social and Psychological Account of a Modern Group that Predicted the Destruction of the World* ¶　　TB/1132

ALVIN W. GOULDNER: Wildcat Strike ¶ TB/1176

FRANCIS J. GRUND: Aristocracy in America: *Social Class in the Formative Years of the New Nation* △ TB/1001

KURT LEWIN: Field Theory in Social Science: *Selected Theoretical Papers* ¶ △ *Edited with a Foreword by Dorwin Cartwright*　TB/1135

R. M. MAC IVER: Social Causation TB/1153

ROBERT K. MERTON, LEONARD BROOM, LEONARD S. COTTRELL, JR., Editors: Sociology Today: *Problems and Prospects* ¶　Vol. I TB/1173; Vol. II TB/1174

ROBERTO MICHELS: First Lectures in Political Sociology. *Edited by Alfred de Grazia* ¶ ○　TB/1224

BARRINGTON MOORE, JR.: Political Power and Social Theory: *Seven Studies* ¶　TB/1221

BARRINGTON MOORE, JR.: Soviet Politics — The Dilemma of Power: *The Role of Ideas in Social Change* ¶　　　　　　TB/1222

TALCOTT PARSONS & EDWARD A. SHILS, Editors: Toward a General Theory of Action　TB/1083

JOHN H. ROHRER & MUNRO S. EDMONSON, Eds.: The Eighth Generation Grows Up ¶　TB/3050

KURT SAMUELSSON: Religion and Economic Action: *A Critique of Max Weber's The Protestant Ethic and the Spirit of Capitalism.* ¶ ○ *Trans. by E. G. French. Ed. with Intro. by D. C. Coleman*　TB/1131

PHILIP SELZNICK: TVA and the Grass Roots: *A Study in the Sociology of Formal Organization* TB/1230

GEORG SIMMEL et al.: Essays on Sociology, Philosophy, and Aesthetics. ¶ *Edited by Kurt H. Wolff* TB/1234

HERBERT SIMON: The Shape of Automation △ TB/1245

PITIRIM A. SOROKIN: Contemporary Sociological Theories: *Through the First Quarter of the 20th Century* TB/3046

MAURICE R. STEIN: The Eclipse of Community: *An Interpretation of American Studies*　TB/1128

FERDINAND TÖNNIES: Community and Society: *Gemeinschaft und Gesellschaft. Translated and edited by Charles P. Loomis*　TB/1116

W. LLOYD WARNER & Associates: Democracy in Jonesville: *A Study in Quality and Inequality* TB/1129

W. LLOYD WARNER: Social Class in America: *The Evaluation of Status*　TB/1013

RELIGION

Ancient & Classical

J. H. BREASTED: Development of Religion and Thought in Ancient Egypt　　　TB/57

HENRI FRANKFORT: Ancient Egyptian Religion TB/77

G. RACHEL LEVY: Religious Conceptions of the Stone Age and their Influence upon European Thought. △ *Illus. Introduction by Henri Frankfort*　TB/106

MARTIN P. NILSSON: Greek Folk Religion TB/78

ALEXANDRE PIANKOFF: The Shrines of Tut-Ankh-Amon.△ *Edited by N. Rambova. 117 illus.* TB/2011

ERWIN ROHDE: Psyche Vol. I TB/140; Vol. II TB/141

H. J. ROSE: Religion in Greece and Rome △ TB/55

Biblical Thought & Literature

W. F. ALBRIGHT: The Biblical Period from Abraham to Ezra　　　　　　TB/102

C. K. BARRETT, Ed.: The New Testament Background: *Selected Documents* △　TB/86

C. H. DODD: The Authority of the Bible △ TB/43

M. S. ENSLIN: Christian Beginnings △　TB/5

M. S. ENSLIN: The Literature of the Christian Movement △　　　　　　TB/6

JOHN GRAY: Archaeology and the Old Testament World. △ *Illus.*　　　　TB/127

JAMES MUILENBURG: The Way of Israel: *Biblical Faith and Ethics* △　TB/133

H. H. ROWLEY: The Growth of the Old Testament △　　　　　　TB/107

G. A. SMITH: The Historical Geography of the Holy Land △　　　　　　TB/138

D. WINTON THOMAS, Ed.: Documents from Old Testament Times △　　　TB/85

WALTHER ZIMMERLI: The Law and the Prophets: *A Study of the Meaning of the Old Testament* △ TB/144

The Judaic Tradition

LEO BAECK: Judaism and Christianity. *Trans. with Intro. by Walter Kaufmann*　TB/823

SALO W. BARON: Modern Nationalism and Religion　　　　　　JP/18

MARTIN BUBER: Eclipse of God: *Studies in the Relation Between Religion and Philosophy* △　TB/12

MARTIN BUBER: For the Sake of Heaven △ TB/801

MARTIN BUBER: Hasidism and Modern Man △ TB/839

MARTIN BUBER: The Knowledge of Man: *Selected Essays.* △ *Edited with an Introduction by Maurice Friedman. Translated by Maurice Friedman and Ronald Gregor Smith*　TB/135

MARTIN BUBER: Moses: *The Revelation and the Covenant* △　　TB/827

MARTIN BUBER: The Origin and Meaning of Hasidism △　　　　　　TB/835

MARTIN BUBER: Pointing the Way. △ *Introduction by Maurice S. Friedman*　TB/103

MARTIN BUBER: The Prophetic Faith TB/73

MARTIN BUBER: Two Types of Faith: *the interpenetration of Judaism and Christianity* ○ △　TB/75

ERNST LUDWIG EHRLICH: A Concise History of Israel: *From the Earliest Times to the Destruction of the Temple in A. D. 70* ○ △　TB/128

7

8

JOHN MACQUARRIE: The Scope of Demythologizing: Bultmann and his Critics △   TB/134

PERRY MILLER & T. H. JOHNSON, Editors: The Puritans: A Sourcebook of Their Writings   Vol. I   TB/1093
   Vol. II   TB/1094

JAMES M. ROBINSON et al.: The Bultmann School of Biblical Interpretation: New Directions? Volume 1 of Journal of Theology and the Church, edited by Robert W. Funk in association with Gerhard Ebeling   TB/251

F. SCHLEIERMACHER: The Christian Faith. △ Introduction by Richard R. Niebuhr   Vol. I   TB/108
   Vol. II   TB/109

F. SCHLEIERMACHER: On Religion: Speeches to Its Cultured Despisers. Intro. by Rudolf Otto   TB/36

PAUL TILLICH: Dynamics of Faith △   TB/42

PAUL TILLICH: Morality and Beyond   TB/142

EVELYN UNDERHILL: Worship △   TB/10

Christianity: The Roman and Eastern Traditions

DOM CUTHBERT BUTLER: Western Mysticism: The Teaching of Augustine, Gregory and Bernard on Contemplation and the Contemplative Life § ○ △   TB/312

A. ROBERT CAPONIGRI, Ed.: Modern Catholic Thinkers I: God and Man △   TB/306

A. ROBERT CAPONIGRI, Ed.: Modern Catholic Thinkers II: The Church and the Political Order △   TB/307

THOMAS CORBISHLEY, S. J.: Roman Catholicism △   TB/112

CHRISTOPHR DAWSON: The Historic Reality of Christian Culture   TB/305

G. P. FEDOTOV: The Russian Religious Mind: Kievan Christianity, the 10th to the 13th Centuries   TB/370

G. P. FEDOTOV, Ed.: A Treasury of Russian Spirituality   TB/303

ÉTIENNE GILSON: The Spirit of Thomism   TB/313

DAVID KNOWLES: The English Mystical Tradition △ TB/302

GABRIEL MARCEL: Being and Having: An Existential Diary. △ Introduction by James Collins   TB/310

GABRIEL MARCEL: Homo Viator: Introduction to a Metaphysic of Hope   TB/397

GUSTAVE WEIGEL, S. J.: Catholic Theology in Dialogue   TB/301

Oriental Religions: Far Eastern, Near Eastern

TOR ANDRAE: Mohammed: The Man and His Faith § △   TB/62

EDWARD CONZE: Buddhism: Its Essence and Development. ○ △ Foreword by Arthur Waley   TR/58

EDWARD CONZE et al., Editors: Buddhist Texts Through the Ages △   TB/113

ANANDA COOMARASWAMY: Buddha and the Gospel of Buddhism. △ Illus.   TB/119

H. G. CREEL: Confucius and the Chinese Way   TB/63

FRANKLIN EDGERTON, Trans & Ed.: The Bhagavad Gita   TB/115

SWAMI NIKHILANANDA, Trans. & Ed.: The Upanishads: A One-Volume Abridgment △   TB/114

HELMUT WILHELM: Change: Eight Lectures on the I Ching △   TB/2019

Philosophy of Religion

NICOLAS BERDYAEV: The Beginning and the End § △ TB/14

NICOLAS BERDYAEV: Christian Existentialism: A Berdyaev Synthesis. Ed. by Donald A. Lowrie △   TB/130

NICOLAS BERDYAEV: The Destiny of Man △   TB/61

RUDOLF BULTMANN: History and Eschatology: The Presence of Eternity ○   TB/91

RUDOLF BULTMANN AND FIVE CRITICS: Kerygma and Myth: A Theological Debate △   TB/80

RUDOLF BULTMANN and KARL KUNDSIN: Form Criticism: Two Essays on New Testament Research. △ Translated by Frederick C. Grant   TB/96

MIRCEA ELIADE: The Sacred and the Profane   TB/81

LUDWIG FEUERBACH: The Essence of Christianity. § Introduction by Karl Barth. Foreword by H. Richard Niebuhr   TB/11

ÉTIENNE GILSON: The Spirit of Thomism   TB/313

ADOLF HARNACK: What is Christianity? § △ Introduction by Rudolf Bultmann   TB/17

FRIEDRICH HEGEL: On Christianity: Early Theological Writings. Ed. by R. Kroner & T. M. Knox   TB/79

KARL HEIM: Christian Faith and Natural Science △ TB/16

IMMANUEL KANT: Religion Within the Limits of Reason Alone. § Intro. by T. M. Greene & J. Silber   TB/67

K. E. KIRK: The Vision of God: The Christian Doctrine of the Summum Bonum § △   TB/137

JOHN MACQUARRIE: An Existentialist Theology: A Comparison of Heidegger and Bultmann. ○ △ Preface by Rudolf Bultmann   TB/125

PAUL RAMSEY, Ed.: Faith and Ethics: The Theology of H. Richard Niebuhr   TB/129

EUGEN ROSENSTOCK-HUESSY: The Christian Future or the Modern Mind Outrun   TB/143

PIERRE TEILHARD DE CHARDIN: The Divine Milieu ○ △   TB/384

PIERRE TEILHARD DE CHARDIN: The Phenomenon of Man○△   TB/383

Religion, Culture & Society

JOSEPH L. BLAU, Ed.: Cornerstones of Religious Freedom in America: Selected Basic Documents, Court Decisions and Public Statements. Revised and Enlarged Edition   TB/118

C. C. GILLISPIE: Genesis and Geology: The Decades before Darwin §   TB/51

KYLE HASELDEN: The Racial Problem in Christian Perspective   TB/116

WALTER KAUFMANN, Ed.: Religion from Tolstoy to Camus: Basic Writings on Religious Truth and Morals. Enlarged Edition   TB/123

JOHN T. MC NEILL: A History of the Cure of Souls TB/126

KENNETH B. MURDOCK: Literature and Theology in Colonial New England   TB/99

H. RICHARD NIEBUHR: Christ and Culture △   TB/3

H. RICHARD NIEBUHR: The Kingdom of God in America   TB/49

RALPH BARTON PERRY: Puritanism and Democracy   TB/1138

PAUL PFUETZE: Self, Society, Existence: Human Nature and Dialogue in the Thought of George Herbert Mead and Martin Buber   TB/1059

WALTER RAUSCHENBUSCH: Christianity and the Social Crisis. ‡ Edited by Robert D. Cross   TB/3059

KURT SAMUELSSON: Religion and Economic Action: A Critique of Max Weber's The Protestant Ethic and the Spirit of Capitalism. ¶ ○ △ Trans. by E. G. French. Ed. with Intro. by D. C. Coleman   TB/1131

TIMOTHY L. SMITH: Revivalism and Social Reform: American Protestantism on the Eve of the Civil War △   TB/1229

ERNST TROELTSCH: The Social Teaching of the Christian Churches ○ △   Vol. I TB/71; Vol. II TB/72

NATURAL SCIENCES AND MATHEMATICS

Biological Sciences

CHARLOTTE AUERBACH: The Science of Genetics Σ △   TB/568

MARSTON BATES: The Natural History of Mosquitoes. Illus.   TB/578

A. BELLAIRS: Reptiles: Life, History, Evolution, and Structure. △ Illus.   TB/520

LUDWIG VON BERTALANFFY: Modern Theories of Development: An Introduction to Theoretical Biology TB/554

LUDWIG VON BERTALANFFY: Problems of Life: An Evaluation of Modern Biological and Scientific Thought △   TB/521

HAROLD F. BLUM: Time's Arrow and Evolution   TB/555
JOHN TYLER BONNER: The Ideas of Biology. Σ △ Illus.
TB/570
A. J. CAIN: Animal Species and their Evolution. △ Illus.
TB/519
WALTER B. CANNON: Bodily Changes in Pain, Hunger,
Fear and Rage. Illus.   TB/562
W. E. LE GROS CLARK: The Antecedents of Man: Intro. to
Evolution of the Primates. ᵒ △ Illus.   TB/559
W. H. DOWDESWELL: Animal Ecology. △ Illus.   TB/543
W. H. DOWDESWELL: The Mechanism of Evolution. △ Illus.
TB/527
R. W. GERARD: Unresting Cells. Illus.   TB/541
DAVID LACK: Darwin's Finches. △ Illus.   TB/544
ADOLF PORTMANN: Animals as Social Beings. ᵒ △ Illus.
TB/572
O. W. RICHARDS: The Social Insects. △ Illus.   TB/542
P. M. SHEPPARD: Natural Selection and Heredity. Illus.
TB/528
EDMUND W. SINNOTT: Cell and Psyche: The Biology of
Purpose   TB/546
C. H. WADDINGTON: How Animals Develop. △ Illus.
TB/553
C. H. WADDINGTON: The Nature of Life: The Main Prob-
lems and Trends in Modern Biology △   TB/580

Chemistry

J. R. PARTINGTON: A Short History of Chemistry. △ Illus.
TB/522

Communication Theory

J. R. PIERCE: Symbols, Signals and Noise: The Nature
and Process of Communication △   TB/574

Geography

R. E. COKER: This Great and Wide Sea: An Introduction
to Oceanography and Marine Biology. Illus.   TB/551
F. K. HARE: The Restless Atmosphere △   TB/560

History of Science

MARIE BOAS: The Scientific Renaissance, 1450-1630 ᵒ △
TB/583
W. DAMPIER, Ed.: Readings in the Literature of Science.
Illus.   TB/512
A. HUNTER DUPREE: Science in the Federal Government:
A History of Policies and Activities to 1940 △ TB/573
ALEXANDRE KOYRÉ: From the Closed World to the Infinite
Universe: Copernicus, Kepler, Galileo, Newton, etc. △
TB/31
A. G. VAN MELSEN: From Atomos to Atom: A History of
the Concept Atom   TB/517
O. NEUGEBAUER: The Exact Sciences in Antiquity TB/552
HANS THIRRING: Energy for Man: From Windmills to
Nuclear Power △   TB/556
STEPHEN TOULMIN & JUNE GOODFIELD: The Architecture of
Matter ᵒ △   TB/584
STEPHEN TOULMIN & JUNE GOODFIELD: The Discovery of
Time ᵒ △   TB/585
LANCELOT LAW WHYTE: Essay on Atomism: From Democ-
ritus to 1960 △   TB/565

Mathematics

E. W. BETH: The Foundations of Mathematics: A Study
in the Philosophy of Science △   TB/581
H. DAVENPORT: The Higher Arithmetic: An Introduction
to the Theory of Numbers △   TB/526
H. G. FORDER: Geometry: An Introduction △   TB/548
S. KÖRNER: The Philosophy of Mathematics: An Intro-
duction △   TB/547
D. E. LITTLEWOOD: Skeleton Key of Mathematics: A
Simple Account of Complex Algebraic Problems △
TB/525
GEORGE E. OWEN: Fundamentals of Scientific Mathe-
matics   TB/569
WILLARD VAN ORMAN QUINE: Mathematical Logic TB/558
O. G. SUTTON: Mathematics in Action. ᵒ △ Foreword by
James R. Newman. Illus.   TB/518
FREDERICK WAISMANN: Introduction to Mathematical
Thinking. Foreword by Karl Menger   TB/511

Philosophy of Science

R. B. BRAITHWAITE: Scientific Explanation   TB/515
J. BRONOWSKI: Science and Human Values. △ Revised and
Enlarged Edition   TB/505
ALBERT EINSTEIN et al.: Albert Einstein: Philosopher-
Scientist. Edited by Paul A. Schilpp   Vol. I TB/502
Vol. II TB/503
WERNER HEISENBERG: Physics and Philosophy: The Revo-
lution in Modern Science △   TB/549
JOHN MAYNARD KEYNES: A Treatise on Probability. ᵒ △
Introduction by N. R. Hanson   TB/557
KARL R. POPPER: Logic of Scientific Discovery △ TB/576
STEPHEN TOULMIN: Foresight and Understanding: An
Enquiry into the Aims of Science. △ Foreword by
Jacques Barzun   TB/564
STEPHEN TOULMIN: The Philosophy of Science: An In-
troduction △   TB/513
G. J. WHITROW: Natural Philosophy of Time ᵒ △ TB/563

Physics and Cosmology

JOHN E. ALLEN: Aerodynamics: A Space Age Survey △
TB/582
STEPHEN TOULMIN & JUNE GOODFIELD: The Fabric of the
Heavens: The Development of Astronomy and Dy-
namics. △ Illus.   TB/579
DAVID BOHM: Causality and Chance in Modern Physics. △
Foreword by Louis de Broglie   TB/536
P. W. BRIDGMAN: The Nature of Thermodynamics
TB/537
P. W. BRIDGMAN: A Sophisticate's Primer of Relativity △
TB/575
A. C. CROMBIE, Ed.: Turning Point in Physics   TB/535
C. V. DURRELL: Readable Relativity. △ Foreword by Free-
man J. Dyson   TB/530
ARTHUR EDDINGTON: Space, Time and Gravitation: An
Outline of the General Relativity Theory   TB/510
GEORGE GAMOW: Biography of Physics Σ △   TB/567
MAX JAMMER: Concepts of Force: A Study in the Founda-
tion of Dynamics   TB/550
MAX JAMMER: Concepts of Mass in Classical and Modern
Physics   TB/571
MAX JAMMER: Concepts of Space: The History of
Theories of Space in Physics. Foreword by Albert
Einstein   TB/533
G. J. WHITROW: The Structure and Evolution of the Uni-
verse: An Introduction to Cosmology. △ Illus. TB/504

10